2nd National Edition

W9-CED-079

SIMPLE WILL BOOK

how to prepare a legally valid will

by Attorney Denis Clifford

NOLO PRESS ⬥ **BERKELEY**

YOUR RESPONSIBILITY WHEN USING A SELF-HELP LAW BOOK

We've done our best to give you useful and accurate information in this book. But laws and procedures change frequently and are subject to differing interpretations. If you want legal advice backed by a guarantee, see a lawyer. If you use this book, it's your responsibility to make sure that the facts and general advice contained in it are applicable to your situation.

KEEPING UP TO DATE

To keep its books up to date, Nolo Press issues new printings and new editions periodically. New printings reflect minor legal changes and technical corrections. New editions contain major legal changes, major text additions or major reorganizations. To find out if a later printing or edition of any Nolo book is available, call Nolo Press at (510) 549-1976 or check the catalog in the Nolo News, our quarterly newspaper.

To stay current, follow the "Update" service in the Nolo News. You can get the paper free by sending us the registration card in the back of the book. In another effort to help you use Nolo's latest materials, we offer a 25% discount off the purchase of any new Nolo book if you turn in any earlier printing or edition. (See the "Recycle Offer" in the back of the book.)

This book was last revised in: **OCTOBER 1992.**

Second Edition:	September 1989
Fifth Printing:	October 1992
Editor:	Stephen Elias
Production:	Stephanie Harolde
Book Design:	Jackie Clark
	Terri Hearsh
Cover Painting:	Denis Clifford
Illustrations:	Mari Stein
Index:	Sayre Van Young

ACKNOWLEDGMENTS

Thanks to all those friends who helped me put this book together:

Naomi Puro, Kay Corbett, Carol Pladsen, Catherine and Paul Clifford, Marilyn Putnam (for all her help through the years), and all my Nolo colleagues—Toni Ihara, Stephanie Harolde, David Cole, Keija Kimura, Glenn Voloshin, Barbara Hodovan, John O'Donnell, Catherine Jermany, Jack Devaney, Ann Heron, Amy Ihara, Kate Thill, Bob Bergstrom, Christine Leefeldt, Julie Christianson, and Mari Stein. Special thanks to Steve Elias, Mary Randolph and Jake Warner for their brilliant and tireless editing of the manuscript. Also, I want to extend special thanks to Dorcas Moulton, for her help with the cover painting, and especially to Jackie Clark, who prepared so many drafts of the manuscript so well, and so cheerfully.

Finally, my thanks and appreciation to the many readers whose comments and suggestions have helped improve the book in many ways.

CONTENTS

CHAPTER 1

HOW TO USE NOLO'S WILL BOOK

A.	Introduction to the Second Edition	1/1
B.	The Human Element	1/2
C.	Dying Without a Will	1/2
D.	What Can You Accomplish In Your Will?	1/2
E.	How to Proceed Through Nolo's Will Book	1/3
F.	A Look at a Basic Will	1/4
G.	Estate Planning: Do You Need More Than a Will?	1/4
H.	Will You Need a Lawyer?	1/7
I.	This is a Workbook	1/8

CHAPTER 2

WILLS — AN OVERVIEW

A.	Basic Legal Requirements for Making a Valid Will	2/1
B.	What Happens If You Die Without a Will?	2/3
C.	Types of Wills	2/3
D.	What You Can't Do In Your Will	2/5
E.	What Happens After You Die	2/6
F.	A Note About Will Writing Vocabulary	2/6

CHAPTER 3

CHOOSING YOUR EXECUTOR OR PERSONAL REPRESENTATIVE

A.	Criteria for Choosing Your Executor or Personal Representative	3/1
B.	Naming Your Executor	3/3

CHAPTER 4

WHAT PROPERTY IS YOURS TO GIVE BY WILL? — OWNERSHIP LAWS

A.	Introduction	4/1
B.	Property You Cannot Dispose of by Your Will	4/3
C.	Gifts to Charities	4/3
D.	Marital Property Ownership Laws	4/4
E.	Marital Property in Community Property States	4/5
F.	Marital Property in Common Law States	4/9
G.	When Spouses Move from State to State	4/13

CHAPTER 5
INVENTORY YOUR PROPERTY

A.	How to Complete Your Property Chart	5/2
B.	Your Property Chart	5/6

CHAPTER 6
DECIDING WHO YOU WANT TO GET YOUR PROPERTY

A.	Basic Terminology	6/2
B.	Explanations and Commentary Accompanying Gifts	6/2
C.	Restrictions on Gifts	6/4
D.	Divorce	6/4
E.	Disinheritance	6/4
F.	Shared Gifts	6/5
G.	Naming Alternate Beneficiaries	6/7
H.	Beneficiary Chart	6/9
I.	Establishing a Survivorship Period	6/16
J.	Simultaneous Death	6/16
K.	Life Estates	6/17
L.	Property You No Longer Own at Your Death	6/18
M.	When You Have Insufficient Liquid Assets to Pay Your Cash Gifts	6/18

CHAPTER 7
CHILDREN

A.	Providing For Your Minor Children	7/1
B.	Custody of Your Minor Child	7/2
C.	Leaving Property to Your Children	7/5
D.	Leaving Property to Other's Children	7/18
E.	Your Children of Any Age	7/22

CHAPTER 8
ESTATE PLANNING BASICS

A.	Probate	8/2
B.	Do You Need To Avoid Probate?	8/3
C.	Why Wills Are Necessary	8/3
D.	Probate Avoidance Methods	8/4
E.	Estate Planning to Reduce Taxes	8/6
F.	Estate Planning Designed to Place Controls on Property	8/9
G.	Planning for Incapacity: The Durable Power of Attorney	8/10
H.	Estate Planning—Summing Up	8/11

CHAPTER 9
LAWYERS, TYPING SERVICES AND DOING YOUR OWN LEGAL RESEARCH

A.	Do You Need a Lawyer?	9/1
B.	Working With a Lawyer	9/1
C.	Doing Your Own Research	9/4

CHAPTER 10

AN OVERVIEW OF THE WILLS YOU
CAN DRAFT USING THIS BOOK

A.	How to Proceed	10/1
B.	Basic Form Wills	10/1
C.	Assemble-It-Yourself Wills	10/3
D.	Formalities	10/4

CHAPTER 11

BASIC WILLS

A.	Introduction	11/1
B.	To Complete Your Basic Will	11/1
C.	What Is Included In a Basic Will Form	11/3
D.	Sample Completed Basic Will	11/10
F.	Basic Will Forms	11/20

CHAPTER 12

ASSEMBLE THE CLAUSES WILL

A.	How to Prepare Your Own Will	12/1
B.	Making Substantive Changes in	12/3
C.	Prepare Your Will—Clause By Clause	12/4
D.	Checklist	12/33
E.	Next Steps	12/33

CHAPTER 13

FORMALITIES OF WILL DRAFTING

A.	Type Your Will	13/1
B.	Staple Your Will	13/2
C.	Requirements for Signing and Witnessing Your Will	13/2
D.	'Self-Proving' Wills: Using a Notary Public	13/3
E.	After Your Will Is Completed	13/4

CHAPTER 14

CHANGING OR REVOKING YOUR WILL

A.	Revising and Updating Your Will	14/1
B.	Making Simple Changes in Your Will by Codicil	14/2
C.	Codicil Form	14/3
D.	Revoking Your Will	14/3

GLOSSARY

CHAPTER 1

HOW TO USE

NOLO'S WILL BOOK

A.	Introduction to the Second Edition	1/1
B.	The Human Element	1/2
C.	Dying Without a Will	1/2
D.	What Can You Accomplish In Your Will?	1/2
E.	How to Proceed Through Nolo's Will Book	1/3
F.	A Look at a Basic Will	1/4
G.	Estate Planning: Do You Need More Than a Will?	1/4
H.	Will You Need a Lawyer?	1/7
I.	This is a Workbook	1/8

A. Introduction to the Second Edition

THIS BOOK ENABLES YOU TO WRITE your own will, valid in every state except Louisiana. If you're temporarily residing outside the United States for work, study, travel or military service, you can also use the Will Book to make a valid will.

This second edition keeps *Nolo's Simple Will Book* current with the latest developments affecting will drafting. For example, an increasing number of states have adopted the Uniform Transfers to Minors Act. In states where it's applicable, the Act can provide a handy method for leaving property to a minor through your will. Using the Act, you simply appoint an adult custodian to manage property you leave the child. The custodian functions free of court supervision. The book explains, in depth, when it's

sensible for you to use the Act, and when another method for leaving property to a minor (such as a children's trust) is preferable. The book also contains thorough instructions and the forms necessary to actually make gifts to minors in your will by using the Act. Other major changes in this second edition include an expanded and revised chapter on children, and up-to-date revisions of the chapter on estate planning.

Using Nolo's Will Book, you can safely prepare your own will, in all normal situations, without the services of a lawyer. You will accomplish all major will-making goals, including specifying who gets your property, and how your children will be provided for. By following the detailed instructions on witnessing and other formalities, you can be sure your will is legal. Fortunately, as you'll see, it isn't hard to make a simple legal will.

B. The Human Element

THE ACT OF MAKING A WILL may seem minor indeed in the face of the overwhelming emotional force and mystery of death. The larger questions and meanings are appropriately left for philosophers, clergy, poets, and, ultimately, to you. For many, death surely is a painful subject to think about, to talk about, and, often, to plan for. The ancient Greeks believed the inevitability of death could best be faced by performing great deeds. Christian religions offer the promise of eternal life; preparing for death means preparing to "meet your maker." Other cultures have prepared for death in a wide variety of ways.

However you choose to prepare, spiritually, for death, many practical matters must be dealt with. For example, your property will have to be given to someone, or some institutions. It's no denigration of death, or life, for you to be concerned with the wisest, most desirable distribution of your property. Writing a will is an act of concern, or love, to insure that the people (and organizations) you care for receive the property you want them to have.

Though most people are aware that they need a will, the majority of Americans (about 66% according to a recent article by Consumer Reports magazine) don't have one. Why? No one knows for sure, but here are some likely reasons:

- The legal establishment has managed to mystify the process of writing a will. People fear that "making it legal" is a terribly complicated task, and are therefore frightened of writing a will themselves for fear of making mistakes.
- People believe that if they go to a lawyer to have a will prepared, they'll be charged a substantial fee. There's considerable basis for this fear. Fortunately, by using this book most people can safely leave their own property to family members, friends and organizations without paying a lawyer.
- Lurking beneath many people's failure to make a will is the superstitious fear that thinking about a will, or preparing one, may somehow hasten death. Though this fear is plainly irrational, it's often a major cause of people putting off writing a will.

C. Dying Without a Will

LET'S PAUSE FOR A MOMENT and consider what happens if you die without a will. If you don't make a will, or use some other valid legal method to transfer your property after you die, the law of your state will cause your property to be distributed to your spouse and children. If you have neither, your property will go to your other close relatives according to a statutory formula. If you have no relatives who qualify under law to inherit your property, it will go to your state (this is called "escheating"—one of my favorite legal words). Similarly, in the absence of a will, state court judges determine who'll care for your children and their property, and also who'll supervise the distribution of all of your property. Unfortunately, it's highly unlikely that these results would be what you would have chosen if you'd taken the time to write your will.

D. What Can You Accomplish In Your Will?

"ESTATE"[1] IS THE LEGAL TERM for all the property you own. You have an estate whether you're wealthy or impoverished. In your will, you can leave your property, or your "estate," in almost any way you want.

Many people worry that the gifts they want to make in their will may not turn out to be legally binding. This worry is expressed in many ways, such as:

"I'm concerned about legal requirements. How can I make gifts so that I know my wishes will be followed? What's the right language to use to leave my property?"

"I want to make many specific gifts to family and friends. I have pictures, mementos, heirlooms, antiques. How can I insure that the proper people get them, and that no one else can claim them?"

Using the Will Book, you can be sure that all gifts you make in your will are legally binding. To accomplish this, you need only state your intentions in plain written English. The Will Book contains all the

---

[1]A thorough will-drafting vocabulary is contained in the Glossary at the end of this book.

necessary technical language to enable most of you to leave your property as you desire.

VOCABULARY—GIFTS

Throughout this book, except where otherwise indicated, the word "gift(s)" is used to mean any property left by your will, whether left to individuals or institutions. Sometimes, in legalese, lawyers distinguish between "devises"—gifts of real estate (real property) and "bequests"—gifts of personal property (everything but real estate). The Will Book uses the word "gift" to cover both types of property.

Using this book, you can safely:
- Leave your personal property and your home and other real estate to your spouse, children, grand-children, other relatives, friends, organizations/charities, or anyone else you desire;
- Provide for an alternate person or organization to inherit your real restate and personal property if the first person you pick to receive the property fails to survive you;
- Leave your partner (mate/lover) as much of your property as you wish if you're not married but live with them.

Of course, by making a will you can do far more than make gifts of property. Generally, using a will from this Will Book, you can:

- Revoke all previous wills;
- Forgive debts owed to you when you die;
- Nominate a personal guardian to care for your child or children, should you die before they reach age 18, in circumstances where the other natural or adoptive parent is unable, unwilling, or incompetent to care for them;
- Leave property to minor children, including your own;
- Choose the best method for managing property you leave to a minor or young adult. For minors, this means deciding between a children's trust, a gift using the Uniform Transfers to Minors Act, or leaving the property directly to a minor, to be

supervised by the property guardian you name in the will;
- Appoint your executor, the person who handles your property after you die, who'll make sure the terms of your will are carried out;
- Provide for what happens to your property in the event of the simultaneous death of your spouse or mate;
- Disinherit anyone you want to, except that state law restricts your power to disinherit your spouse; and
- Provide for what happens to your body after you die.

E. How to Proceed Through Nolo's Will Book

THE WILL BOOK IS DESIGNED FOR YOU to read sequentially, chapter-by-chapter. Each chapter takes you through the next steps necessary for you to draft your will. Here's a brief synopsis of what you'll cover:

Chapter 2 contains a general overview of wills—how they work and what you can do in yours.

In Chapter 3 you'll learn about executors and choose the persons who will serve as your executor, and alternate executor, should your first choice be unable or unwilling to serve.

In Chapter 4 you'll review the property ownership laws that apply to your state and make an accurate determination of exactly what property is in your estate.

In Chapter 5 you'll inventory and list your property.

In Chapter 6 you'll specify who are to be your "beneficiaries," or inheritors.

Chapter 7 discusses several considerations that will affect you if you have your own children, or plan to leave property to any minors. You can skip this section if you're not a parent, and you don't intend to leave property to any minor children. If you have children, however, or are considering gifts to any minors, Chapter 7 is essential reading.

Chapter 8 covers the basics of estate planning, including avoiding probate, minimizing death taxes, and using trusts. Estate planning can help insure that your relatives and friends get as much of your property as possible after you die, by avoiding needless payments to governments and lawyers.

Chapter 9 discusses lawyers—how to decide if you need one to review your will, or for estate planning, and how to locate a good one, if necessary.

Chapter 10 contains a discussion of the differences between Chapter 11 wills (basic form wills) and Chapter 12 wills (where you assemble pre-drafted clauses), so you can properly choose the approach that's best for you.

Chapter 11 provides six sample basic wills[2] for certain standard situations. If your needs allow, you can use one of these forms to prepare your own will.

Chapter 12 provides you with more options for drafting your will, including a variety of clauses you may need or want. It allows you to assemble these clauses in a number of different combinations and custom-tailor a will to meet your specific needs.

Chapter 13 covers the formalities necessary to prepare (execute) a valid will in your state, from typing to signing and witnessing requirements.

Chapter 14 covers what you need to do after your will has been executed, from where to store it to how often to review it.

---

[2]The French philosopher Rabelais accomplished the task of writing a one-sentence will, as follows: "I have nothing, I owe a great deal, and the rest I leave to the poor."

F. A Look at a Basic Will

SEEING A COMPLETED BASIC WILL drafted from a form in Chapter 11 should help you understand that you really can safely write your own will. At this point, some technical phrases or terms may not be crystal clear to you, but rest assured that every clause and term will be thoroughly explained before you actually begin drafting yours.

Let's take as our example Jane Martinez, a single woman in her mid-thirties. June has never been married and has no children. She has a close relationship with her life companion Michael, has several good friends, and a cherished older sister, Martha Dougherty.

Jane's major assets are the expensive tools she uses in her woodworking business, her sports car, and $15,000 in savings. She also values her extensive library, several pieces of jewelry and one Thomas Hart Benton etching she inherited from her aunt. After proceeding through the Will Book, Jane prepared the following will. This example is complete except for the formula language defining the executor's powers (called "boilerplate" by lawyers), and the witnessing clause. These are omitted here to save space. In all wills prepared from the forms in Chapter 11 or Chapter 12, both must be included.

G. Estate Planning: Do You Need More Than a Will?

ONE ISSUE YOU'LL RESOLVE in the course of using this book is whether a will is the only practical arrangement you'll need, or want, to prepare for your death. Although a will is an indispensable part of any estate plan, many people determine they should make some additional preparation, which can include:

WILL OF JANE MARTINEZ

I, Jane Martinez, a resident of Monclair, Essex County, New Jersey, declare that this is my will.

1. I revoke all wills and codicils that I have previously made.

2. I am not married.

3. I make the following gifts of cash:

- I give $5,000 to my good friend Amy Wolpren, or, if she doesn't survive me by 45 days, to my sister Martha Dougherty.

- I give $5,000 to my good friend John McGuire, or, if he doesn't survive me by 45 days, to my sister Martha Dougherty.

- I give $5,000 to my life companion Michael Francois, or, if he doesn't survive me by 45 days, to my sister Martha Dougherty.

4. I make the following specific gifts of personal property:

- I give all my woodworking tools and business interest in Martinez Fine Woodworking and my car to my life companion, Michael Francois, or, if he fails to survive me by 45 days, to my sister Martha Dougherty.

- I give my Thomas Hart Benton etching to my sister Martha Dougherty or, if she fails to survive me by 45 days, to her daughter, Anita Dougherty.

- I give my gold jewelry and my books to my good friend Jessica Roettingern, or, if she fails to survive me by 45 days, to my sister Martha Dougherty.

5. I give my residuary estate, i.e., the rest of my property not otherwise specifically and validly disposed of by this will or in any other manner, to my sister Martha Dougherty, or, if she fails to survive me by 45 days, to Michael Francois.

If any beneficiary of a shared residuary or specific gift made in this will fails to survive me by 45 days, the surviving beneficiaries of that gift shall equally divide the deceased beneficiary's share. If all beneficiaries of a shared residuary or specific gift fail to survive me by 45 days, that gift shall pass in equal shares to the alternate beneficiaries named to receive that gift. If the alternate beneficiaries named by this will to receive a specific gift don't survive me by 45 days, that gift shall become part of my residuary estate.

6. I nominate Michael Francois as executor of this will to serve without bond. If Michael Francois shall for any reason fail to qualify or cease to act as executor, I nominate Martha Dougherty as executor, also to serve without bond. I direct that my executor take all actions legally permissible to have the probate of my estate done as simply as possible, including filing a petition in the appropriate court for the independent administration of my estate.

[This clause is completed by the standard Nolo executor's powers provisions contained in all sample wills. See example on page 11/14.]

I subscribe my name to this will this 8th the day of October, 1986, at Montclair, Essex County, New Jersey, and do hereby declare that I sign and execute this instrument as my last will and that I sign it willingly, that I execute it as my free and voluntary act for the purposes therein expressed, and that I am of the age of majority or otherwise legally empowered to make a will, and under no constraint or undue influence.

Jane Martiner
_____

[Will completed by the witnesses signing the the witness clauses. See Basic Will I in Chapter 11.]

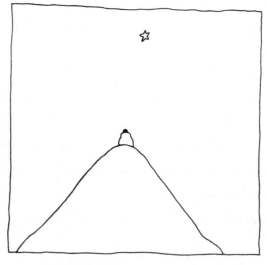

THE MYSTERY OF IT ALL

- Preparing for the possibility that they'll become incapacitated and unable to make medical or financial decisions for themselves. The simplest and wisest method to prepare for this contingency is to prepare a "durable power of attorney"[3] (discussed in Chapter 8, Section G), naming a person you choose to have legal authority to act for you if you ever become incapacitated.
- Arranging for the most efficient and economical ways of transferring your property before or after you die. This kind of estate planning is primarily concerned with two problems: reducing death taxes and reducing probate costs and delays.
- The basics of estate planning are covered in Chapter 8. Estates worth less than $600,000 aren't subject to federal estate tax (absent large gifts during life), so death taxes aren't a concern for many people. Probate, very simply, is the court process wills must go through. Standard methods for avoiding probate, including living trusts and joint tenancy, are discussed in Chapter 8.
- Handling a personal need. Many personal situations require more sophisticated estate planning. Spouses in second or subsequent marriages often want to provide for the other spouse, but also insure that the bulk of their property is preserved for the children from an earlier marriage. One common way to accomplish this is by use of what's called a "marital life estate" trust. Another common problem is the need for parents of a disadvantaged child to provide for that child, at the same time that they preserve his eligibility for the government benefits. These concerns are discussed briefly in Chapter 8 and in more detail in *Plan Your Estate With a Living Trust* (Clifford, Nolo Press). However, to actually prepare one of these trusts, you'll usually need to see a lawyer.

For many of you, a will is all you need, or want. A will has the advantage of being the simplest estate planning device, the easiest to prepare. Many young people want to be certain their desires regarding their property will be carried out if they die; they also know it's statistically highly unlikely that they'll die for years. So they decide to postpone the cost and hassles of full-scale estate planning until their autumnal years. A will is all they need for now.

Similarly, the primary estate planning goal of many young couples is to insure to the best of their abilities that their minor children are well provided for and cared for, especially if both parents should die together. A will allows parents to accomplish this by naming both personal and property guardians for the children. Later, of course, this same couple may well want to engage in more extensive estate planning if they accumulate considerable property through the years.

Finally, many people, no matter what their age or health, simply don't want the bother and cost of extensive estate planning. They may say, "Yes, I guess I should do some full-scale estate planning, but I never get around to it." Fortunately, preparation of a simple will achieves their basic goal of distributing their property as they see fit, with as little disturbance to themselves as possible. In other words, if you're waiting, or procrastinating about preparing a comprehensive estate plan, be sure you at least have a will.

If you don't know now whether you want more than a will, relax. As you work through the Will Book, you'll take stock of your situation, and learn enough about estate planning so you can make an informed decision about what you need.

H. Will You Need a Lawyer?

MOST PEOPLE CAN MOST DEFINITELY DRAFT their own will without any aid except this book. The will-making process doesn't inherently necessitate a lawyer. After all, for most people making a will involves absolutely no conflict with others, which is the usual reason for hiring an attorney. Only occasionally does a will require the sort of complex legal maneuvering that can necessitate a lawyer's skills.[4]

On the other hand, a will typing service can help you use this book and type your will in an attractive final format. For this type of assistance, contact the

---

[3]Nolo Press publishes *The Power of Attorney Book*, containing all the information and forms you need to prepare your own durable power of attorney.

[4]Ambrose Bierce defined a lawyer as "one skilled in circumvention of the law."

National Association for Independent Paralegals at (800) 542-0034.

Finally, you should know that no state law requires that a will be prepared or approved by a lawyer.

You also may be interested to know that even if you hire a lawyer to draft your will, the lawyer will most probably prepare it by using a standard attorney's form book containing the same types of clauses you'll find here, with the addition of considerable unnecessary legal-sounding verbiage. Very likely, this standard form has been input into a computer or computerized typewriter, so all that's left to be done is to type in your name, the names of the people you want your property to go to, and other necessary information, and then to print out the document.

Some members of the legal establishment have tried to frighten the public with horror stories of disasters that befell some benighted person whose self-drafted will didn't achieve his goals. A renowned lawyer once remarked that anyone who can take out his own appendix can write his own will. This analogy is false. An accurate one is that if you can prepare your own income tax form, preparing your own will should present you with no problems, unless yours is an unusual situation (I flag these throughout the book). In other words, drafting a valid will takes intelligence and common sense, not sophisticated skills.

Nevertheless, you shouldn't approach the task of will drafting with a rule against consulting a lawyer, or at least having one review your work. Some people's situations are complicated and do call for legal assistance. If you want to impose controls over a piece of land for the next two generations, that requires a lawyer. And I've already mentioned that a lawyer will be needed to prepare a marital life estate trust or to provide for a disadvantaged child. The Will Book doesn't show you how to prepare any trust, except for a simple trust for property you leave to your own minor children designed to delay the age at which they take the property you leave them. Finally, if you believe some family members will challenge your will because you disinherit them, you should consult a lawyer to see how you can best prepare in advance to counter this challenge.

 This is the symbol you'll see throughout the Will Book when reference to a lawyer is suggested. Though you'll find quite a few of these symbols in the book, you'll probably not be affected by any of them. Use of lawyers is discussed in detail in Chapter 9.

If you do determine at some stage that you want a lawyer's assistance, this book will still be helpful in a number of ways. First, by having become knowledgeable about wills, and by preparing a draft of what you want, you may substantially reduce the lawyer's fee. Second, you'll be better able to determine if a lawyer is dealing with you in a straightforward way, or is trying to bamboozle you into an overly complicated and expensive approach with fancy talk.

One piece of advice. In a will, you're expressing your own intentions. No one else can know those intentions. Sometimes, when people think, or fear, that they need a lawyer, what they're really doing is longing for an authority figure (or believing one is required) to tell them what to do. By buying this book you've demonstrated that you're not willing to turn such basic decisions as the distribution of your own property over to someone else. Good. Keep that firmly in mind when considering whether you actually need a lawyer's help.

I.   This is a Workbook

FINALLY, PLEASE TREAT THE WILL BOOK as a workbook, not a book to cherish unmarked. It's specifically designed to help you actively prepare your will. You'll be engaged in the processes necessary to prepare your will throughout the book—writing down factual information, making notes, recording your decisions. A number of worksheets are provided to help you do this. You can leave the worksheets in the book while using them, or tear them out (they're perforated), or photocopy them and work on the copies. This, of course, is up to you. So, take out a pencil, eraser and some scratch paper (in case you need more room than the worksheets provide), and get ready. Without further ado, as speakers at ceremonial dinners say, let's now learn more of what a will is and what a will can do.

CHAPTER 2

WILLS — AN OVERVIEW

A. Basic Legal Requirements for Making a Valid Will   2/1

B. What Happens If You Die Without a Will?   2/3

C. Types of Wills   2/3

D. What You Can't Do In Your Will   2/5

E. What Happens After You Die   2/6

F. A Note About Will Writing Vocabulary   2/6

A. Basic Legal Requirements for Making a Valid Will

THE LEGAL REQUIREMENTS TO DRAFT A VALID WILL aren't nearly as complicated as most people fear. Read what follows carefully and you will be reassured.

1. The Law That Governs Your Will

Generally, a will is valid in any state in the U.S. where you die, if it was valid under the laws of the state (or country) where the will writer was "domiciled" when the will was made.[1] Your domicile is where you have your home. This means your principal home, where you spend most of your time, as opposed, say, to a summer home. You can only have one domicile.

Prepare your will in, and for, the state of your domicile, even if you work in another state.

 If there's any doubt in your mind about which state is your permanent home (for example, if you divide your time roughly equally between houses in two states, or if you're in the military and live off base) and how that might affect your will, check with an attorney.

What happens if you move to another state? The short answer is that you should review your will in light of the new state's laws, especially property ownership laws (see Chapter 14 for a discussion of what to look for). Fortunately, you'll probably determine that your original will remains valid.

2. Age Requirements

To make a will you must either be:

- 18 years of age or older (except 19 in Wyoming and 19 for real estate in Alabama); or

---

[1]Also, if your will is valid in the state where you die, it's legally immaterial that it was invalid in the state where it was prepared.

• Living in one of those few states that permit younger persons to make a will if they're married, in the military, or otherwise considered "emancipated."

 Don't make a will if you're under 18 unless you've checked with a lawyer.

3. Mental State

You must be of "sound mind" to make a valid will. The fact that you're reading and understanding this book is, as a practical matter, sufficient evidence that you meet this test. The legal definitions of "sound mind" are mostly elaborations of common sense. Thus, the standard interpretations include that the person making the will (called the "testator" in legalese):

• Must know she's making a will and what a will is;
• Has the capacity to understand the relationship between herself and those persons who would normally be provided for in the will;
• Has the ability to understand the nature and extent of her property;
• Has actual knowledge of the nature of the act she's undertaking; and
• Has the capacity to form an orderly scheme of distributing her property.

In reality, a person has to be pretty far gone before a court will rule that she lacked the capacity to make a valid will. For example, forgetfulness or even the inability to recognize friends don't by themselves establish incapacity. Also, it's important to remember that there's normally no affirmative burden to prove to a court that the will writer was competent. It's presumed that the will writer was of sound mind, unless someone challenges this in a court proceeding—which is rarely done.

A will can also be declared invalid if a court determines that it was procured by "fraud" or "undue influence." This usually involves some evil-doer manipulating a person of unsound mind to leave all, or most, of his property to the manipulator.

 If you suspect there's even a remote chance someone will challenge your will on the basis of your mental competence, be sure to see a lawyer. For example, if you plan to leave the bulk of your property to someone you know is disliked and mistrusted by most of your family, work with a lawyer to minimize the possibility of a lawsuit, and maximize the chances your side will prevail if there is one.

4. Technical Requirements

To be valid, a will must comply with the technical will drafting requirements of your state's law. In general, these requirements, which are very similar in all states, except Louisiana, are less onerous than many people imagine.

The technical requirements sufficient for a will to be valid in every state, except Louisiana, are:
• The will must be typewritten (in Section C, I discuss oral and handwritten wills that are valid in some states), and expressly state that it's your will;
• The will must have at least one substantive provision. The most common substantive provisions dispose of some, or all, of your property by making gifts to whoever you want to have it. However, you can also have a valid will that only appoints a personal guardian for your minor children and doesn't dispose of any property.
• You must appoint at least one executor.[2] This person (called a "personal representative" in some states) is responsible for supervising the distribution of your property after your death and seeing that your debts and taxes are paid;
• You must date and sign the will.

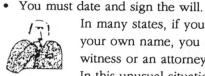 In many states, if you're too ill to sign your own name, you can direct that a witness or an attorney sign it for you.

In this unusual situation, you should have a lawyer's assistance, especially if substantial amounts of property are involved. It could always be claimed that someone too ill to sign her name

---

[2]Nevertheless, in most states, even if you fail to name an executor in an otherwise valid will, a court will appoint one and then enforce the will.

wasn't mentally competent. In any subsequent court challenge to the will, the lawyer's testimony that you appeared to be in full possession of your faculties could be very important.

• The will must be witnessed by at least two, or, in some states, three, witnesses who don't inherit under the will. This means that the witnesses watch you sign your will, and then sign it as your witnesses. Witness requirements are covered in detail in Chapter 13, Section C2.

Those are all the basic technical requirements. There's no requirement that a will be notarized. In many states, though, if you and your witnesses sign an affidavit (sworn statement) before a notary public, you can help simplify the court procedures required for the will after you die (called "probate"). This use of notarization is called a "self-proving" will and is covered in Chapter 13, Section D.

A will doesn't need to be recorded or filed with any government agency, although it can be in a few states.

B. What Happens If You Die Without a Will?

LET'S LOOK A LITTLE DEEPER into what would happen if you die without a will or other legal device to transfer your property. In legalese, this is called dying "intestate." Unfortunately, most Americans die intestate. Among the famous people who've died without a valid will are Presidents Abraham Lincoln, Andrew Johnson, and U. S. Grant, as well as Howard Hughes and Pablo Picasso.

Since you bought this book, I won't bother with sermons on how foolish it would be for you to die intestate. However, it can be illuminating to understand what dying without a will involves. If you didn't make provisions for what happens to your property when you die, your state law, called "intestacy law," makes them for you. Here's how intestacy laws work:

• A court petition must be filed to have your property distributed under the intestacy laws.

• A judge will appoint an administrator, whose main qualification may be that he's a crony of the judge, to supervise the distribution of your property and hire the probate lawyer.

• Your property (after payment of administrator's, attorney's, and other fees) will be divided as state law mandates. Basically, your property will be parceled out between your closest family members, in different proportions depending upon your family situation and the specifics of state law.

Obviously, the division of property according to state intestacy laws is highly unlikely to coincide with your exact personal desires. If you want to distribute any of your property to friends or organizations, intestacy won't do it. Normally, you don't even insure that your spouse receives all your property if you die intestate since, under the laws of most states, your property (or some of it) will be divided between your spouse and children or other relations. Further, if you're living with a domestic partner to whom you aren't married, absent a contract, that person can't receive any of your property if you die intestate.

• If you have minor children, a judge will appoint a guardian for them to manage any property they receive through the intestacy laws.

In sum, dying intestate is as unwise as it is unnecessary.

C. Types of Wills

THERE ARE THREE BASIC KINDS OF WILLS: typed,[3] handwritten and oral. More complicated wills, such

---

[3]These include wills drafted on a computer using a program like *WillMaker* (Nolo Press) or other will-drafting programs, which are printed out.

as joint wills and contracts to make a will, are generally not advisable for the reasons discussed on the next page. Reciting your gifts, or all the terms of your will, on videotape isn't a legal substitute for a valid will.

1. The Typed 'Witnessed' Will

This is the conventional will, the kind this book enables you to prepare. Once prepared, it must be properly signed and witnessed. The typed or "formal" will is the kind familiar to courts, and is what most people mean when they speak of a will. (Specific typing requirements for your will are covered in Chapter 13, Section A.)

One version of a typed will is a statutory will, which is valid in some states, including California, Michigan, Wisconsin and Maine, and under consideration in the legislatures of several others. A statutory will is a printed, fill-in-the-blanks, check-the-boxes form. In theory, statutory wills are an excellent idea—inexpensive, easy to complete, and thoroughly reliable. Unfortunately, in practice statutory wills are so limited they aren't useful for most people. The main reason for this is that the choices provided in the statutory forms as to how property can be left are quite limited. And because these statutory forms cannot legally be changed, you simply can't customize them to fit your situation. For example, the California Statutory Will allows you to give your automobile, and all household property, including jewelry, as one gift. You cannot divide up this property if you want to. The California Statutory Will is primarily useful only to people who are married. Even if you're a married Californian, if you want to leave some of your property, beyond a few cash gifts, to relatives, friends, etc., the statutory will is not very useful.

2. The Holographic or Handwritten Will

A holographic (handwritten) will must be written, dated and signed entirely in the handwriting of the person making the will. It needn't be witnessed. Holographic wills are recognized by about 25 states. They are definitely not recommended and not covered in this book. Holographic wills are a poor idea because probate courts traditionally have been very strict when examining them after the death of the will writer. One reason for this is that since handwritten wills are normally not witnessed, they're often thought to be less reliable. For this reason, they can be more difficult to get through the probate process because of the need to prove that the will was actually written in the deceased person's handwriting.

3. The Nuncupative Will

This is an oral will. It's valid only in a minority of states. Generally, oral wills, even where valid, are acceptable only if made under special circumstances, such as the will maker's imminent danger of death or if made while on active duty with the U.S. military.

4. Joint Wills

A joint will is one typed document made by two people, who are usually married. Each leaves everything to the other when the first one dies, and then the will goes on to specify what happens to the property when the second person dies. In effect, a joint will prevents the surviving person from changing his mind regarding what should happen to the other's property after the first person dies. Joint wills typically tie up property for years, pending the second death. Also, it can be unclear whether the survivor can revoke any part of the will. For these reasons, I don't recommend this type of will. A couple can use the Will Book to prepare two separate wills, which can accomplish most of the sensible goals of a joint will, without its limits and dangers. If the spouses' goal is to insure that property will ultimately go to children of prior marriage(s), a marital life estate trust is a better way to achieve this (see Chapter 8, Section F).

 If the joint will is regarded as a contract between the two makers, both must consent for a revocation to be effective. This is a potential source of litigation. Be sure and see an attorney if you're considering a joint will.

5. Contracts to Make a Will

A contract to make a will (and leave certain property to the other party to the contract) is valid but not wise. A contract in which you agree to leave your car to Fred will take precedence over a subsequent will (one that breaches the contract) that doesn't mention Fred and leaves the car to Sam. The usual case in which such contracts are made is where someone provides services—care, live-in nursing, etc.—in return for an agreement that the person receiving the care will leave all or some of her property to the person providing the care. Most lawyers prefer to establish a trust for these situations. Tying up your property so you cannot change your will isn't desirable for more reasons than I can list here. Most financial advisors advise against signing a contract to leave property in a will.

 If you want to know more about drafting a trust for these purposes, see a lawyer.

6. The Living Will

A "living will" isn't a will at all, but a document where the writer states that she wants a natural death and doesn't want her life artificially prolonged by use of life support equipment. "Living wills," which are also sometimes called "Directive to Physicians," are valid in most states. Generally, a better way to provide binding instructions regarding use of life support systems is by use of a durable power of attorney (see Chapter 8, Section G) that is valid in most all states.

D. What You Can't Do In Your Will

AS WAS DISCUSSED IN CHAPTER 1, you can give away your property in your will in almost any conceivable way you desire. You can leave all you've acquired to your family, a foundation, your favorite grandchild, your lover, or in trust for your cats. You can leave bequests to non-citizens. You can exclude, or disinherit, anyone you want to, within the limits of your state's laws on family rights (see Chapter 4).

There are, however, a few limitations on what you can do in a will. You cannot:

- Attempt to encourage or restrain certain types of conduct of your beneficiaries. For example, you cannot make a gift contingent on the marriage, divorce, or change of religion of a recipient. You can, however, make a gift contingent on other behavior, i.e., "to John, if and when he goes to college." In general, however, the Will Book discourages making contingent gifts, for reasons discussed in more detail in Chapter 6, Section C.
- Use a will to leave money for an illegal purpose.
- Require your executor to hire any particular attorney to handle the probate of your will. Probate is the process in which a will is submitted to a court, debts paid, and the property ordered distributed as the will directs. While the executor is responsible for seeing that this process is properly carried out, most of the work is typically done by a lawyer (or, more realistically, her secretary).[4] The will writer can informally indicate his preference for a particular attorney, and the executor presumably will follow that request, but

---

[4]In California, you can handle a probate without a lawyer by using *How to Probate An Estate* by Nissley (Nolo Press).

the executor cannot be legally bound to do so, no matter what the will says or the testator wants.

Perhaps the most basic limitation on your power to use a will to distribute property is based on the requirement that for a will to be effective as to any particular item of property, you must own it at your death. In other words, a will isn't binding until your death. Before then, you can give away, or sell, any asset mentioned in your will. Of course, if you do give away, or sell, property that you've specified in your will, you should rewrite your will to reflect the change.

Also, a will can't dispose of property that you've legally bound yourself to transfer by other means. For example, as discussed in Chapter 8, property held in joint tenancy or in a living trust, as well as the proceeds of life insurance or IRAs, isn't subject to a will.

E. What Happens After You Die

AFTER YOU DIE, YOUR PROPERTY will be transferred as your will directs, and the other provisions of your will will be carried out. Here's the normal sequence.

- Your executor (called a "personal representative" in some states) locates your will, which you should have stored in a safe, but accessible place.
- The executor hires an attorney for the probate proceeding, unless no probate is required (see Chapter 8 for a discussion of probate and situations where it isn't required).
- If probate is required, the lawyer (or your executor acting without a lawyer) handles the probate court proceeding.
- The probate court officially confirms the executor, issuing her legal authority to conduct the estate's business in what's traditionally called "letters of administration."
- The probate court appoints the persons you named in your will to be guardians for the person of your minor children (see Chapter 7 for how you can best control this).

- The executor manages your estate during the probate process, handling (usually without the need for court approval) any problems that arise and paying your debts, including any income, state and federal death taxes.
- Money or property left to a trust created in your will gets distributed to the designated trustee.
- Once probate is completed, your property is distributed as your will directs. Completing probate generally takes at least four months and often as long as a year. Once the proceeding is completed, further creditor's claims against the dead person's estate aren't valid.

F. A Note About Will Writing Vocabulary

IN THESE FIRST TWO CHAPTERS, you've been presented with some of the basic lingo lawyers and courts use when discussing wills. Learning this vocabulary and the simple concepts behind it is a significant step towards gaining the self-reliance necessary to write your own will. It's easy to be intimidated and uncomfortable when we don't know what attorneys are talking about. This obfuscation is often consciously, even cynically, used to keep people dependent on lawyers, particularly with a subject like will drafting.

This book contains a Glossary at the end of the book that defines all the important terms for writing your will and making estate-planning decisions. If you're unsure of the meaning of any legal term used in the text, please turn to the Glossary to aid your understanding.

CHAPTER 3

CHOOSING YOUR EXECUTOR
OR PERSONAL REPRESENTATIVE

A. Criteria for Choosing Your Executor or Personal Representative   3/3
B. Naming Your Executor   3/4

IT'S TIME TO GET STARTED making decisions about your will. The first decision you'll make is who shall serve as your executor, and successor executor, in case, for any reason, your original choice can't serve. An executor is called a "personal representative" in some states, but for simplicity's sake, I'll only use the term "executor."

As you know by now, your executor is the person you name in your will to have legal responsibility for handling your property and distributing it as your will directs. If your will must go through probate, your executor has the authority to hire a probate attorney. If your will is exempt from probate (see Chapter 8, Section B), your executor is the sole person who'll supervise distribution of your property.

Obviously, the executor has an important job. Indeed, your executor is legally entitled to a fee for his services, payable from your estate. The fee scale varies from state to state, ranging from a fixed percentage of the probate estate (the total value of the property passing through probate) to "reasonable compensation." In reality, an executor often waives the fees, especially if he's a substantial inheritor of the estate. You should discuss the question of fees with the person you choose for your executor, to be sure the two of you are in agreement.

Your executor's powers and responsibilities are, in very general terms, defined by state law. In addition, all the will forms in this book contain a standard clause defining extensive powers of the executor appointed in that will. This clause is set out in Chapters 11 and 12. When you read this list, the duties may seem so awesome and burdensome that you doubt anyone would want the job, let alone be able to manage it. Fortunately, in reality an executor's job isn't usually difficult. It's the probate attorney (in truth, mostly her secretary and staff) who normally handles the legal details involved in the transfer of your property, unless the executor chooses to handle this himself. With a well drafted will, the transfers themselves are almost always routine. In other words, the people/organizations you specified to receive your property get it without problems. Usually the executor just checks in with the probate attorney occasionally, signs legal papers, pays your final bills and any death taxes (with estate funds), and makes sure your property actually goes to who's named in the will to receive it.

A. Criteria for Choosing Your Executor or Personal Representative

THE MOST IMPORTANT CRITERION in naming an executor is to choose someone you trust completely. Once you have accomplished this, there's no reason to also require him to post a financial guarantee (called a "bond") to insure that all duties are properly carried out. This is especially true when you realize that the cost of buying the bond must be paid for by your estate. So all wills in the Will Book state that no bond is required of any executor.

If at all possible, your executor should reside in your state fairly close to where you live. Some states require that cash bonds be posted for executors who live out of state, even if you provide that this isn't necessary in your will. In any case, because of paperwork and other administrative responsibilities, which may include making one or more appearances in court, it's not sensible to name someone who resides far away from the property and location of the probate proceeding as executor.

Many people name as executor someone who benefits substantially under the will. This makes sense as an executor who has an interest in how your property is distributed is likely to do a conscientious job. Often this person is a close family member, spouse or an adult child.

You also want to be sure to name someone who's willing to do the job. Obviously you should discuss this with your executor, and receive his consent to serve before finalizing your decision.

Finally, you want to name someone who's healthy and likely to be around after your death. To be safe, you should always select at least one successor executor to serve if your first choice cannot.

For many people the choice of executor is obvious—their spouse, or mate. Others select a best friend or close family relation. If there's no obvious person who comes to mind as your executor, you have to work through your possible selections, using your common sense to decide who would be the wisest choice. Do remember, however, that human concerns are usually more important than technical "expertise."

What about naming a corporate executor, such as a bank? I strongly recommend against it in most circumstances. Your executor is your personal representative in the distribution of your property after your death. You want someone human, with genuine concern, not an institution, to do the job. If your most trusted friend is your banker, name him as executor, but not the bank itself.

However, special circumstances may compel the naming of a corporate or professional executor. For example, if you're actively involved in running a business, and your executor will be responsible for continuing that business, at least for a while, you'll want someone with business acumen or experience. If you can't find any person you know and trust to take on this major responsibility, you'll have to select a professional management firm. Banks often provide this service, as do a number of other companies, such as private trusts, which specialize in the area. One possibility is to name a trusted person and a professional management company, as co-executors. Just remember, though, this is a last resort.

What about choosing co-executors? While it's simpler to choose one executor, there's no rule that says you must. There are occasionally sensible reasons for choosing two. Sometimes those reasons are personal—a parent names both children as co-executors, so as not to appear to favor one. Or the reasons can be practical—your preferred choice for executor lives out of state, and you want at least one executor who lives in your state, who'll be nearby.

Naming co-executors raises some potential problems. Suppose one becomes unavailable? Under the terms of wills you can make using this book, the remaining original executor serves alone. In case both original executors are unavailable, you should, however, name a successor executor.

Another problem that can arise as a result of naming co-executors is that they may disagree. Should this occur, the disagreement will be resolved by the probate court. Of course, it's wise to appoint people who can work together so as to minimize the possibility of this happening.

Another alternative to dealing with the potential problems caused by naming co-executors is to custom draft will provisions to deal with them in advance. For example, if you think that co-executors are likely to disagree in particular areas, you can provide that one has the right to override the other. Or, if you don't want one co-executor to serve as your sole executor if the other becomes unavailable, you can provide for a substitute co-executor. Because these are unusual needs, I recommend that you consult a lawyer to review the necessary language you've drafted regarding co-executor's powers.

Note: If you do choose co-executors, you'll need to use the "assemble-the-clauses" format of Chapter 12 rather than the simpler format of Chapter 11.

 Because of coordination problems, I advise against naming more than two executors. If you have personal reasons why you feel you want three or more executors, discuss this with an attorney.

If you own real estate in another state than the one you're living in, you may want to name a separate executor (called an "ancillary executor") to handle matters in that state. This is because separate estate distributions proceedings must be initiated in the state where real property is located. For instance, if you're living in Nebraska when you die, but own some real estate in Iowa, there will be probate proceedings in both states.

 If you do wish to appoint an ancillary executor, see an attorney.

You may decide to appoint your executor to act in other capacities for you. For example, if you decide to prepare a durable power of attorney (see Chapter 8, Section G), you may authorize your executor to be the person to make financial and health care decisions for you if you become incapacitated. Or, if you create a trust for your minor children, you may well want your executor to be the trustee too. Before that choice is finalized in your will, you'll have become familiar with durable powers of attorney and trusts for children, and you'll have discussed all this with the person you choose as executor, and received his or her agreement to your plans.

B. Naming Your Executor

GET YOUR PENCIL READY. Here you list the name and address of your choice for your executor, and then successor executor. How you'll actually put this into your will is explained in Chapter 11 or 12.

NAMING A SINGLE EXECUTOR

_____
Executor's Name

_____
Executor's Address

_____
Successor Executor's Name

_____
Successor Executor's Address

NAMING CO-EXECUTORS

_____
First Co-Executor's Name

_____
First Co-Executor's Address

_____
Second Co-Executor's Name

_____
Second Co-Executor's Address

_____
Successor Executor

_____
Successor Executor's Address

CHAPTER 4

WHAT PROPERTY IS YOURS TO

GIVE BY WILL?—OWNERSHIP LAWS

A. Introduction   4/1
B. Property You Cannot Dispose of by Your Will   4/3
C. Gifts to Charities   4/3
D. Marital Property Ownership Laws   4/4
E. Marital Property in Community Property States   4/5
F. Marital Property in Common Law States   4/9
G. When Spouses Move from State to State   4/13

A. Introduction

TO PREPARE YOUR WILL, YOU FIRST NEED to figure out what you own, what it's worth, and what you owe. You'll do this in the next chapter. But before you do, it's important that you review the rules governing property ownership discussed in this chapter. There are several principle reasons for doing this. One is that obviously you can't leave property you don't own. In addition, you want to be sure you're not violating any law by giving away property you do own.

What you own is determined by state property ownership laws. Many readers, married or single, will find these laws raise no problems for them. If, as you read the preliminary sections of this chapter, you learn that your property situation is simple, you can skip the rest and move on to Chapter 5.

1. Unmarried People

If you're single, have no minor children and own all your property outright, with no shared ownership, you should have little problem with any state law ownership issues. You're free to leave your property to whatever people or institutions you wish. However, if you own any property in shared ownership—such as property in joint tenancy[1] tenancy in common,[2] or in partnership—you'll need to understand how this shared ownership affects your right to give away this property by your will.

Insurance, pensions and retirement accounts where you have named a beneficiary are other types

---

[1]Joint tenancy is a form of property ownership by two or more persons where surviving owners automatically inherit the share of a dead owner. This important estate planning concept is discussed in more detail in Chapter 8.

[2]Tenancy in common is, basically, all shared property ownership except joint tenancy, tenancy by the entirety, and community property. This concept is also discussed in Chapter 8.

of property that can't be disposed of by will. I discuss these in Section B, below.

Before you decide that as a single person you can safely skip most of this chapter, do be sure you're single. A surprising number of people aren't absolutely sure whether they're married or not. Problems with making this determination commonly occur in three circumstances:

- Many people have been told, have heard, or somehow believe they're divorced, but have never received a final divorce decree to confirm it. If you're in this situation, call the court clerk in the county where the divorce was supposed to have occurred and get the records. If you can't track down a final decree of divorce, it's best to assume you're still married;

- A great number of people believe they're married by common law. Most aren't. Common law marriages are valid only in the following states.[3]

Alabama	Ohio
Colorado	Oklahoma
District of Columbia	Pennsylvania
Georgia	Rhode Island
Idaho	South Carolina
Iowa	Texas
Kansas	Utah
Montana	

Even in these states, merely living together isn't enough to create a common law marriage; you must intend to be married.

 Some people don't know if their divorce is legal. This is particularly true of Mexican and other out-of-country divorces where only one person participated. This is a complicated area and beyond the scope of this book. If you have any reason to think that your former spouse might claim to be still married to you at your death, see a lawyer. In the meantime, for the purposes of making your will, assume you're still married.

---

[3]In New Hampshire, common law marriage exists if a couple has lived together for at least three years, and one dies without leaving a will.

2. Married People

Married people's property ownership situations are often more complex than single people's because spouses typically own property together. In community property states (see Section E below), spouses typically share property ownership even though only one spouse's name is on the title slip or deed. In addition, as is discussed in detail in Section F below, in the 41 non-community property states, one spouse usually has a legal right to take a portion of the other's property at death even if that spouse attempts to leave it to someone else.

While these issues are important, there is no reason to become anxious about them. Indeed, if you and your spouse plan to leave all, or the great majority, of your property to each other, it may not be crucial to understand who legally owns each item of property. After all, as long as the survivor will get it all, what's the difference? However, in general, you should know who owns what, and in what proportion, before you make your will. Otherwise, your intentions as to who should inherit your property other than your spouse may be substantially frustrated. How to determine what each spouse owns is covered in detail in Sections D through G of this chapter.

Divorce Note: If you get divorced, is your will automatically revoked as to your (now) former spouse? Not necessarily. The answer depends on which state you live in. In a majority, divorce does automatically revoke a will's provisions as to a former spouse. But in a few states, divorce doesn't revoke the will as to the former spouse. Worse, in several others, divorce revokes the entire will. The moral here is simple: Regardless of the state you live in, if you get divorced, redo your will.

B. Property You Cannot Dispose of by Your Will

AS MENTIONED, THERE ARE CERTAIN TYPES OF PROPERTY you cannot give away by your will, because that property is owned in a form where a legally binding disposition has already been made. If you try to give these types of property through your will, that gift will be void and of no effect. So it's obviously important that you clearly understand what property cannot be subject to your will. Fortunately, as you'll see, most of these restrictions are obvious.

1. Property Where You Have Already Designated a Named Beneficiary or Beneficiaries

The most common example here is life insurance. You cannot give your life insurance proceeds via a will to someone different than the beneficiary(ies) you specified in your policy.

Other types of property where you normally name beneficiaries outside of will provisions include pension plans, retirement benefits (public, corporate or private, such as IRAs), and certain bank accounts where you name a beneficiary to receive the account when you die. These are commonly called "pay-on-death" accounts or "Totten Trusts" and are discussed in Chapter 8, Section D(2).

2. Property Transferred by Joint Tenancy or a Living Trust

This heading refers to property transferred by estate planning devices (see Chapter 8) designed to avoid probate. The two primary methods are joint tenancy and living (inter vivos) trusts.

Joint tenancy is a form of shared ownership of property in which the surviving owner(s) automatically own the interest of a deceased owner. If you attempt in your will to leave your share of joint

tenancy property to someone other than the surviving owner(s), that gift is void and has no effect.[4]

A living trust is a trust created while you're alive, not after you die (i.e., not created by your will). To put it simply, a trust is an arrangement by which property is formally given to a trustee (who can be the owner of the property), who is responsible for managing the property for the benefit of someone else, called a "beneficiary." Property you transfer to a living trust cannot subsequently be disposed of by your will unless the living trust is terminated by you prior to your death.

3. Property Controlled By Binding Contractual Agreements

Property specifically controlled and limited by a contract cannot be disposed of in violation of that contract's terms. A common example is a partnership interest. The partnership agreement (a contract) may impose limits on your ability to dispose of your interest by will. For example, the surviving partners may have the right to buy a deceased partner's interest at a "fair market value." The deceased partner can, of course, specify in her will who is to receive the money obtained from this sale.

C. Gifts to Charities

HERE'S ANOTHER BIT OF LAW YOU MAY NEED TO KNOW regarding legal limits on your ability to give away your property—restrictions on gifts to charities. These laws are a holdover from centuries past. It used to be that gifts to charitable institutions (e.g., churches, hospitals, educational institutions) couldn't be made:
1. within a certain time prior to death (e.g., within a year), or
2. in excess of a certain percentage of a total estate. These rules were enacted primarily to discourage churches and other charitable organizations from using unfair means, such as promising elderly people a place in heaven, to fill their own coffers

---

[4]Unless all joint tenants die simultaneously, discussed in Chapter 6, Section J.

at the expense of a surviving family. While most states have entirely done away with these restrictions, a few haven't. These are:

District of Columbia	Mississippi
Florida	Montana
Georgia	Ohio
Idaho	

 If you're in one of these states, you should check with an attorney if you desire to leave a large part of your estate (certainly more than half) to a charitable institution, especially if you believe your spouse or children will object or that you may not have too long to live at the time you make your will. However, if you're leaving a relatively small percentage of your estate to charity, you needn't worry about these restrictions no matter where you live.

D. Marital Property Ownership Laws

AS NOTED, MANY ISSUES OF PROPERTY OWNERSHIP at death involve marriage rights and laws. Why is marriage so crucial to the rules covering how you can leave your property (by the way, why don't they mention this in romantic Hollywood movies or love songs)? For two reasons:

• First, your spouse may already own some property you believe is yours.

• Second, your spouse may have rights to inherit a share of your property, whether you like it or not.

In both situations, state law determines what is yours to leave by will and what is not. This means that if you're married (this includes everyone who hasn't received a final decree of divorce or annulment), it's important that you understand the marital property laws:

• Of the state where you're domiciled (permanently living, i.e., your home), and

• Of any state where you own real estate. This is important because the marital ownership laws applicable to real estate are the laws of the state where the real estate itself is located, no matter where you live.

 A valid prenuptial contract can vary the normal marital property law of your state as you and your spouse agree in the contract. If you have such a contract and are in doubt as to how its provisions affect your right to leave property in your will, see a lawyer.

States can be broadly divided into two types for the purpose of deciding what is in your estate when you die:

COMMUNITY PROPERTY STATES	COMMON LAW STATES
Arizona	All other states
California	(and the District of
Idaho	Columbia) except
Nevada	Louisiana
New Mexico	
Texas	
Washington	
Wisconsin[5]	

If you live (or own real estate) in a community property state, you should read Section E. If you live (or own real estate) in a common law state, you should read Section F. Most readers needn't read both sections. If you have moved, while married, from a community property state to a common law state, or vice versa, also read Section G of this chapter.

---

[5]Although the terminology is different, Wisconsin has adopted a marital property act much like those found in community property states.

E. Marital Property in Community Property States

REMINDER: ONLY MARRIED PEOPLE who live or own real estate in a community property state need read this section.

The basic rule of community property law is simple: During a marriage all property acquired by either spouse is owned in equal half shares by each spouse, except for property received by one spouse by gift or inheritance. This marital property concept derives from the ancient marriage laws of some European peoples, including the Visagoths, passing eventually to Spain, and through Spanish explorers and settlers, to some Western states. In a somewhat different form, this concept has been adopted by Wisconsin.

The other type of ownership possible in community property states is "separate property," that is, property owned entirely by one person. A married person residing in a community property state can own separate property. For example, property owned before a marriage remains separate property even after the marriage. Also, property can be given as "separate property" to one spouse by a will or gift.

Thus, in community property states, what you own typically consists of all of your separate property and one-half of the property owned as community property with your spouse. Together, this is the property you can leave in your will. Obviously, then, it's extremely important that you know what property falls in the community property category and what is legally classifiable as your separate property.

For many couples who have been married a number of years, determining what is community property and what is separate is relatively easy. The lion's share is community, as most, or all, property owned before marriage is long gone and neither spouse has inherited or been given any substantial amount of separate property. Still, even if you believe this is your situation, I recommend that you take a moment to read the next few pages to be sure.

1. Community Property Defined

The following property is community property:

- All employment income received by either spouse during the course of the marriage;[6]
- All property acquired with employment income received by either spouse during the course of the marriage (but not with income received during a permanent separation);
- All property which, despite originally being separate property, is transformed into community property under the laws of your state. This transformation can occur in several ways, including when one spouse makes a gift of separate property to the community (e.g., changing the deed of a separately-owned home to community property) or when separate property gets so mixed together with community property that it's no longer possible to tell the difference (lawyers call this "commingling").

The one major exception to these rules is that all community property states, except Washington, allow spouses to treat income earned after marriage as separate property if they sign a written agreement to do so and then actually keep it separate (as in separate bank accounts). Most people don't do this, but it does happen.

2. Separate Property Defined

All property owned by either spouse prior to marriage, or property one spouse receives after marriage by gift[7] or inheritance, is separate property as long as the spouse in question keeps this property separate and doesn't mix (commingle) it with community property. As mentioned, if commingling occurs, separate property may turn into community property.

There are some differences between community property states regarding classification of certain types

---

[6]This generally only refers to the period when the parties are living together as husband and wife. From the time spouses permanently separate, most community property states consider newly-acquired income and property as the separate property of the spouse receiving it.

[7]Community property can be transformed into separate property and vice versa by means of gifts between spouses. Further, one spouse's separate property can be given to the other spouse as his separate property. The rules for how to do this differ from state to state. The trend is to require that this sort of gift be made in writing.

of property. One of the biggest is that in California, Arizona, Nevada, New Mexico and Washington, any income from separate property during a marriage is also separate property. In Texas and Idaho, income derived from separate property during a marriage is considered community property.[8]

Pension Note: Generally, pensions are considered to be community property, at least the proportion of them attributable to earnings during the marriage. However, certain major federal pension programs, including Social Security and Railroad Retirement, aren't considered community property because federal law considers them to be the separate property of the employee. Military and private employment pensions, on the other hand, are considered to be community property.

3. Examples Illustrating Community and Separate Property Ownership

Many, indeed most, married couples have little difficulty determining what is community property. But if there's any confusion or uncertainty, it's best to resolve it while both spouses are still living. After you discuss and resolve any problems, you should write out and sign a "Marital Property Agreement" setting forth your determinations.[9]

Here are some examples to help you and your spouse better understand how community property principles apply to your property.

[8]Wisconsin's statutes on this point are confusing; if this point matters to you, see a Wisconsin lawyer.
[9]Sample agreements for Californians are contained in *California Marriage and Divorce Law* by Warner, Ihara & Elias (Nolo Press).

Example 1: You're living in a community property state and your property consists of the following:

- A computer inherited by your spouse during marriage;

- A car you purchased prior to marriage;

- A boat, owned and registered in your name, which was purchased during your marriage with your income;

- A family home, which the deed states that you and your wife own as "husband and wife" and which was also purchased with your earnings.

Your net "estate" (all the property you're free to give away at death) consists of the car, one-half the boat and one-half your equity in your family home. Why? The car was yours before the marriage and is thus separate property; the boat was purchased with community property income (i.e., income earned during the marriage); and the home was both purchased with community property income and is owned as husband and wife. The computer, on the other hand, was inherited by your spouse and is therefore her separate property.

Example 2: James is married to Sue Ellen. They have three minor children, Peter (15), Sharon (12) and Pilar (10). James and Sue Ellen live in Arizona, a community property state. They own approximately $50,000 equity in a house (with a market value of $150,000) as "husband and wife" and a joint tenancy savings account containing $15,000. James separately owns a fishing cabin in Colorado worth $12,000, which he inherited from his father, and an Austin Healy sports car worth approximately $10,000, which he purchased before he was married. In addition, James owns several expensive items received as gifts, including a Leica 35mm SLR camera ($1,000), a stamp collection ($8,500) and a custom-built computer ($12,000).

Note: Remember, gifts and inheritances received by one spouse after marriage are the separate property of that spouse.

Using *Nolo's Simple Will Book,* James makes the
following property disposition:
- His one-half interest in the community property
  home to Sue Ellen (valued at $25,000, or one-half
  of the equity);
- His separate property fishing cabin to Sue Ellen;
- His separate property Austin Healy to his brother
  Bob;
- His separate property camera to his daughter
  Sharon;
- His separate property stamp collection to his
  daughter Pilar, and
- His separate property computer to his son Peter.

James makes no provision for his share of the
joint tenancy savings account since this passes automatically to Sue Ellen because of her "right of
survivorship" (see Chapter 8).

In addition, James would want to appoint someone as "personal guardian" for the minor children in
the event he and Sue Ellen die simultaneously or for
some other reason Sue Ellen is unable to perform this
task. This is discussed in Chapter 7.

For those of you who may have more complex
ownership problems, let's look deeper into how
community property laws operate. Again, you won't
need to pursue this subject any further if:
1. You're clear about which of your property is
   separate property and which is community
   property; or
2. You and your spouse are leaving all or most of
   their property to each other, in which case it
   doesn't make any real difference as to whether
   property is classified as separate or community.

However, if neither is true for you, then it's
important to read further.

4. Community/Separate Property Ownership Problems

In some situations, determining what is community
property and what is separate property is neither
obvious nor easy. Divorce courts churn out an endless
stream of decisions regarding the nuances of
community property rules. Here are several potential
problem areas:

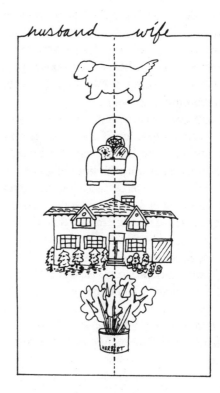

COMMUNITY   PROPERTY

Appreciated Property: In most community
property states when the separate property of one
spouse goes up in value the appreciation is also
separate property. However, if one spouse owns
separate property before a marriage, but both spouses
contribute to the costs for maintaining or improving
that property during the marriage, and the property
has substantially appreciated in value, it can be
difficult to determine what percentage of the current
value of the property is separate property and what is
community property.

The most common instance of this is a house
originally owned by one spouse. Then for a length of
time, say 10 or 30 years, both spouses pay, from
community funds, the costs for maintaining the house
(mortgage, insurance, upkeep, etc.). Over the length
of the marriage, the value of the house grows tremen-
dously. How can the spouses determine what portion
of the present value is community property? Basically,
the spouses can accomplish this by agreeing on any

division they decide is fair. If they do, they should reduce this understanding to writing. If you can't do this on your own, see a lawyer. Resolving this issue is especially important if either of the spouses plan to leave a substantial portion of the house to someone other than the other spouse.

Businesses: Family-owned businesses can create difficult problems, especially if the business was owned in whole or part before marriage by one spouse and grew later. As with home ownership, the basic problem is to figure out whether the increased value is community or separate property. Lawyers normally approach the problem like this: if both spouses work in the business, then the increase in value that the business undergoes during such period is usually community property. However, if only the spouse who originally owned the business as separate property works in it, it is often not so clear whether the increase in value of a business was due to the work of that spouse (community property) or whether the separate property business would have grown just as much anyway. If the latter is true, the increase in value could be separate property in most community property states, except Texas and Idaho, where it would also be community property.

 If you plan to leave your share of the business to your spouse, or in a way your spouse approves of, you have no practical problem. However, if your view of who owns the business is different than that of your spouse, and you don't see eye to eye on your estate plans, it's important to get professional help.

Monetary Recovery for Personal Injuries: As a general matter, personal injury awards or settlements are the separate property of the spouse receiving them, but not always. In some community property states, this money is treated one way while the injured spouse is living and another way upon his death. Also, the determination as to whether it's separate or community property can vary when the injury is caused by the other spouse. In short, there is no easy way to characterize this type of property.

 If a significant amount of your property came from a personal injury settlement and you and your spouse don't agree as to how it should be left, you'll want to check the specifics of your state's law.

Borrowed Funds: Generally, all community property is liable for debts incurred on behalf of the marriage (i.e., the community). A spouse's separate property is usually responsible for that spouse's separate debts, as would be the case if a spouse used a separate property business as collateral for a loan to expand that business. In addition, each spouse's one-half share of the community property is normally liable to pay that spouse's separate property debts. Unfortunately, it isn't always easy to determine whether a particular debt was incurred for the benefit of the community or only for the benefit of one spouse's separate property. Further, in some states such as California one spouse's separate property may be liable for debts for food, shelter and other common necessities of life incurred by the other spouse.

 If you're worried about what debts your estate may be liable for, see a lawyer.

SEPARATE PROPERTY

5. Additional Resources

Good sources of information if you're interested in pursuing this subject further are *Community Property Law in the United States,* by W. S. McClanahan (Bancroft Whitney, 1982) and *California Marriage and Divorce Law,* by Ralph Warner, Toni Ihara, & Stephen Elias (Nolo Press).

F. Marital Property in Common Law States

COMMON LAW STATES

Alabama	Maryland	Oklahoma
Arkansas	Massachusetts	Oregon
Connecticut	Michigan	Pennsylvania
Colorado	Minnesota	Rhode Island
Delaware	Mississippi	South Carolina
Florida	Missouri	South Dakota
Georgia	Montana	Tennessee
Hawaii	Nebraska	Utah
Illinois	New Hampshire	Vermont
Indiana	New Jersey	Virginia
Iowa	New York	West Virginia
Kansas	North Carolina	Wyoming
Kentucky	North Dakota	District of Columbia
Maine	Ohio	

In common law states, there is no rule that property acquired during a marriage is owned by both spouses. Common law principles are derived from English law, where in feudal times the husband owned all marital property and a wife had few legal property ownership rights and couldn't will property.

To protect a spouse from being disinherited and winding up with nothing after her spouse's death, common law states give a surviving spouse legal rights to a certain portion of the other's estate. These laws are discussed in Section F(2). If you plan to leave your spouse more than 50% of your property, these laws won't apply to you and you can skip or skim that part of this chapter.

In common law states the property you own, whether married or not, consists of:

a. Everything held separately in your name if it has a title slip, deed or other legal ownership document; and

b. Everything else you have purchased with your property or income.

Thus, in these states the key to ownership for many types of valuable property is whose name is on the title. If you earn or inherit money to buy a house, and title is taken in both your name and your spouse's, you both own the house. If your spouse earns the money but you take title in your name alone, you own it.[10] If title is in her name, she owns it.

If there is no title document to the object (say a new computer), then the person whose income or property is used to pay for it owns it. If joint income is used, then ownership is shared (generally considered to be a tenancy in common, unless a written agreement provides for a joint tenancy or tenancy by the entirety).[11]

SEPARATE PROPERTY

---

[10]Despite the general rule stated here, the courts in most states will not allow a manifest injustice to occur. Thus, if property earned by one spouse ends up in the other spouse's name, the courts may find some way (called "using their equity powers") to straighten the matter out so that justice is done. This often comes up at divorce. For example, under "Equitable Distribution" law of most common law property states, the court has power to divide marital property fairly (often equally) no matter what the ownership document says.

[11]As previously discussed, property held in joint tenancy (often abbreviated "JTWROS" or "WROS," which means "joint tenancy with right of survivorship") or tenancy by the entirety (a form of joint tenancy for married persons valid in some states), passes to the surviving joint tenant when the other joint tenant dies. This is called the "right of survivorship." Property held in tenancy in common doesn't automatically pass to the surviving tenant(s) in common. Instead, the portion belonging to the deceased owner passes under the terms of that person's will, or alternate estate planning device such as a living trust.

1. Examples of Property Ownership Rules in Common Law States

Example 1: Wilfred and Jane are husband and wife and live in Kentucky, a common law property state. They have five children. Shortly after their marriage, Wilfred wrote an extremely popular computer program that helps doctors diagnose a variety of ills. Wilfred has received annual royalties averaging about $100,000 a year over a ten-year period. During the course of the marriage, Wilfred used the royalties to purchase a car, yacht and mountain cabin, all registered in his name. The couple also own a house as joint tenants. In addition, Wilfred owns a number of family heirlooms. Over the course of the marriage, Wilfred and Jane have maintained separate savings accounts. Jane's income (she works as a computer engineer) has gone into her account and the balance of Wilfred's royalties has been placed in his account (that now contains $75,000).

Wilfred's property (his estate) would consists of the following:

- One-hundred percent of the car, yacht and cabin, since there are title documents listing all this property in his name. Were there no such documents, Wilfred would still own them because they were purchased with his income;

- One-hundred percent of the savings account because it is in his name alone;

- The family heirlooms;

- One-half of the interest in the house.[12] However, if the house was in Wilfred's name alone, it would be his property, even if purchased with money he earned during the marriage, or even if purchased with Jane's money.

Example 2: Martha and Scott, husband and wife, both worked for thirty years as school teachers in rural Michigan, a common law property state. They had two children, Harry and Beth, both of whom are grown with families of their own. Scott recently died. Generally, Scott and Martha pooled their income. They jointly purchased such items as a house, worth $100,000 (in both their names as joint tenants), cars (one in Martha's name, worth $5,000 and one in Scott's, worth $3,000), a share in a vacation condominium, worth $13,000 (in both names as joint tenants), and some of the household furniture. Each maintained a separate savings account (approximately $5,000 in each), and they also had a joint checking account with a right of survivorship, containing $2,000.

Scott spent several thousand dollars equipping a darkroom he built in the basement. Hoping that son Harry would take up his photography hobby, Scott placed the entire contents of the darkroom in a revocable living trust (see Chapter 8, Section C(2)) which passed them to Harry upon Scott's death, but which left Scott in control during his life. The remaining property left at Scott's death consisted of antiques and heirlooms that both Martha and Scott inherited from their families.

Several years before his death, Scott used the Will Book to make a will leaving his real estate and some personal property to Martha and the rest of his personal property to Beth. After his death, Martha automatically owned the house and condominium because the property was owned in joint tenancy. Again remember, where property is in joint tenancy or tenancy by the entirety, you cannot use a will to leave it to anyone other than the other joint tenant(s).[13] For the same reason, the joint checking account with an automatic right of survivorship went to Martha outside of the will. Similarly, Harry received the darkroom equipment under the terms of the living trust. Beth received Scott's savings account (regardless of the source of the funds) and the specific heirlooms and antiques that were left to her.

---

[12]Although the house is in Wilfred's estate, it would go to Jane independent of the will because of its joint tenancy status.

[13]However, in many states you can unilaterally (by yourself, without permission from the other joint tenant) terminate a joint tenancy prior to death and then leave your share of the jointly-owned property as you see fit.

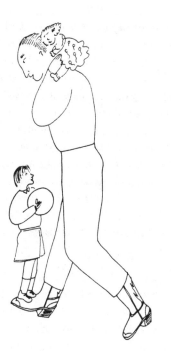

2. Family Protection in Common Law States

If you plan to leave your spouse one-half or more of your property in your will, you can skip this discussion and proceed to Chapter 5. Otherwise, read on for important information.

At first glance, it would seem there is no problem for married people in common law states when it comes to deciding what property you can leave and to whom. If your name is on the title document, or the property was acquired with your funds in the absence of such title, you own it and can leave it by will to the beneficiary of your choice, right? No, not when it comes to disinheriting a spouse. Suppose, for example, one spouse owns the house, the car and most of the possessions, including the bank accounts, in his name alone and leaves it all to a stranger (or, worse, a lover). The stranger could then kick the surviving spouse out of the house, empty the bank accounts, and so on. Of course, this rarely happens. But just in case, all common law property states have some way of protecting the surviving spouse from being completely, or even substantially, disinherited.While many of these protective laws are similar, they do differ in detail. In fact, no two states are exactly alike.

A SMIDGEN OF HISTORY

Hundreds of years ago, the English courts, confronted with the problem of a few people disinheriting their spouses, developed the rules called "dower" and "curtesy." These are fancy words for the sensible concept that a surviving wife or husband who isn't adequately provided for in a spouse's will automatically acquires title to a portion of the deceased spouse's property by operation of law. "Dower" refers to the interest acquired by a surviving wife, while "curtesy" is the share received by a surviving husband. When the United States was settled, most states adopted these concepts. To this day, all states except those that follow the community property ownership system still retain some version of dower and curtesy, although some states have dropped the old terminology. These, of course, aren't needed in community property states because each spouse already owns one-half of all property acquired from the earnings of either during the marriage.

a. Family Allowances

Some states in both categories (common law and community property) provide protection devices such as "family allowances" and "probate homesteads." These vary greatly from state to state. They may entitle the decedent's immediate family to a few hundred dollars or up to nearly $20,000. They may also give the spouse or minor children the right to live in the family home—or inherit it.

b. The Spouse's Minimum Share

In most common law property states, a spouse is entitled to one-third of the property left in the will. In a few, it's one-half. The exact amount of the spouse's minimum share often depends on whether or not there are also minor children and whether or not the spouse has been provided for outside the will by trusts or other means (see Section 3 below).

A SPOUSE'S POWER TO WAIVE STATUTORY INHERITANCE RIGHTS

In a number of states, a spouse has the legal ability to waive her or his rights to a statutory inheritance from the other spouse's estate. The waiver must be in writing. It can be done either before marriage, in a prenuptial agreement, or after marriage, in a postnuptial agreement.[15] The effect of a valid waiver is that one spouse receives whatever property the other decides to leave her or him by will, which can be far less than the statutory inheritance amount.

Statutory inheritance rights are often waived in second or subsequent marriages. Particularly if both spouses have a comfortable amount of their own property, neither may be concerned with inheriting from the other. And one or both spouses may want their property to go to other inheritors, particularly children from prior marriages.

Absent a valid spousal waiver, what happens if the person making the will leaves nothing to her spouse or leaves less than the spouse is entitled to under state law? In most states, the surviving spouse has a choice. He can either take what the will provides (called "taking under the will"), or reject the gift and instead take the minimum share allowed by the law of the particular state. Taking the share permitted by law is called "taking against the will."

Example: Leonard's will gives $50,000 to his second wife, June, and leaves all the rest of his property, totalling $400,000, to be divided between his two children from his first marriage. June can elect to take against the will and receive her statutory share of Leonard's estate, which will be far more than $50,000.

When a spouse decides to "take against the will," the property that is taken must of necessity come out of one or more of the gifts given to others by the will. In other words, somebody else is going to get less. In the above example, the children will receive much less than Leonard intended. You should understand, therefore, that if you don't provide your spouse with

---

[15] It's generally considered gauche to bring up the subject during the wedding ceremony. (Just kidding!)

---

at least his statutory or "intestate"[16] share under your state's laws, your gifts to others may be seriously interfered with.

Put bluntly, unless there's an agreement to the contrary, if you don't wish to leave your spouse at least one-half of your estate, and haven't otherwise generously provided for him or her outside of your will, your estate may be heading for a legal mess and you should see a lawyer.

3. The 'Augmented' Estate

In many common law states, the share that the surviving spouse is entitled to receive is measured by what that spouse receives both under the terms of the will and outside of the will by transfer devices such as joint tenancy and living trusts. This is called the "augmented" estate.

Example: Alice leaves her husband, Mike, $10,000 and her three daughters $100,000 each in her will. However, Alice also leaves real estate worth $500,000 to Mike by a living trust. The total Mike receives from this augmented estate, $510,000, is more than one-half of Alice's total property, so he has nothing to gain by taking against the will.

While the augmented estate concept is actually rather complicated (I've simplified it here), its purpose is clear and easy to grasp. Basically, all property of a deceased spouse, not just the property left by will, is considered in determining whether a spouse has been left his statutory share. This means that in determining whether a surviving spouse has been adequately cared for, the probate court will look to see the value of the property the spouse has received outside of probate, as well as counting the value of the property that

---

[16] As mentioned in Chapter 2, a person who dies without a will is said to have died "intestate." When this happens, there are a whole set of rules in each state about who gets what. The share that someone gets under these rules is their "intestate share." As mentioned above, in most states, a surviving spouse's intestate share depends on whether or not there are children. It typically varies between one-third and two-thirds of the probate estate.

passes through probate. This makes sense because many people devise ways to pass their property to others outside of wills, to avoid probate fees.

4. Chart of Family Law Protection in Common Law States

The chart on page 4/14 provides a cursory outline of the basic rights that states give to the surviving spouse. I don't attempt to set out the specifics of every state's law here. Also, please realize that many states' laws are quite complex in this area.

 If this issue is significant to you, see a lawyer.

States which clearly allow a spouse to waive his or her statutory rights to inherit from the other spouse's estate are identified on the chart by this symbol: •

G. When Spouses Move from State to State

WHAT HAPPENS WHEN A HUSBAND AND WIFE ACQUIRE PROPERTY in a non-community property state but then move to a community property state? California and Idaho (community property states) treat the earlier acquired property as if it had been acquired in a community property state. The legal jargon for this type of property is "quasi-community property." The other community property states don't recognize the quasi-community property concept and instead go by the rules of the state where the property was acquired.[16] Thus, if you and your spouse moved from any non-community property state into California or Idaho, all of your property is treated according to community property rules (see Section E above). However, if you moved into any of the other community property states from a common law state, you'll need to assess your property according to the rules of the state where the property was acquired.

 The opposite problem exists when couples move from a community property state to a common law state. Here each spouse generally retains his one-half interest in the property accumulated while they were married in the community property state. However, the reasoning of the courts in dealing with the problem hasn't been totally consistent. Accordingly, if you have moved from a community property state to a common law state, and you and your spouse have any disagreement or confusion as to who owns what, you'll need to check with a lawyer.

---

[16]Arizona and Texas recognize quasi-community property for dissolution (divorce) purposes, but not for will purposes.

I.   SURVIVING SPOUSE RECEIVES RIGHT TO ENJOY A PORTION (USUALLY 1/3RD) OF DECEASED SPOUSE'S REAL PROPERTY FOR THE REST OF HIS OR HER LIFE

- Connecticut   Rhode Island   Vermont
- Kentucky   South Carolina   West Virginia

II. SURVIVING SPOUSE RECEIVES PERCENTAGE OF ESTATE

a) FIXED PERCENTAGE

• Alabama	1/3 of augmented estate
• Alaska	1/3 of augmented estate
• Colorado	1/2 of augmented estate
• Delaware	1/3 of estate
District of Columbia	1/2 of estate
• Florida	30% of estate
• Hawaii	1/3 of estate
Iowa	1/3 of estate
• Maine	1/3 of augmented estate
• Minnesota	1/3 of augmented estate
• Montana	1/3 of augmented estate
• Nebraska	1/2 of augmented estate
• New Jersey	1/3 of augmented estate
• North Dakota	1/3 of augmented estate
• Oregon	1/4 of estate
• Pennsylvania	1/3 of augmented estate
• South Dakota	1/3 of augmented estate
Tennessee	1/3 of estate
• Utah	1/3 of augmented estate

b) PERCENTAGE VARIES IF THERE ARE CHILDREN
   (USUALLY 1/2 IF NO CHILDREN, ONE-THIRD IF CHILDREN)

Arkansas	• Missouri
Illinois	New Hampshire
• Indiana	• New York
Kansas	• North Carolina
• Maryland	Ohio
Massachusetts	Oklahoma
• Michigan	Virginia
Mississippi	• Wyoming

III. ONE YEAR'S SUPPORT, PLUS FURNITURE

Georgia

Note: States which clearly allow a spouse to waive his or her statutory rights to inherit from the other spouse's estate are identified on the chart by this symbol: •

CHAPTER 5

INVENTORY YOUR PROPERTY

A. How to Complete Your Property Chart   5/2

B. Your Property Chart   5/6

NOW THAT YOU UNDERSTAND how state property ownership laws affect you, it's time to focus on the basic job of inventorying your property. For some people with small estates or who keep all this information in their heads, this will be easy. And of course, if you plan to leave all of your property to one person, you simply don't need a detailed list of all of your property. Similarly, if you plan to make only one, or few, individual gifts and leave all the rest of your property to one person, you may not need to make a detailed list of your property.

Example: Jane wants to leave all of her woodworking tools and equipment to her friend Alice, her car to her friend Amy, and everything else she owns (that includes stocks, jewelry, money, market funds and personal household possessions) to her sister Mary. There's no reason for Jane to list each item of property she's giving to her sister.

In sum, if you find that you already know to whom you want to give what you own, you can skim, or even skip, this chapter and move quickly through the next one, where you'll name your beneficiaries. However, more typically, if you own many pieces of property and wish to divide it among several (or more) people and organizations, you'll want to carefully list both everything you own and everything you owe. A careful use of this inventory chart is also recommended if you suspect your net worth might subject you to federal estate taxation. If you want to get a better handle on this, see Chapter 8.

Listing your property means recording all your property (your assets) and your debts (your liabilities) on the chart provided in Section B of this chapter for use later when you make specific gifts in your will.[1] To help you do this, the property chart is divided into two sections, appropriate labeled "Assets" and "Liabilities." Each of these sections is then further divided into four categories designed to help you identify and value your property. Take a look at the chart now to get acquainted with how it works.

---

[1]As you complete this chart, it may occur to you that your property, ownership documents and other important papers are spread all over the place. Leaving this kind of mess at your death is almost guaranteed to make life miserable for your executor. Therefore, along with making your will, it's wise to adopt a coherent system to list and organize all your property. A convenient way to do this is to use *For the Record,* Nolo's computer recordkeeping program that allows you to easily keep track of all your legal, financial and personal records.

A. How to Complete Your Property Chart

BEFORE FILLING OUT THE PROPERTY CHART, please read the following brief discussion.

Category 1. Identify and Describe Your Property

The first category of the Assets section of the property chart is for listing your property. There are no rules that require your property to be listed in any particular form or legal language, either in the chart or in your will. The whole point is to be clear about what property you own.

1. Identify Your Personal Property

Your personal property consists of all your property except real estate. This includes your liquid assets (cash, savings accounts, etc.), all your business property (except business real estate), including "intellectual property" like copyrights, patents or trademarks, and all other non-real estate possessions you own.

You need to identify the property in sufficient detail so that there can be no question as to what the gift consists of. Let's look at some common types of personal property.

a. Bank Accounts

You can list bank accounts by any means sufficient to identify them. If you have more than one account, it makes sense to list the account number: "Bank account #78-144212-8068 at Oceanside Savings, Market St. Branch."

If you only have one account, you can identify it by bank name: "Savings Account at Bay Savings Bank."

b. Personal Possessions

Valuable Items: Items of personal property that have significant monetary, personal or sentimental value should be separately identified:

- "My collection of 19th century American coins"
- "My 1986 Mercedes Automobile, License # 123456";
- "My Tiffany lamp";
- "My gold earrings with the small rubies in them";
- "The Daumier print captioned 'Les beaux jours de la vie.'"

PORTRAIT OF AUNT ZELDA

Less Valuable Items: If you're like most people, you have all sorts of minor personal items you don't want to bother itemizing. To deal with these, you can simply list all items in a certain category (e.g., "all my tools," "all my dolls," or baseball cards, or records, or machines and equipment). Or you can simply include miscellaneous items in household furnishings and possessions.

c. Household Furnishings and Possessions

Aside from valuable items already listed, other household furnishings and possessions—from your clothes to the washer-dryer—can be listed generally: "All my household furnishings and possessions (at 12 High Street, Chicago, Illinois)"

d. Stock Accounts and Money Market Accounts

These need to be listed clearly enough so there's no question what property is referred to:

- "The money market account #6D-32 2240001, at International Monetary Inc."

- "All stock and any other assets in account #144-16-4124, at Smith Barney & Co."
- "100 shares of General Motor common stock."
- Certificate of Deposit, No. 10235, Lighthouse Savings and Loan Association, Ventura, CA.

e. Business Interests

Remember, "personal property" includes all business interests (except, of course, any real estate, which is dealt with under the real estate clause below). For many people in business for themselves, the business is their most valuable asset.

Solely-owned businesses can be listed simply by name:

"The Funjimaya Restaurant";

"The King of Hearts Bakery."

Your ownership of a shared business can be listed as:

"All my interests in the Ben-Dee partnership";

"All my shares of X Corporation."

Warning on Leaving an Interest In a Shared Business: In many cases, you can leave a solely-owned business as easily as any other property. For example:

"I give the Ace Pharmacy to my husband, George Malone, or, if he doesn't survive me, to my children, Andrew Malone and Alexis Malone."

 However, often an interest in a shared-ownership business cannot be left so simply. First, the co-owners, partners, or corporate shareholders may well have ownership, buy-out, and/or management rights that must be considered. Second, there's always the practical problem of trying to insure continuity, or survival, of the business, which often takes far more planning than deciding who to leave ownership to. If you face these problems, see a lawyer.

2. Identify Your Real Property

To describe real property, simply list its address or location. This is normally the street address, or condominium apartment number. If there's no post office address, as in the case if you own undeveloped land, simply describe the real property in normal language (e.g., my 120 acres in Lincoln County near the town of Douglas). You don't need to use the legal description from the deed.

It often happens that real property contains items that are properly classified as personal property. For instance, farms are often sold with tools and animals. If you intend your real property gift to include this personal property, indicate generally what this consists of. It's best to generally specify the large ticket items (e.g., tractor, cattle, etc.) and refer generally to the rest of the items as "personal property."

Example 1: "My 240 acre truck farm in Whitman County with all tools, animals, machines and other personal property found there at my death, except for the two bulls (that I'll give to my son, Fred)."

Example 2: "My fishing cabin on the Wild River in Maine and all the fishing gear, furniture, tools and other personal property I keep there."

Category 2. State How Your Property Is Owned

As discussed in detail in Chapter 4, it's important to identify any property that you own jointly with someone else and determine exactly how much of it you own so you know exactly what property you can transfer by will. Or, to reverse the point, it's important that you understand what property isn't eligible to be included in your will because it's owned by someone else.

Here are the major types of property ownership and the symbols you should use to record your ownership on the chart. If you have any questions about any of these, refer to Chapter 4.

1. Property You Can Leave By Will

Sole Ownership (S.O.): Property you own solely and outright. This generally includes all property in your name in common law property states (Chapter 4, Section F) and all your separate property in community property states (Chapter 4, Section E).

Tenancy in Common (T.C.): Property held in shared ownership that isn't joint tenancy or tenancy by the entirety (see Chapter 8, Section D). If the ownership deed doesn't specify the type of shared ownership, it's tenancy in common. You can leave your portion of property held as tenants in common in your will, unless restricted by a contract (such as a partnership agreement).

Community Property (C.P.): In community property states, property acquired during a marriage. You can leave your one-half share of community property to whomever you want to have it. See Chapter 4, Section E. The other one-half of the community property already belongs to your spouse and you have no power to provide for it in your will.

2. Property You Cannot Transfer By Will

Joint Tenancy (J.T.) and Tenancy by the Entirety (T.E): As previously described in Chapter 4, Section B, you cannot normally will any property owned in joint tenancy (often abbreviated as "JTWROS," meaning "joint tenancy with right of survivorship") or tenancy by the entirety. The reason for this is that the share of the first tenant to die must go to the surviving tenant(s). (For more on joint tenancy and tenancy by the entirety, see Chapter 8.) Joint tenancy and tenancy by the entirety must be spelled out in an ownership document. It's never presumed.

In the rare case of simultaneous death of joint tenants, or tenants by the entirety, the property is divided into as many shares as there are joint tenants. Then the shares are divided as if each of the tenants survived the other. So, if you want to be extra thorough, you can make provision in your will for what happens to your share of joint tenancy or tenancy by the entirety property in the event you and the other joint tenants die simultaneously. In this case, you can give your share of the joint tenancy property like any other gift you make to whomever you want (see Chapter 6).

Living Trust Property (L.T.): Property you own that you have transferred to a living trust. This property cannot be transferred by will unless you terminate the living trust (see Chapter 4, Section B and Chapter 8).

Insurance Pensions, etc. (I.P.): Insurance policies pensions and other benefits with a named beneficiary(ies), such as an IRA, or a KEOGH (see Chapter 4, Section B). You can't leave these types of property in a will.

Bank Account Trusts (B.A.T.): Bank trust accounts (sometimes called "Totten Trusts" or "Pay on Death Accounts") where you have named beneficiary(ies) to take the funds when you die. You can't leave these funds in your will unless you terminate the trust (see Chapter 8).

Most people will be able to quickly determine the legal categories their property falls into. However, occasionally, to be sure about the ownership status of a particular piece of property you may have to do some work. For example, you may have to dig out the deed to your house or stock certificates to clarify if you own property in joint tenancy or not. Never guess! If you're not sure how you own an item of property, take the time to find out. Do this even if it means you have to check real property records at the recorder's office or do similar detective work.

If you live in a community property state and are married you may have more difficult problems concerning property ownership as discussed in Chapter 4, Section E. Be sure to resolve them. For example, if you're unsure whether a $10,000 bank account is community property or your separate property, bear in mind that it matters a great deal how you and your spouse characterize it, assuming you can agree in writing.

 If your conclusions about your gifts or the value of your net estate depend heavily on characterizations of property about which you're uncertain, you should seek advice from a lawyer or accountant. Otherwise you may end up leaving property you don't own, or fail to dispose of property that you do.

Category 3. List the Percentage of Shared Property You Own

In this third category, list the percentage of each item of shared property you own. You should have just figured this out as part of filling in the information for Category 2. People who own property as tenants in common should be particularly careful, however. Since you can own any percentage of that property— from 1% to 99%—it's important you know what portion is yours. Also, this information is necessary to determine the net value of your property for tax purposes.

If the property is community property or a tenancy by the entirety, the ownership is automatically 50-50. If it's held in joint tenancy, all joint tenants own equal shares. Thus, if there are two joint tenants, the ownership is 50-50; if there are three, each owns one-third, and so on.

Category 4. Estimate the Net Value of Your Property

In this category list the "net value" of your property. Net value means your equity in your share of the property, (i.e., the market value of your share, less your share of any encumbrances on it, such as a mortgage on a house or the loan amount due on a car). Doing this not only helps you determine the value of what you have to give away in your will, but also tells you whether you're likely to be subject to death taxes, especially federal estate taxes (see Chapter 8).

Example: If you own a house with a market value of $250,000 as tenants in common with your brother and you each own half, you would compute the value of your share by first subtracting the amount of any mortgages, deeds of trust, liens, past due taxes, etc. from the market value to arrive at the total equity in the property. If you assume that there's a $100,000 mortgage and no other debts, this means that the total equity is $150,000. As you own half of the property, it follows that your share is worth $75,000.

Obviously, listing the net value of your property involves making estimates. Doing this is fine; there's no need to burden yourself with seeking absolutely precise figures. Remember, your death taxes, if any, will be based on the net value of all your property when you die, not its current worth. For example, if you think your solely owned house is worth about $200,000, your car $5,000, and your stamp collection would fetch $2,000 if you put an ad in a philatelist's journal, use those numbers. If these items are owned as community property with your spouse or in joint tenancy with your brother, divide each of these amounts in half to determine the value of your share. It's a most unusual case indeed where you'd need an appraiser to give you a valuation of any of your property at this stage.[2] At most, take a few minutes time to investigate what any particular item of property is worth.

B. Your Property Chart

REMEMBER, THIS CHART IS PURELY FOR YOUR CONVENIENCE. It can be as messy as you need to make it, as long as you know what's on it when you select your beneficiaries in Chapter 6 and draft your will from Chapters 11 or 12.

After you list all of your property, take a moment to review whether each item can be left by your will. To be sure your conclusions are correct, review the discussion under Category 2 above. Then, for each item you can leave by will, mark a W in the box. Doing this can make it quick and easy to refer back to this chart later when it comes time to actually make your will.

---

[2]Appraisals may be necessary for tax and probate purposes after you die.

PROPERTY WORKSHEET

I. Assets

Column 1 Description of Your Property	Column 2 Type of Shared Ownership	Column 3 Percentage You Own	Column 4 Net Value of Your Ownership
A. Liquid Assets			
1. cash (dividends, etc.)			
2. savings accounts			
3. checking accounts			

Column 1 Description of Your Property	Column 2 Type of Shared Ownership	Column 3 Percentage You Own	Column 4 Net Value of Your Ownership
4. money market accounts			
5. certificates of deposit			
6. mutual funds			
7. trust income			

Column 1 Description of Your Property	Column 2 Type of Shared Ownership	Column 3 Percentage You Own	Column 4 Net Value of Your Ownership

B. Other Personal Property
(all your property except liquid assets, business interests including patents and copyrights, and real estate — houses, buildings, apartments, etc.)

1. listed (private corporation) stocks and bonds

2. unlisted stocks and bonds

3. government bonds

Column 1 Description of Your Property	Column 2 Type of Shared Ownership	Column 3 Percentage You Own	Column 4 Net Value of Your Ownership
4. automobiles and other vehicles, including planes, boats and recreational vehicles			
5. precious metals			
6. household goods			
7. clothing			

Column 1 Description of Your Property	Column 2 Type of Shared Ownership	Column 3 Percentage You Own	Column 4 Net Value of Your Ownership
8. jewelry and furs			
9. art works, collectibles and antiques			
10. tools and equipment			
11. valuable livestock/animals			

Column 1 Description of Your Property	Column 2 Type of Shared Ownership	Column 3 Percentage You Own	Column 4 Net Value of Your Ownership
12. money owed you (personal loans, etc.)			
13. vested interest in profit sharing plan, stock options, etc.			
14. limited partnerships			
15. vested interest in retirement plans, IRAs, death benefits, annuities			

Column 1 Description of Your Property	Column 2 Type of Shared Ownership	Column 3 Percentage You Own	Column 4 Net Value of Your Ownership
16. life insurance			
17. miscellaneous (any personal property not listed above including trust property you can leave to others))			
C. Business Personal Property			
1. patents, copyrights, trademarks and royalties			

Column 1 Description of Your Property	Column 2 Type of Shared Ownership	Column 3 Percentage You Own	Column 4 Net Value of Your Ownership
2. business ownerships (partnerships, sole proprietorships, corporations, etc.; list separately and use a separate sheet of paper if you need to elaborate)			
name and type of business			
_____	_____	_____	_____
_____	_____	_____	_____
_____	_____	_____	_____
name and type of business			
_____	_____	_____	_____
_____	_____	_____	_____
_____	_____	_____	_____
3. miscellaneous receivables (mortgages, deeds of trust, or promissory notes held by you; any rents due from income property owned by you; and payments due for professional or personal services or property sold by you that are not fully paid by the purchaser)			
_____	_____	_____	_____
_____	_____	_____	_____
_____	_____	_____	_____

D. Real Estate

Column 1
Description of Your Property

Column 2
Type of Shared Ownership

Column 3
Percentage You Own

Column 4
Net Value of Your Ownership

address _____

address _____

address _____

Column 1 Description of Your Property	Column 2 Type of Shared Ownership	Column 3 Percentage You Own	Column 4 Net Value of Your Ownership
address			
address			
			$ ____

E. TOTAL NET VALUE OF ALL YOUR ASSETS

II. Liabilities (what you owe)

Many of your liabilities will already have been accounted for because you listed the net value of your property in Part I of this chart. For example, to determine the net value of your interest in real estate, you deducted the amount of all mortgages and encumbrances on that real estate. Similarly the value of a small business is the value after business debts and other obligations are subtracted. For th s reason, the only liabilities you need list here are those not previously covered. Don't bother with the small stuff (such as the phone bill, or what you owe on your credit card this month), which changes frequently. Just list all major liabilities not previously accounted for, so you can get a clearer picture of your net worth.

Column 1 To Whom Debt Is Owed	Column 2 Net Amount of Debt You Owe

A. Personal Property Debts

1. personal loans (banks, major credit cards, etc.)

2. other personal debts

Column 1 To Whom Debt Is Owed	Column 2 Net Amount of Debt You Owe

B. Taxes (include only taxes past and currently due. Do not include taxes due in the future or estimated estate taxes)

_____

_____

_____

_____

C. Any other liabilities (legal judgments, accrued child support, etc.)

D. TOTAL LIABILITIES [excluding those liabilities already deducted in Section I]

III. NET WORTH [Total Net Value of All Your Assets (Section I. E.) minus Total Liabilities (Section II. D.)]

CHAPTER 6

DECIDING WHO YOU WANT
TO GET YOUR PROPERTY

A.	Basic Terminology	6/2
B.	Explanations and Commentary Accompanying Gifts	6/2
C.	Restrictions on Gifts	6/4
D.	Divorce	6/4
E.	Disinheritance	6/4
F.	Shared Gifts	6/5
G.	Naming Alternate Beneficiaries	6/7
H.	Beneficiary Chart	6/9
I.	Establishing a Survivorship Period	6/15
J.	Simultaneous Death	6/16
K.	Life Estates	6/17
L.	Property You No Longer Own at Your Death	6/17
M.	When You Have Insufficient Liquid Assets To Pay Your Cash Gifts	6/18

NOW IT'S TIME TO RECORD YOUR CHOICES of who gets the property you listed in Chapter 5. This includes all children you want to make gifts to. To help you do this, I provide a chart on which you'll be asked to designate beneficiaries and alternate beneficiaries to receive the following types of gifts:

- Cash (including all money in bank and money market accounts);
- Specific personal property items, including business interests, stocks, mutual funds;
- Forgiveness of debts (a type of gift);
- Specific real property items; and
- The rest of your estate (called your "residuary estate").

When you draft your will in Chapter 11 or Chapter 12, you'll use the information from this chart to guide you in your property disposition.

Deciding who is to receive your property is the heart of preparing your will. Normally it involves making personal decisions, not legal ones. For most people, it's satisfying to make gifts[1] to those they care about. And, of course, it can be very satisfying to know you've arranged to give property you cherish to people who'll value it as much as you do. Before you decide what property you want to give to which

---

[1]For a fascinating exploration of the meanings of giving, read *The Gift: Imagination and the Erotic Life of Property*, by Lewis Hyde (Random House).

persons, some general information about leaving property in a will is in order.

A. Basic Terminology

THERE ARE SEVERAL BASIC LEGAL TERMS INVOLVED in deciding who is to receive your property. Let's define each briefly.

Beneficiary: The person(s) or organization(s) you name to receive your property.

Example: "I give $10,000 to my cousin Sean O'Reilley."

Alternate Beneficiary: A person or organization you name to receive a gift if the original beneficiary doesn't receive it (usually because that original beneficiary predeceases the will writer or doesn't survive her by some number of days designated in the will).

Example: "I give all my shares of Zeta Corporation to my cousin Sean O'Reilley, or, if he doesn't survive me by 45 days, to his daughter Barbara O'Reilley."

Barbara O'Reilley is your alternate beneficiary.

Specific Gift:[2] Specifically identified property which you give to a named beneficiary, such as the stock in the previous example. You already listed your property in Chapter 5.

Residue or Residuary Estate: What remains of your property after all specific gifts are made. The will writer's costs for death taxes, probate, and last debts are often specifically made payable from the residuary estate under the terms of the will. Some wills make few specific gifts and simply leave the bulk of their property in the residue.

Residuary Beneficiary: The person(s) and/or organization(s) you name to receive the residue of your property after your specific gifts are distributed and your debts, taxes, probate and attorney fees are paid.

---

[2]To remind you, I use the word "gift" instead of the terms "bequest" and "devise" to mean any property passed under a will.

Example: "I give my residuary estate to Caleb Hamilton."

Survivorship Period: The period of time specified in a will that a beneficiary (usually including alternate beneficiaries and the residuary beneficiary) must survive the will writer in order to legally inherit the gift. Between 45 and 180 days is a common survivorship period.

B. Explanations and Commentary Accompanying Gifts

WITH VERY FEW LIMITS, YOU CAN WILL YOUR PROPERTY however you choose. Most people simply leave their worldly goods to family, friends, and perhaps some charities. However, more inventive gifts are also possible. If you wish, you can leave some money for friends to throw a party every year on your behalf, or to sponsor a series of jazz (or classical or western) concerts. An anonymous benefactor of the college I went to earned my life-long gratitude by endowing the milk supply in the dining hall, so all us milk lovers could always have as much as we wanted.

If you wish, you can also provide commentary on your gifts. For example:[3]

I give _____ $10,000 _____ to my veterinarian, Dr. Surehands, for all her kind and competent treatment of my pets over the years _____

_____ or, if ___ Dr. Surehands ___ doesn't survive me by 45 days, to _____ .

---

[3]When I provide examples in this chapter, I employ the same format you will be using when you actually draft your will in Chapters 11 or 12. This format includes some predetermined language and underlined blank spaces where you enter information.

I give _my outboard motor_ to _my good friend Hank Pike, who always enjoyed fishing with me on the lake._

_____ or, if _Hank_ doesn't survive me by 45 days, to _____.

EXPLAINING YOUR GIFTS TO YOUR CHILDREN

You can divide up your property among your children as you see fit (unless a minor child is entitled to some money or property; see Chapter 4). If your children are already responsible adults, your prime concern will likely be about fairness—given the circumstances and the children's needs. Often this will mean dividing your property equally among your children. Sometimes, however, a parent decides to distribute property in differing shares for one of a number reasons: the special health or educational needs of one child, the relative affluence and stability of another, the fact that one child has previously been given money, or even because the parent is estranged from a child.

Doing this can sometimes raise serious worries—a child who receives less property may conclude that you cared for him or her less. To deal with this, you may wish to explain your reasons for dividing your property unequally. You can either explain your reasons in your will, or prepare a letter to accompany your will which expresses these reasons. For example:

I give my residuary estate, i.e., the rest of my property not otherwise specifically and validly disposed of by this will or in any other manner, to _40% each to my son Charles and my daughter Diane and 20% to my son Tim_ or if _any of them_ fails to survive me by 45 days, _their share shall be divided equally between the survivors. I love all my children deeply and equally. I give 20% to Tim because he received family funds to go through medical school, so it is fair that my other two children receive more of my property now._

A will can be a place for expressing your final sentiments, fond or not so fond. Short of libel,[4] the scope of your remarks is limited only by your imagination. I know of wills in which the writers expressed at some length their love for a mate, children and friends.

By contrast, Benjamin Franklin's will left his son William, who was sympathetic to England during our Revolution, only some land in Nova Scotia, and stated, "The fact he acted against me in the late war, which is of public notoriety, will account for my leaving him no more of an estate that he endeavored to deprive me of." And then there was the German poet Heinrich Heine, who wrote a will coldly leaving his property to his wife on the condition that she remarry, so that "there will be at least one man to regret my death." William Shakespeare cryptically left his wife his "second best bed," a bequest that has intrigued Shakespearean scholars for centuries.

If you decide you want to express some sentiments in your will, it's fine to do it in your own words, whenever it seems appropriate.

1. Gifts to a Married Person

When you make a gift to someone who's married, the gift is that person's individual or separate property if you make the gift only in his or her name. For example: "I give my antique clock to Mary Kestor."

This means Mary would be entitled to keep the entire gift in the event of divorce (assuming the gift had been kept separate, i.e., not commingled with other shared marital property so that the gift could no longer be separately identified). If you want to emphasize this intent, you can say: "I give my antique clock to Mary Kestor as her separate property."

By contrast, if you wish to make a gift to a married couple, simply make it in both their names. For example: "I give my silver bowl to Edna and Fred Whitman." Again, you can provide emphasis by stating: "I give my silver bowl to Mr. and Mrs. Fred Whitman, as husband and wife."

---

[4]If you libel someone in your will, your estate can be liable for damages. If you want to say something disparaging in your will, check it with a lawyer.

2. Forgiveness of Debts

One type of gift you can make in your will is to forgive a debt, i.e., release the person who owes you the debt from responsibility to pay it. Any debt, written or oral, can be forgiven. If you're married and forgiving a debt, be sure you have full power to do so. If the debt was incurred while you were married, you may only have the right to forgive half the debt (especially in community property states) unless your spouse agrees in writing to allow you to forgive his or her share of the debt as well. To forgive debts you'll need to use Chapter 12 to draft your will rather than Chapter 11.

C. Restrictions on Gifts

1. Legal Restrictions

There are only a very few legal restrictions on your power to leave property in your will. While these rarely apply, let's be extra cautious and review them briefly:

- Some felons, and anyone who unlawfully caused the death of the person who wrote the will, cannot be inheritors;
- You cannot attempt to encourage or restrain some types of conduct of your beneficiaries. For example, you cannot make a gift contingent on the marriage, divorce, or change of religion of a recipient;
- You cannot validly leave money for an illegal purpose, e.g., to establish the Institute for the Encouragement of Drug Addiction.

2. Restrictions Imposed by the Simple Will Book

 In addition to the preceding legal prohibitions on gifts, the *Simple Will Book* further limits the types of gifts you can make. Specifically, complex shared gifts, such as those discussed in Section F below, require the help of a lawyer. Probably more

significant, gifts where a beneficiary only gets the use of the property during his or her life (discussed in Section K), cannot be made by the use of the *Simple Will Book*. The desire to make a life estate gift is fairly common. It occurs when a person in a second or subsequent marriage wishes to leave property to a surviving spouse for that spouse's life only. Then, when that spouse dies, the property goes to other spouse's children from a prior marriage. For each of these types of gifts, the help of an attorney is essential.

Also, you cannot make a conditional gift using the *Simple Will Book*. For example, you cannot leave money to a nephew, Ed, if he goes to veterinary school, but, if he doesn't, to your niece Polly. The reason for this is that I believe most conditional gifts create far more problems than they solve. To continue the example of Ed, the potential animal doctor, here are just a few problems inherent in this approach: How soon must Ed go to veterinary school? What happens if he applies in good faith but fails to get in? Who decides if he's really studying? What happens to the money before Ed goes to veterinary school?

 In any situation where you want to impose conditions on a gift, someone must be responsible for being sure the conditions are fulfilled. The best way to do this is by leaving the property in a trust to be managed by a trustee. Aside from property left to your children in a simple children's trust designed to delay the age at which they inherit property to an age older than eighteen (see Chapter 7), you cannot impose these types of controls on property by using the *Simple Will Book*. Unfortunately, the types of trusts necessary to exercise such control aren't available in a self-help law format, and require the assistance of a lawyer.

D. Divorce

AS PREVIOUSLY MENTIONED, IN SEVERAL STATES a final judgment of divorce (or annulment) doesn't automatically revoke any gift made by your will to your former spouse. In a few others, it may revoke the entire will. Therefore, after a divorce you should revoke your old will[5] and make a new one. It isn't necessary to specifically disinherit a former spouse; simply leaving this person out of your will achieves the same result. Of course, if you want to emphasize your feelings, you can specifically state in your new will that your former spouse is to receive nothing from your estate.

E. Disinheritance

IN THE GREAT MAJORITY OF STATES following the common law property ownership systems, you cannot fully disinherit a spouse. These states' laws allow a surviving spouse to claim a portion of a deceased spouse's estate, no matter what the deceased spouse's will provides (this is discussed in more detail in Chapter 4, Section F). And a minor child may be entitled to inherit from you. Otherwise, you can disinherit anyone you want to. If you decide, however, to disinherit a child, or grandchild of a deceased child,[6] you must do so expressly by specifically declaring your intention in your will (e.g., "I disinherit my son, Nero, and declare he shall receive nothing from my estate"). In other words, unlike the situation with all other people, merely leaving a child (or child of a deceased child) out of your will doesn't "disinherit" that child (see Chapter 7, Section D). Again, anyone else can be disinherited simply by omitting to name him or her as a beneficiary.

Note: If you want to disinherit a child or child of a deceased child, prepare your will from Chapter 12 rather than one of the Chapter 11 form wills. Or put another way, use a Chapter 11 will only if you plan to leave at least some property to all your children and the children of any of your deceased children.

You may have heard that some lawyers recommend leaving $1 to relatives you want to disinherit. Is this legally necessary? No. There's generally no need to mention a relative, or anyone else, in your will only to leave them one dollar. If, however, you think a relative

might try to contest your will, you might leave that relative $1, to make it absolutely clear you did consider her and wanted to give no more. This same approach may be used if you don't wish to provide substantially for a child (or child of a deceased child) but don't want to disinherit him or her explicitly. This issue is specifically addressed in Chapter 7.

F. Shared Gifts

IF YOU LEAVE ALL YOUR PROPERTY IN A SERIES OF GIFTS, each designated to go to one person or organization, you don't need to worry about the troubling questions that can arise in making a shared gift and should skip this section and go on to Section G of this chapter. Because of the difficulties shared gifts can create, you should avoid making them, if possible. But what if you really do wish to leave your antique music box, or your wonderful '55 T-Bird convertible or your one major asset, your house, to all three of your children? Let's look at the problems you face when you leave one piece of property to more than one person.

1. Percentage of Ownership

The first question that arises with shared gifts is what percentage of ownership each beneficiary gets. If you want the gift shared equally, simply say so:

I give the property commonly known as _____ _1123 Elm St., Centerville_ _(my house)_____ to _my three children, Anne,_ _Rob and Tony in equal shares_

or, if _they_____ doesn't survive me by 45 days, to _my brother Fred_____.

If you don't specify the shares, it's presumed that you intended equal shares. You can, of course, divide ownership up in any way you decide:

---

[5]This is easily done by a sentence in the new will.

[6]You can disinherit all your grandchildren with parents (i.e., your children) who are alive simply by omitting those grandchildren from your will.

I give the property commonly known as _____
W 11th St (my house) and all furniture, rugs, appliances and household goods
to *40% to my spouse Mary, 20% to my son John, 20% to my daughter Mildred, and 20% to my brother Tim*
or, if *any of them* doesn't survive me by 45 days, to *the Wildlife Foundation*

If you do this, make sure your numbers add up to 100%.

2. Control

Control is the most basic problem with shared ownership. Suppose the people you've given a gift to disagree about how to use it. To return to the example of the house given to the three children, suppose two want to sell it, and another doesn't. Who prevails?

You can put provisions in your will governing this, e.g., "The house cannot be sold unless all three of my children agree on it." But often other problems follow. If two want to sell the house, but one doesn't, who has to manage the house? Does the house have to be rented at market value? Can the child who wants to keep the house live in it? If she does, must she pay the others any rent? What happens if one child dies? The difficulties of dealing with these types of complications is why I recommend against getting into specifying details of long-term control of property you leave your beneficiaries.

However, in some situations you may be confident your clause covers any problems which can arise. For example, this sort of clause probably doesn't really need a lawyer's review:

I give the property commonly known as *my antique music box,*
to *my three children to share equally. It may not be sold unless all three children agree on that sale (sharing the music box means each child shall retain possession of the music box for four months during each calendar year)*
or, if *any of them* doesn't survive me by 45 days, to *be shared between the survivors.*

If a shared gift is to be divided immediately after your death, problems of control must be resolved promptly. If you think your beneficiaries will agree on division of the property, there's no problem. For example, this sort of clause should cause no difficulties if the beneficiaries cooperate.

I give the property commonly known as *all my household furnishings and possessions equally*
to *my children Mike and Spike*
or, if *one* doesn't survive me by 45 days, to *the other*.

However, if you're worried about conflict, you can appoint someone to resolve any which arise:

I give the property commonly known as *all my household furnishings and possessions equally*
to *my children Mike and Spike, to be divided by them, or if they cannot agree, the equal division shall be made by my executor.*
or, if *one* doesn't survive me by 45 days, to *the other*.

Another way to deal with this situation is to discuss it with the proposed beneficiaries. If there's genuine agreement between them, potential problems are less likely to become real ones. If you conclude there's genuinely no risk of conflict, you can simply make the shared gift without any conditions or directions, leaving it entirely up to the beneficiaries to resolve any problems.

If you don't spell out in your will how these questions are to be resolved (for example, by the executor), and if the beneficiaries can't agree, the courts will decide for you. For example, if co-owners disagree about selling a house, any of them has the right to obtain a court order directing that the house be sold and the proceeds divided among the co-owners.

 In general, you should have any clauses you draft concerning controls over a shared gift reviewed by a lawyer. A lawyer can also tell you the rule that governs shared ownership in the absence of instructions in your will.

G. Naming Alternate Beneficiaries

WHAT HAPPENS IF A PERSON (OR PERSONS) NAMED in your will to receive a gift fails to survive you? Who gets the property? Should you address this contingency in your will? For most people, the answer is "yes." They name alternate beneficiaries to receive gifts if their first choice dies before they do. Doing this is sensible for a number of reasons. Perhaps you've made some gifts to older people, or relatives in poor health who may not survive you. Or you don't want the bother of redoing your estate plan if the unlikely occurs and a younger beneficiary dies before you. Or you're concerned that you might not have time, before your own death, to revise your estate plan after a beneficiary dies.

On the other hand, some people who decide they don't want to worry about their beneficiaries dying before they do decide not to name alternate beneficiaries. This decision is especially likely if the beneficiaries are considerably younger. Also, many people figure that if a beneficiary does die before they do, they'll normally have time enough to modify their will, trust or other document to name a new beneficiary.

Finally, there's another reason why you may choose not to name alternate beneficiaries. All wills prepared from the Simple Will Book provide that if the primary beneficiary fails to survive you by the

period indicated in the will,[7] and you haven't named an alternate beneficiary, the gift becomes part of the residue and goes to your residuary beneficiary. Thus, assuming your residuary beneficiary is the person you want to receive a particular gift if the primary beneficiary dies, you've already named an alternate beneficiary for that gift and don't need to do it a second time. However, when your residuary beneficiary is a person (as opposed to a charity or other institution), it's always wise to name an alternate residuary beneficiary in case your first choice doesn't survive you.

Example: Betsy McCray leaves a gift of $10,000 to her friend Daniel Carlan. Her will names her daughter, Kendell McCray, as her residuary beneficiary, and her other daughter, Sara, as her alternate residuary beneficiary. Betsy doesn't name any specific alternate beneficiary because she wants Kendell or Sara to have the property, if Daniel fails to survive her by 45 days. If this occurs, the $10,000 gift becomes part of the residue. Betsy would enter this information for the gift to Daniel in the Beneficiary Chart in this chapter as follows:

$10,000 to David Carlan
Amount   Beneficiary

(left blank)
Alternate Beneficiary

Assuming you don't want your residuary beneficiary to inherit all of your property should all of the people you've named to inherit your gifts fail to survive you by the period specified in your will, this book offers you the opportunity to name an alternate beneficiary for each gift. There are different considerations for naming alternate beneficiaries for a shared gift than for a gift to a single beneficiary. Because the overwhelming number of readers will prefer to follow my advice and make each gift to a single individual, I'll first tell you how to handle this. Then, in subsec-

---

[7]All wills in Chapter 11 provide for a survivorship period of 45 days. The reason why this survivorship period is chosen is discussed in Section I of this chapter. If you're using Chapter 12 to make your will, you can set this survivorship period yourself.

tion 2 below, I'll show you how the wills in this book help you handle alternate beneficiaries for shared gifts.

1. Alternate Beneficiaries for Individual Gifts

To name an alternate beneficiary for a gift to an individual, simply enter that person's or organization's name on the appropriate line in the worksheet in this chapter. Then, when you make your will using either the Chapter 11 or Chapter 12 approach, you'll follow instructions and transfer this information to the appropriate will clause. Please reassure yourself by turning over a few pages and taking a look at how simple the worksheet really is and that none of this is particularly difficult.

Example 1: Sal Benito decides to leave her antique piano to her brother Tim Jones. In case Tim fails to survive her by 45 days, Sal wants her sister Ruth Jones as alternate beneficiary. At this point, she simply enters this information in the appropriate box on the Beneficiary Chart as follows:

my antique piano _____ to
Item
Tim Jones _____
Beneficiary(ies)
Ruth Jones _____
Alternate Beneficiary(ies)

There's no rule regarding who you should name as alternates for gifts made to individuals; that's up to you. For example, many people will divide the bulk of their property among their children. As an alternate beneficiary for each particular piece of property left to one child should that child fail to survive them by the period specified in the will, these people will name their other child (or children). Others will prefer to deal with this same possibility by designating the children of the deceased child (their grandchildren), or a friend as alternate beneficiaries.

Example 2: Sal Benito prepares a will leaving her house to her son Peter Benito. In case Peter doesn't survive her by 45 days, Sal names her other child, Peggy Abrams, as alternate beneficiary. She would do this on the Beneficiary Chart as follows:

my house at 11 Garden Lane, Boston to
Property Address
Peter Benito _____
Beneficiary(ies)
Peggy Abrams _____
Alternate Beneficiary(ies)

If possible, I advise naming just one person or institution as alternate beneficiary for each gift. If, however, you really do want the gift to go to more than one person should the primary beneficiary fail to survive you by the period specified in the will, you can accomplish this by naming both or all of them. It's best to do this by naming each person individually rather than using a general term such as "all my other children." However, if your child Mary, a beneficiary, has one child and may have more, you can name as alternate beneficiaries (should Mary fail to survive you) "her children, in equal shares."

Example 3: Sal Jones' will leaves her summer home to Ruth Abrams. If Ruth doesn't survive her by 45 days, Sal's will provides that the alternate beneficiaries are "Ruth Abram's children, in equal shares." She would accomplish this on the Beneficiary Chart as follows:

my summer home at Old Forge Pond, New York to
Property Address
Ruth Abrams _____
Beneficiary(ies)
Ruth Abrams' children in equal shares
Alternate Beneficiary(ies)

 All this seems simple enough, and it usually is. However, if you want to move to the next level of contingencies, it can get complicated. To continue with Example 3, suppose Sal wants to consider what happens if both Ruth and one of Ruth's children fail to survive her by the required period. Or Sal wants to impose controls over the gift if Ruth's children receive it because Ruth has failed to survive her. Handling these types of remote contingencies is tricky, and if you want to get in this deep, you'll need to see a lawyer. However, frankly, I think a more sensible way to handle these types of unlikely-to-occur contingencies is to keep your will up to date.

2. Alternate Beneficiaries for Shared Gifts

When it comes to shared gifts, providing an alternate beneficiary is more complicated. The reason is that more than one possibility must be provided for. The best way to appreciate this is to suppose that you leave your house in equal shares to A, B, and C. What happens if B dies? Does the house go equally to A and C, or equally to A, C, and B's children, or does B's share go to another named alternate beneficiary or the residuary beneficiary? And, if this isn't enough complexity for you to think about, consider the question of what happens if A and B, or even A, B and C all fail to survive you by the period specified in the will.

Clearly, a little order is needed so you don't give up and run to a lawyer. The *Simple Will Book* provides this order by simplifying your choices. In all shared gift situations, the wills in this book state that if one of the named beneficiaries dies before you do, the other or others divide(s) that person's share. Thus, to return to the example above, if you make a gift to A, B and C, and B predeceases you, A and C share the entire gift. Only if A, B and C all fail to survive you by the period specified in the will does an alternate named by you in your will take the gift.

Example: Ethel Turk is a widow with three children, Maude, Patricia and Elliot. Ethel leaves her house to all three in equal shares. She names her close friend Mary Rogers as alternate beneficiary. If Maude fails to survive Ethel by the period specified in the will, and Ethel doesn't change her will, Patricia and Elliot will jointly inherit the house and Mary Rogers will inherit nothing. Mary will only get the house if Maude, Elliot

and Patricia fail to survive Ethel by the requisite period and Ethel doesn't change that provision in her will.

 As mentioned above, while the method I provide should meet most people's needs, there are other ways to take care of shared gifts should one of the group of named beneficiaries predecease you. Many of these are quite complicated and are outside the scope of this book. See a lawyer if you need to write a provision for alternate beneficiaries for shared gifts.

H. Beneficiary Chart

OKAY, IT'S TIME TO START TO PIN DOWN who'll receive your property. In the following chart you'll list your property, using descriptions from the chart in Chapter 5.[8] First identify each item of your property you want to give as a distinct gift. Then list a beneficiary or beneficiaries for each item. Use full names and provide extra identification if the names are extremely common or there may otherwise be confusion as to who you mean. You don't normally need to list addresses unless you think the beneficiary might be hard for your executor to find. If you give one item of property to be shared by more than one beneficiary, be sure you've considered the concerns discussed in Section F. After naming your primary beneficiary or beneficiaries, you can put down your choice for an alternate, as outlined in Section G above.

After you go through the first four sections of the Beneficiary Chart and make all specific gifts of personal and real property, name alternate beneficiaries and forgive debts (if desired), you'll use Section 5 to name your residuary beneficiary. This person, or persons, receives all property that you haven't otherwise given away in your will. Some people choose to make only a few specific gifts—heirlooms or cash gifts, for example—and leave the bulk of their estate to spouses or children through a residuary clause. More typically, people will make a number of specific

[8]Of course, if you didn't use this chart because of the simplicity of your desires or property situation, there is no need to return to that chapter.

gifts and name a residuary beneficiary to take what's left over.

1.   Minor or Young Adult Beneficiaries

If you name a minor (a child under 18) as a beneficiary or alternate beneficiary, you'll need to impose some form of adult supervision over that gift. You'll handle that matter in Chapter 7. Here you need only decide who you are making gifts to.

Similarly, you can impose mature supervision over gifts you made to younger adults (for the purpose of the *Simple Will Book,* defined as under age 35) by use of a trust. Again, how you can do this is explained in Chapter 7.

2.   Simple Beneficiary Situation

In many situations in which you plan to leave all of your property to one person, or divided between several, completing the chart will be very easy. Simply list the beneficiary, or beneficiaries, as your residuary beneficiaries. Then, when you complete your will, you won't make any specific gifts at all. All your property will pass under the residuary clause.

Example: "I give my residuary estate . . . to my wife Zelda Hadly, or, if she fails to survive me by 45 days, to my son Joe and daughter Mary in equal shares."

Except in a simple beneficiary situation, before you name a residuary beneficiary, keep in mind that:

1. The residue of your estate may contain a great deal of property. Everything you own at your death that isn't otherwise given away is included in the residue. That includes property you overlook when you make your will, or that you acquire later, or that for some reason cannot go to the persons you specifically willed it to. Also, the value of the residue can increase substantially if the value of residual property (stock or land, for example) goes up.

2. The residue is commonly the first thing to be used to pay for your taxes, debts, and specific monetary gifts if you haven't specified an adequate source of funds to accomplish this. In addition, while

the rule varies from state to state, in most states, any shortfalls in specific gifts of money are made up first from the residue, unless you state in the will a different preference. The same may be true if a spouse is eligible to take against the will and decides to do so (see Chapter 4, Section F).

Note: Chapter 12 contains clauses that allow you to specify that you want any shortfalls in money to be dealt with in other ways.

3.   Completing the Beneficiary Chart

Okay, now it's time to fill in the chart. To do so, follow these steps:

Step 1: Make your cash gifts, specifying the amount, the names of the primary beneficiaries, and the names of the alternate beneficiaries. Make sure the total amount of your cash gifts is in line with the total value of your liquid assets (e.g., bank accounts, bonds, stocks, etc) as described in the Chapter 5 property inventory chart.

Step 2: Turn back to the property chart you prepared in Chapter 5.

Step 3: Transfer each item (or category of items) that you want to make a specific gift of from that chart to this chart according to its item # and a brief shorthand description.

Example: Under item #10 on the Chapter 5 property chart, Tom Jones describes his car as follows: "1968 Mustang Convertible, Red, I.D. # D23769523, Lic. # 1DSF234." Tom transfers that item to this chart as follows: "#10-Mustang."

Step 4: Name primary beneficiary or beneficiaries.

Step 5: Name alternate beneficiary or beneficiaries.

Step 6: If you wish to forgive debts, enter the appropriate information in Part 3 of the chart.

Beneficiary Chart

1.   Specific Cash or Liquid Asset Gifts

_____ to _____
Amount   Beneficiary

_____
Alternate Beneficiary

_____ to _____
Amount   Beneficiary

_____
Alternate Beneficiary

_____ to _____
Amount   Beneficiary

_____
Alternate Beneficiary

_____ to _____
Amount   Beneficiary

_____
Alternate Beneficiary

_____ to _____
Amount   Beneficiary

_____
Alternate Beneficiary

_____ to _____
Amount   Beneficiary

_____
Alternate Beneficiary

_____ to _____
Amount   Beneficiary

_____
Alternate Beneficiary

_____ to _____
Amount   Beneficiary

_____
Alternate Beneficiary

_____ to _____
Amount   Beneficiary

_____
Alternate Beneficiary

_____ to _____
Amount   Beneficiary

_____
Alternate Beneficiary

2. Gifts of Specific Personal Property

_____ to

Item

_____

Beneficiary(ies)

_____

Alternate Beneficiary(ies)

_____ to

Item

_____

Beneficiary(ies)

_____

Alternate Beneficiary(ies)

_____ to

Item

_____

Beneficiary(ies)

_____

Alternate Beneficiary(ies)

_____ to

Item

_____

Beneficiary(ies)

_____

Alternate Beneficiary(ies)

_____ to

Item

_____

Beneficiary(ies)

_____

Alternate Beneficiary(ies)

_____ to

Item

_____

Beneficiary(ies)

_____

Alternate Beneficiary(ies)

_____ to

Item

_____

Beneficiary(ies)

_____

Alternate Beneficiary(ies)

_____ to

Item

_____

Beneficiary(ies)

_____

Alternate Beneficiary(ies)

_____ to

Item

_____

Beneficiary(ies)

_____

Alternate Beneficiary(ies)

_____ to

Item

_____

Beneficiary(ies)

_____

Alternate Beneficiary(ies)

_____ to

Item

_____

Beneficiary(ies)

_____

Alternate Beneficiary(ies)

_____ to

Item

_____

Beneficiary(ies)

_____

Alternate Beneficiary(ies)

_____ to

Item

_____

Beneficiary(ies)

_____

Alternate Beneficiary(ies)

_____ to

Item

_____

Beneficiary(ies)

_____

Alternate Beneficiary(ies)

3. Debts Forgiven

_____ to   _____
Amount Forgiven   Debtor

_____
Date of Loan

_____ to   _____
Amount Forgiven   Debtor

_____
Date of Loan

_____ to   _____
Amount Forgiven   Debtor

_____
Date of Loan

_____ to   _____
Amount Forgiven   Debtor

_____
Date of Loan

_____ to   _____
Amount Forgiven   Debtor

_____
Date of Loan

4. Gifts of Real Estate

_____ to
Property Address

_____
Beneficiary(ies)

_____
Alternate Beneficiary(ies)

_____ to
Property Address

_____
Beneficiary(ies)

_____
Alternate Beneficiary(ies)

_____ to
Property Address

_____
Beneficiary(ies)

_____
Alternate Beneficiary(ies)

_____ to
Property Address

_____
Beneficiary(ies)

Alternate Beneficiary(ies)

_____ to

Property Address

_____

Beneficiary(ies)

_____

Alternate Beneficiary(ies)

_____ to

Property Address

_____

Beneficiary(ies)

_____

Alternate Beneficiary(ies)

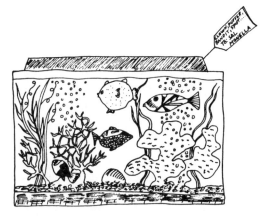

5. Residuary Beneficiary or Beneficiaries (to receive the rest of your estate after all specific gifts are made)

If you name more than one person, or one organization, to share your residue, here's what happens (under all of the wills in this book) if one of these people doesn't survive you by the number of days provided in your will. The surviving named beneficiaries of the shared residue will take the deceased beneficiary's share. In other words, in a shared residue situation, the alternate beneficiary you name will only inherit if all of the people you name to share the residue of your estate fail to survive you by the period specified in your will. This is exactly the same plan as discussed in Section G(2) above and illustrated in the example of Ethel Turk and her three children.

Reminder: It's particularly important to name an alternate residuary beneficiary. You want to be sure

you have a backup, in case your first choice, your residuary beneficiary, fails to survive you. Your residue is your "fail safe" option. If a specific gift can't be made, because the beneficiary (and alternate beneficiary, if you named one) dies before you do, that gift becomes part of your residue. But if your residuary beneficiary predeceases you, and you didn't name an alternate residuary beneficiary, you have no "fail safe" option, and your residue would have to be distributed according to state law.

Enter your choices for residuary and alternate residuary beneficiary in the spaces below.

_____

Residuary Beneficiary's Name

_____

Alternate Residuary Beneficiary

After completing the beneficiary chart, read further in this chapter if you want to know more about:
• Why survivorship periods are a good idea (Section I);
• What happens if you and your spouse die simultaneously (Section J);
• Leaving property to someone for use during his or her life only (called a "life estate") and then having it pass to someone else (Section K);

- Property left in a will that you don't own at death (Section L); or
- What happens if you don't have enough liquid assets to pay each gift (Section M).

I.   Establishing a Survivorship Period

A SURVIVORSHIP PERIOD MEANS THAT A BENEFICIARY, or an alternate beneficiary, must survive the will writer by a specified time period to inherit. One reason for imposing survivorship periods on gifts is to avoid double death taxes and probate costs. If the person to whom you leave property dies soon after you, the property will be included in his estate. The result is that the property you'd hoped the person would use and enjoy merely raises the dollar value of his estate, possibly increasing its taxes and becoming subject to additional probate fees. Also, this property now passes under the terms of your beneficiary's will, rather than being given to someone you've chosen. To avoid all this, most wills set a specific time period by which a beneficiary must survive the will writer.

Example: "I give my 1955 T-Bird to my best friend Anthony, or, if he doesn't survive me by 45 days, to my cousin, Jacques de Paris."

 All basic wills in Chapter 11 have a 45-day survivorship period for your primary beneficiaries. In a Chapter 12 will you have the opportunity to select any reasonable survivorship period you want (or none at all) to apply to all primary beneficiaries. My preference is for relatively short periods, 45 to 60 days, to be sure you haven't tied property up beyond the time practically required to transfer it. If no probate is required, as is often the case for small estates and gifts made to a surviving spouse, property can be transferred to beneficiaries in a matter of days or weeks. But since formal probate often takes at least six months (and sometimes more than one year), there are also sensible arguments for a lengthier survivorship period, say 180 days. If you want to choose a period longer than this, see a lawyer.

J.   Simultaneous Death

MANY COUPLES, MARRIED OR NOT, who will their property to each other wonder what would happen to the property if they were to die in the same accident or occurrence. The usual answer is simple. Assuming a survivorship clause is used (See Section I above), the property left to the other spouse or mate as a primary beneficiary will pass to the alternate beneficiary. If, however, either or both of you leave property to the other and there's no survivorship clause in operation, or there's no alternate beneficiary, what happens?

In the absence of a special clause (called a simultaneous death clause), your property may pass to your spouse (or mate) or vice versa. This means that your spouse's heirs will receive your property or your heirs will receive your spouse's property. Hardly the result that either of you would intend.

To prevent this from happening I recommend the use in a will of a "simultaneous death" clause, providing that when it's difficult to tell who died first, and no survivorship clause covers the gift, the property of each person is disposed of as if he survived the other.

You may ask, "How logically can a simultaneous death provision work? How can I be presumed to have outlived my spouse for purposes of my will, but then she's presumed to have outlived me for purposes of her will?" The answer to this paradox is that, under the law, each of your wills will be interpreted independently of the other. Thus, each provision in your separate wills provides the result each of you would most likely intend.

Example: Martha and George, a married couple, die in a plane wreck. Both their wills have simultaneous death provisions. Thus George's property, which he willed entirely to Martha, doesn't go to her because under the simultaneous death clause, Martha is presumed to have already been dead when George died. George's property goes to whomever he named as alternate or residuary beneficiary. This same process is repeated for Martha's property; it goes not to George but to the alternate beneficiaries.

You'll find a simultaneous death clause in the basic wills for a married couple and for a person living with a lover/mate. It's also included in the "assemble-a-will" approach in Chapter 12.

1. Simultaneous Death of Joint Tenants

What happens if people (spouses or otherwise) who own joint tenancy property die simultaneously? The property is divided into as many equal shares as there are joint tenants. Then a share is given to each owner's estate.

Example: Jim and Mary Smith, owners of a house in joint tenancy, die together in a plane crash. One half of the joint tenancy property is included in Jim Smith's estate. The other half is included in Mary Smith's estate.

Under the wills prepared from the Will Book, your share of any joint tenancy property which becomes part of your estate because of simultaneous death of you and the other joint owners becomes part of your residue and goes to your residuary beneficiary. However, you can specifically name a beneficiary for your share. An example of an express provision would be:

I give _any joint tenancy property which_
_becomes part of my estate_____ to
_____Mary Jones_____ or,
if _Mary Jones_____ doesn't survive me
by 45 days, to _Tim Jones_____ .

Remember, though, that if one joint tenant does survive the other(s), that tenant receives all the joint tenancy property, no matter what your will says.

K. Life Estates

AS PREVIOUSLY MENTIONED, THE WILL BOOK doesn't show you how to create what's called a "life estate." This is property left for the use of one beneficiary for his or her life; when the life beneficiary dies, the property passes to another beneficiary designated by the original will maker. The life beneficiary cannot leave any interest in the property in his will, because he has no interest which survives his death. Because life estates can be important to some people's estate planning needs, let's take a closer look at how they work.

Example: Marilyn James is married to Martin Smith. Marilyn has two grown children from her first marriage. Marilyn's major asset is the house she owns, which she and Martin have lived in for ten years. In Marilyn's will she leaves the house to Martin in a life estate and then to her children. This means Martin has the right to use of the house during his lifetime, but upon his death the life estate terminates and the house goes to Marilyn's children.

The usual way to create a life estate is by a trust (see Chapter 8, Section F). In the above example, Marilyn would need a life estate trust as part of her will to accomplish her desires. Drafting this type of trust may seem simple at first, but it isn't. For example, here are only a few of the questions that can arise:
- Does the surviving spouse, the one with the "life estate" interest, have the right to sell the house and buy another one?
- Suppose the surviving spouse has massive medical bills. Can he borrow money against the house (pledging it as security) to pay the bills?
- Can he rent the house?
- What right do the wife's children have to find out what the husband is doing regarding the house?

All these problems, and more, should be resolved in the language establishing the trust. There are also technical IRS requirements which must be met, and a mistake in complying with these can be disastrous in tax terms. Further, since a trust cannot be changed or amended once the will writer dies and may last for many years, a poorly drafted trust can cause all sorts of problems down the road.

 Life estate trusts are discussed in *Plan Your Estate With a Living Trust* (Nolo Press), but you'll need a lawyer to prepare one. If you do decide you want to see a lawyer to establish a life estate trust, don't just turn the whole matter over to him or her. Carefully sketch out the substance of what you want (and the contingencies you're worried about), before you see the lawyer.

L. Property You No Longer Own at Your Death

A WILL ISN'T BINDING UNTIL THE DEATH OF THE WILL WRITER. Before then, you can give away or sell any property mentioned in your will. Even if the will is never amended or re-written to recognize that you no longer own particular pieces of property, the gift or sale is valid.

But what happens when you do dispose of property and cause a discrepancy between what your will provides and the amount or type of property actually left in your estate when you die? Or putting the same question somewhat differently, what happens if at your death your will leaves people more or different property than is actually available for distribution?

If you've given someone a specific piece of property in your will (say a particular Tiffany lamp) but you no longer own that property when you die, that beneficiary is out of luck. Lawyers call this "ademption." People who don't inherit the property in question are often heard to use an earthier term.

M. When You Have Insufficient Liquid Assets To Pay Your Cash Gifts

A SIMILAR PROBLEM TO THE ONE DISCUSSED ABOVE occurs when there isn't enough money to go around. You might simply spend some of the money you left people in your will. In addition, your debts, taxes, funeral expenses, and probate fees must be paid before your gifts can be made and if all these expenses reduce your estate to less than the amount your cash gifts add up to someone is obviously out of luck. One cause for depletion of the cash in an estate occurs if a resident of a common law state leaves her spouse such a small portion of her estate that the spouse is able to "take against the will" (See Chapter 4, Section F). Another cause is when a will maker fails to either mention or provide for one of his children in his will, thus qualifying the child as an "overlooked" heir who's entitled to a share of the will maker's estate, under law (see Chapter 7).

If your will disposes of more than you have, this necessitates what's called an "abatement" in legalese. "Abatement" works as follows. Absent a specific directive by the will writer (that's you) in the will, the law of each state provides the rules for how the executor of an estate must conduct abatement proceedings. Some states require that property first be taken from the residue and sold; others first require a pro-rata reduction of cash gifts, if possible without the sale of specific objects of property. If property must be sold, unspecified property (i.e., property from your estate's residue) is generally the first to be used, then specific gifts of personal property, then specific gifts of real estate. The details of how different states reduce gifts vary too much to be covered here.

The wills in Chapter 11 allow abatement to be carried out according to the laws of each state. Chapter 12, on the other hand, contains two different abatement clauses. One provides that shortfalls in specific cash gifts are to be made up from the residue.[9] The other provides for pro-rata reduction of all cash gifts if there isn't enough money to pay them in full. If you choose the residue option, and there's a shortage of cash available to pay all cash gifts, the people who receive your residue will lose out first. If the residue is still not sufficient to account for a cash deficit in your estate, the executor is directed to abate in the most equitable (fair) way possible consistent with state law.

Example if Residuary Option Is Chosen: Paul leaves $20,000 to Steve, Stephanie, Barbara and Jack. When he dies there's only $40,000 in cash in his estate. However, Paul's estate also contains a house for which he has named no beneficiary. To pay the full amount of the cash gifts, the house must be sold. The residuary beneficiary takes what's left over after the cash gifts are paid.

Example if Pro-Rata Option Is Chosen: If you pick the pro-rata reduction clause and there isn't enough money to pay for the cash gifts, all cash gifts will be reduced by the same percentage. This percentage is determined by dividing the total amount of cash originally given in the will into the total amount actually available for making gifts.

Example: Robert makes cash bequests of $20,000 to Kate, John, Mary, and Toni. When he dies there's only $40,000 in his estate after debts and burial expenses are paid. The four beneficiaries receive $10,000 each.

If you don't include either clause, any necessary abatement will be conducted in accordance with your state's statutes.

Warning: The subject of what happens if you leave more property in your will than is actually available is far too complex to cover here in any meaningful detail. However, the overall point is simple. Don't give away more than you own, after what you owe and what your estate will need to pay in tax is subtracted. Make a new will whenever your property situation changes significantly.

 If you desire more information about how your property will be distributed in the event an abatement (reduction of gifts) is required (i.e., your estate comes up short), consult an attorney knowledgeable in such matters.

---

[9]The residue, remember, is all of your property that hasn't been specifically described and given to someone by your will.

CHAPTER 7

CHILDREN

A.	Providing For Your Minor Children	7/1
B.	Custody of Your Minor Child	7/2
C.	Leaving Property to Your Children	7/5
D.	Leaving Property to Other's Children	7/18
E.	Your Children of Any Age	7/22

THIS CHAPTER NEED BE READ only if you're concerned with children. In the context of making your will, the word "children" has two meanings. The first is "minors"—those not legal adults. Basically, minors are under age 18. The second meaning is offspring of any age. Parents obviously can have "children" who are themselves adults.

Parents of *minor children* have two concerns: who will raise the children if the parents can't, and who will supervise property the parents (or others) leave for the children? Parents of *adult children* can leave property to these children as simply as to any other adult. However, this isn't always desirable. People leaving property to young adults, often don't want them to be able to receive their property outright until they've reached an age when they can (hopefully) manage money sensibly. These people face a similar problem of providing for the supervision of property as do the parents of minors. So, in parts of Sections C and D, I explain how you can impose age controls on property you leave to younger adult beneficiaries. Section E discusses other concerns applicable to children of any age, including disinheriting children and providing for adopted or out-of-wedlock children.

A. Providing For Your Minor Children

MOST PARENTS OF MINOR CHILDREN are extremely concerned about what will happen to their children if disaster strikes and the parents die unexpectedly. Indeed, creating a legal, and personally chosen, method for handling this grim possibility is the major goal many younger parents want to accomplish by their wills. If both parents are raising the children, the major concern is usually providing for them in case of the simultaneous death of the parents. If only one parent is involved—because the other parent is deceased, has abandoned the child or is unavailable for some other reason—the single parent is similarly anxious to arrange for someone else to care for the child if that parent dies.

Providing for your minor children if you die involves two distinct concerns:

1. Providing Personal Care: Who will raise the children if you can't? In legal terms, this means who will be each child's personal guardian?

2. Providing Financial Care: How can you best provide financial support for your children? What property will be available? Who will handle and supervise it for the children's benefit? And what legal method is best for leaving it to them?

B. Custody of Your Minor Child

IF TWO BIOLOGICAL OR ADOPTIVE PARENTS[1] are willing and able to care for the child, and one dies, the other normally has the legal right to assume sole custody. This is true if the parents are married, divorced, or had never married, as long as both parents are cooperating to raise their children. But what happens if both parents die? Or suppose there's only one parent in the picture, and he dies?

If there's no parent available who's competent and willing to do the job, some other adult must become the minor child's legal manager, unless the child is legally emancipated.[2] This adult is called the child's "personal guardian." In a will, a parent can nominate the person he or she wants to serve as personal guardian for his or her children, if one is needed. This normally means that neither parent is available to take custody of the child. A parent can also nominate an alternate personal guardian, in case the first choice can't serve.

You must name your children's personal guardian in your will. You cannot use other estate planning devices, such as a living trust, for this purpose.

Most people with minor children probably know who they want to name as their child's personal guardian. However, when choosing a personal guardian and alternate personal guardian, remember the obvious: You can't draft someone to parent your kids. Be sure any person you name is ready, willing

---

[1]By "adoptive," I mean people who have legally adopted a child, not people functioning informally as stepparents.

[2]An "emancipated minor" is a minor who has achieved legal adult status. The rules for emancipation are governed by your state's laws; normal grounds are marriage, military service, or the fact that a sixteen- or seventeen-year-old is living independently with the authority of a court "emancipation" order. Emancipation is uncommon. Most importantly, for this book's purposes, you cannot emancipate your child in your will.

and able to do the job. Also, if two parents are involved, they should agree on who they want to appoint. And it's best not to name a couple as joint managers, even if they'll likely function that way. Doing this raises many potential problems, including what happens if the couple splits up.

If you're determined to appoint joint personal guardians, see a lawyer.

If a child's parents die, the person named as a minor's personal guardian in their wills doesn't become the legal guardian until formally appointed by a court. The judge has the authority to name someone other than the parent's choice if she's convinced it's in the best interests of the child. Children aren't property, and naming a personal guardian in a will doesn't have the same automatically-binding effect as a provision giving a lamp to a beneficiary. However, if no one with a superior claim contests the right, or competence, of your choice for your child's personal guardian, a court will almost certainly confirm this person. In practice, a court rarely rejects an unopposed nominee, and only if there are grave and provable reasons, such as alcoholism, or a serious criminal background. A responsible parent won't, of course, select a guardian with such problems.

For some parents, appointing a personal guardian for their minor child is, unfortunately, not cut-and-dried. If the parents are separated or divorced, one parent may not want the other to obtain custody of the child, believing someone else would be a better choice to raise the child. In other situations, parents want to name different personal guardians for different children. If you don't face one of these problems, and are confident you can now safely name your child's personal guardian and alternate guardian, proceed to Section B(3) to enter your choices. However, if you have any doubts or questions, read the material immediately below before making your choice.

1. Naming Someone to Be the Personal Guardian in Place of the Other Parent

Even if you do not want the other parent to obtain custody of your child if you die, if that parent seeks custody, he or she will usually be granted it—usually, but not always.

In an age when many parents live separately, predicaments like the following are, sadly, common:

"I have custody of my three children. I don't want my ex-husband, who I believe is emotionally destructive, to get custody of our children if I die. Can I choose another guardian?"

"I have legal custody of my daughter and I've remarried. My present wife is a much better mother to my daughter than my ex-wife, who never cared for her properly. What can I do to make sure my present wife gets custody if I die?"

"I live with a man who's been a good parent to my children for six years. My mother doesn't like this person because we aren't married and would try to get custody of the kids if I die. What can I do to see that my mate gets custody?"

There's no definitive answer to these types of questions. The personal guardian you name in your will can seek custody of the children even if the other parent is alive. However, if you die while the child is still a minor and the other parent disputes your choice in court, the judge's decision will very likely grant custody to the other natural parent, unless this parent has:

a. abandoned the child,[3] or

b. is unfit as a parent.

It's usually difficult to prove that a parent is unfit, absent serious problems such as alcohol abuse or mental illness. The fact that you don't like or respect

the other parent is never enough, by itself, to deny custody. But if you honestly believe the other natural parent is incapable of properly caring for your children, or simply won't assume the responsibility, here's how to proceed:

Step 1: Name the person you want to be your child's personal guardian in your will.

Step 2: Explain, in your will, why you're making your choice.

Example: Liz, the custodial parent of Amanda, has remarried Brad, who has raised Liz's child with her since the child was a year old. Amanda's father (Liz's ex) has no interest in Amanda and hasn't taken care of her for years. So Liz specifies in her will that if she dies, she wants Brad to be appointed guardian of Amanda. She includes a paragraph that gives the date Brad began caring for Amanda, describes how he has functioned as a parent, and states that Amanda's father has neither taken any interest in the child nor paid any child support for nine years.

This statement in the will can be very helpful to Brad's efforts to be appointed personal guardian, if Liz dies before Amanda reaches 18. Unlike a natural or adoptive parent, a stepparent[4] isn't legally presumed to be the best guardian for a child. However, unless Amanda's natural father contests Liz's specification of Brad as guardian, it will probably be honored. And even if the natural father does seek custody, it may well not be granted to him. Brad can file a custody suit, asserting that the ex-husband legally "abandoned" his child, and use Liz's will as evidence that granting him custody will be in Amanda's best interest.

---

[3]This normally means not providing for or visiting the child for an extended period. "Abandonment"must be declared in a court proceeding, where a judge finds that a parent has substantially failed to contact or support a child for an extended period of time, usually (depending on state law) at least a year or two. Abandonment can be declared at a guardianship hearing if, after your death, the other parent, who hasn't visited or supported for an extended period, contests your choice in your will of someone else to serve as guardian.

[4]Brad could become Amanda's legal father through a formal legal action known as a stepparent adoption, which could be routinely accomplished if her biological father were willing to relinquish his parental rights or a court terminated those rights, because the biological father had legally abandoned the child by failing to support or visit her for an extended period. Once an adoption has taken place, the adoptive parent has all the legal rights and responsibilities of a natural parent. This can be done in California without a lawyer by using *How To Adopt Your Stepchild in California,* by Frank Zagone and Mary Randolph (Nolo Press).

Step 3: If you think there's any reasonable possibility the other parent, or any relative or "friend," will contest your nomination for your children's personal guardian, discuss the details of your situation with a lawyer who specializes in family law. If there's a disputed custody proceeding after your death, a judge has wide discretion in deciding how much weight, if any, to give to written statements about your child's custody you made before you died. A knowledgeable lawyer can help you prepare your best case in advance.

2. Naming Different Personal Guardians for Different Children

In your will, you can name different personal guardians for different children. This can be desirable, especially if all children don't share the same two biological parents.

Example: Melissa has a 15-year-old daughter, Irene, from a first marriage, and two-year-old twins from her second marriage to Alfonso. Irene's father abandoned her years ago. Irene doesn't get along well with Alfonso. Melissa uses her will to name her friend Nancy, who is close to Irene, to be Irene's personal guardian, should something happen to her. When it comes to the twins, their father, Alfonso, would of course have custody of them if Melissa dies. Similarly, Melissa would have custody of the twins if Alfonso dies. Melissa and Alfonso both name Alfonso's mother, Ellie, as personal guardian for the twins, to serve if both parents die simultaneously. Ellie, who already often cares for the twins, is not particularly close to Irene, and wouldn't want the additional responsibility of caring for her.

---

3. Name the Personal Guardian for Your Minor Children

Okay, enough background. In the space below, record your choice(s) for personal guardian of your children. You do not need to name the other parent as a personal guardian. To remind you, the guardian you name will normally serve only if both parents cannot care for the child. You should also name an alternate guardian in case your original choice can't serve. Later on, you'll insert your choices in your will when you draft it from Chapter 11 or Chapter 12.

The basic wills in Chapter 11 allow you to name one personal guardian for all of your children. This will be satisfactory to most people but, as noted above, there may be reasons why you want to name different personal guardians for different kids. You'll need a Chapter 12 will to do this.

NAME ONE PERSONAL GUARDIAN FOR ALL YOUR CHILDREN

_____

Personal Guardian

_____

Alternate Personal Guardian

NAME DIFFERENT PERSONAL GUARDIANS FOR DIFFERENT CHILDREN

_____

Personal Guardian
Personal Guardian for _____

_____

(children's names)

_____

Alternate Personal Guardian for these children

_____

Personal Guardian
Personal Guardian for _____

_____

(children's names)

_____

Alternate Personal Guardian for these children

---

4. State Why You Chose the Personal Guardian(s)

In the space below, you can state why you chose who you did to be your children's personal guardian(s). As noted, a statement is wise if your circumstances are unusual and you believe your choice might be challenged. Any statement you draft here must be entered in a Chapter 12, assemble-it-yourself will, rather than by using one of the basic wills from Chapter 11.

Here's an example of such a statement:

"I have nominated my companion, Peter Norris, to be the guardian of my daughter, Melissa, because I know he would be the best guardian for her. For the past six years Peter has functioned as Melissa's parent, living with me and her, helping to provide and care for her, and loving her. She loves him and regards him as her father. She hardly knows her actual father, Tom Delaney. She hasn't seen him for four years. He has rarely contributed to her support or taken any interest in her."

_____

_____

_____

_____

_____

C. Leaving Property to Your Children

WHEN YOU FILLED OUT YOUR BENEFICIARY CHART in Chapter 6, you listed your children to whom you wanted to leave gifts, and you indicated what type of beneficiary you wanted each to be. You can, of course, make gifts to any of your children, whether minors or adults, as any type—as a primary beneficiary, or an alternate beneficiary, and/or as your residuary beneficiary or alternate residuary beneficiary. For instance, it's common to name one's spouse as primary beneficiary of major gifts, with the couple's children as alternate beneficiaries, to receive the property only if the spouse fails to survive the will writer. Or, a parent may make a few small gifts to friends as direct beneficiaries and leave the bulk of her estate equally to her three children as her residuary beneficiaries.

As is explained in Section E of this chapter, you must give something in your will to each of your children, or expressly disinherit any child you don't want to be entitled to receive any of your property. If you don't, state law may require that they automatically inherit a substantial portion of your state.

If you make any gifts to a minor child, it's important to understand that minors cannot legally own property outright, free of supervision, beyond a minimal amount—in the $2,500 to $5,000 range, depending on the state. An adult must be legally responsible for managing any significant amount of property owned by a minor child. Therefore, a vital part of preparing your will is arranging for responsible supervision of any property your minor children might own. This includes all property you leave them, and any other property they might acquire, by gift, as beneficiary of an insurance policy, inheritance, or their own work, that doesn't come with a built-in adult supervisor. This chapter shows you how to provide for such supervision should you die before the minor reaches 18.

No supervision is legally required for gifts received by any competent child over 18. However, many parents don't want to risk allowing their children to be able to receive substantial amounts of property outright while they're comparatively young. So this section also shows you how your will can impose supervision over gifts you make to your children, whether they are now minors or young adults, so that they won't receive these gifts outright until they've reached an age you've chosen.

LEAVING PROPERTY TO YOUR SPOUSE FOR THE BENEFIT OF YOUR CHILDREN

One informal way for parents of minor children or young adults to provide for the supervision of property for the benefit of the children is for each to give it outright in their wills to the other parent, with an understanding that it is to be used for their children's benefit. This approach makes sense if the parents completely trust each other, but doesn't work well if the other parent is out of the picture or financially imprudent. Also, leaving property to the other parent won't handle the adult supervision problem if both of you die simultaneously. If you named your minor or young adult children as alternate beneficiaries for property left first to your spouse, you need to provide a method in your will for adult supervision of any property your children might inherit. Nor will leaving property to the other spouse handle any property your minor children acquire from some other source that doesn't come with built-in supervision. So, if you have any minor or young adult children, even if you give all property to the other parent and name the children only as alternate beneficiaries, you should also provide in your will for some method for adult supervision for any property they do happen to inherit.

1. Methods of Providing for Adult Supervision Over Gifts to Your Children

There are three different methods that may be possible for you to use in your will to provide for adult supervision for gifts to your children.

a. Method 1: The Uniform Transfers to Minors Act[5]

The states that have adopted the Uniform Transfers to Minors Act (UTMA) are listed on page 7/8. If your state isn't on this list, it's not possible for you to leave property to your minor children in your will by this method, and you should skip ahead to Method 2, "The Children's Trust."

[5]Uniform laws, as the name states, are standardized laws created by a legal commission. However, when it adopts a uniform law, a state legislature can make changes in the "uniform"version.

UNIFORM TRANSFERS TO MINORS ACT (UTMA) DEFINED

The UTMA authorizes you to provide for adult supervision of gifts you make to a minor by appointing a "custodian" and "successor custodian" in your will to supervise that minor's gifts until any remaining property must be turned over to the child outright at the age the UTMA specifies. As the chart above shows, this is either 18 or 21, depending on the state, except that, in a few states, a will writer can vary the statutory age to another age within a set range.

In states where the custodian supervises a child's gifts until the child becomes 21 (or up to 25 in California), the UTMA can be used for gifts to young adults under the age of termination, as well as for gifts made to minors.

The authority of the custodian to supervise the gift is defined in the UTMA, and is very broad. Basically, the custodian has complete discretion to control and use the property as she determines is in the children's interest. Normally, no court supervision is required.

If you live in a state that hasn't adopted the UTMA, it's theoretically possible that you can use the law of another UTMA state to make gifts to a minor in your will. If the minor, or custodian, or the gift property resides in that other UTMA state when you die, your will can validly use that state's laws. The problem is that you can't know, now, where a minor, or custodian, or gift (except real estate) will be when you die. So, if you reside in a non-UTMA state, and try to use this method, you are obligating yourself to keep your will up-to-date on where the minor or custodian resides, and even then you could never be sure they would still reside there on the date of your death. Given the fact that you can accomplish the task of providing supervision for property given to minors in your will by an alternate method—namely, the children's trust—I believe it's unwise to use the Uniform Transfers to Minors Act unless you reside in a UTMA state.

If you live in a UTMA state, whether or not it's sensible for you to use the UTMA for gifts you make in your will to your children usually depends on the size of the gift, and the age a child must reach under your state's law for the custodian to turn the gift over to the child.

- States that permit the gift to be turned over when the child becomes 21 or older. In these states, using the UTMA provides dual benefits: First, should you die while the child is a minor, or before she's 21 (or up to 25 in California), the custodian can manage the property free of court supervision; second, the child doesn't receive what remains of the gift until she's reached 21, the normal age for completing, or nearly completing, college. Thus in these states, using the Act is often sensible for gifts primarily intended for college education, i.e., gifts in the $50,000-$100,000 range. Depending on the college the child attends, amounts of this size will be fairly rapidly expended for the child's education and living needs. Since there isn't likely to be much left by the time the child becomes 21, there's little sense in tying the property up beyond that age.

Note: California and Nevada sensibly allow the will writer to choose an age between 18 and 25 which the child must reach before the gift is released to him. Because of this flexibility to have a custodian provide management until the child becomes 25, residents of these states can often use the Act for larger gifts to their minor children, whether intended for college or graduate education, or other purposes.

- States that require the gift to be turned over to the child when he becomes 18. In these states, the benefit of using the UTMA is solely that the custodian is free from court supervision should you die while the child is a minor. Because any remaining gift property must be turned over to the child once he becomes 18, using the UTMA is normally sensible only for smaller gifts. What is a "smaller gift" can be a subjective decision. Certainly, gifts of $5,000 or less are smaller gifts. You can sensibly decide that a gift between $5,000 and, say, $50,000 is a smaller gift, if you're willing to have the gift turned over to the child when he becomes 18.

It's also possible, although not common, for a parent to leave a large amount of property, worth over $50,000, to a minor child, and be willing to allow that child to receive the property outright at age 18. But for most large gifts, parents normally want to impose management to last until the child reaches some age older than 18, at which point she is entitled to receive the gift free of supervision.

b. Method 2: The Children's Trust

A children's trust is valid in all states. The main advantage of a children's trust over the UTMA is that it allows you to specify the exact age each child must reach before receiving outright property you left him or her in your will.

CHILDREN'S TRUST DEFINED

A children's trust is a legal entity you create in your will. In the trust, you appoint an adult as trustee, to have the responsibility of managing property you've left the beneficiary, or beneficiaries, you name here (your child or children). You also appoint a successor trustee in case your first choice can't serve. Your will sets out the trustee's duties and powers, and the beneficiary's rights. In the children's trusts included in this book, the trustee can spend trust money for the child's living needs and educational and medical expenses. During the existence of the trust, the trustee must file state and federal tax returns for the trust. The trustee isn't normally subject to court supervision.

In a children's trust, you specify the age each child must reach for the trustee to end that child's trust and give him or her what's left of the trust property outright.

Many parents don't want to risk having large amounts of property turned over to their children when they reach 18 and become legal adults, or even when they're 21 or 25. By creating a children's trust in a will, a parent can provide that property is supervised for the benefit of a child until she reaches an age when she can (the parent hopes) sensibly manage money.

The children's trusts in the will forms in this book state that each child's trust ends when that child becomes 35, unless you have specified a different age, between 18 and 35, for that trust to end. We selected age 35 as the absolute cut-off age for each child to receive his or property because these trusts are primarily "children's" trusts and are not designed for the lifetime management of property. Age 35 seemed like the most sensible dividing line between "young adults" and "fully mature adults" (or, youth and middle age).

STATES THAT HAVE ADOPTED THE UNIFORM TRANSFERS TO MINORS ACT

State	Gift Must be Released When Minor Reaches Age	
Alabama	21	
Alaska	18	(can be extended up to 25)
Arizona	21	
Arkansas	21	(can be reduced to no lower than 18)
California	18	(can be extended up to 25)
Colorado	21	
District of Columbia	18	
Florida	21	
Georgia	21	
Hawaii	21	
Idaho	21	
Illinois	21	
Indiana	21	
Iowa	21	
Kansas	21	
Kentucky	18	
Maine	18	(can be extended up to 21)
Maryland	21	
Massachusetts	21	
Minnesota	21	
Missouri	21	
Montana	21	
Nevada	18	(can be extended up to 25)
New Hampshire	21	
New Jersey	21	(can be reduced to no lower than 18)
New Mexico	21	
North Carolina	21	(can be reduced to no lower than 18)
North Dakota	21	
Ohio	21	
Oklahoma	18	
Oregon	21	
Rhode Island	18	
South Dakota	18	
Tennessee	21	
Utah	21	
Virginia	18	(can be extended to 21)
Washington	21	
West Virginia	21	
Wisconsin	21	
Wyoming	21	

If you want a child's trust to last beyond age 35, review your situation with a lawyer. While you do have the power to extend the age beyond 35, you should evaluate why you want to choose an older age. If your children aren't able to manage money by age 35, they may never be, and you'll need a more sophisticated trust. (See Chapter 8, Section D.)

Although the children's trusts in the will forms in this book are designed to manage property inherited by minors, they can also be used to impose age controls on property left to your younger adult children. Thus, if you use your will to make a gift to your 22 year old son, you could provide in a children's trust that he wouldn't be entitled to receive the gift outright until he became a set age, such as 28, 30 or 35.

If you die before a child has reached the age you've specified for him or her to receive trust property outright (or age 35, if you didn't), the trust becomes operational. The trustee manages the trust property and can spend it for the beneficiary's "health, support, maintenance and education." The trustee is given broad discretion to interpret these terms.

• When to use a children's trust.

If the Uniform Transfers to Minors Act isn't applicable in your state, a children's trust is usually the best way to make any gifts above roughly $25,000 to your minor child. If you leave property worth less than $25,000 to a minor child, the annual cost of administering the trust (such as the cost of preparing and filing state and federal, trust income tax returns, and any fees charged by the trustee) will eat up an unacceptably large percentage of the property. If you don't set up a trust for a gift under $25,000, it will be managed by the property guardian you name in your will. (See Section C(1)(c) below.)

If you live in a non-UTMA state and establish a children's trust, the crucial decision is at what age each child should receive his or her trust property outright. That usually depends on how much property you give the child. If the gift is in the $25,000 to $50,000 range, and you intend that the money be used for college, it's often sensible to specify that children's trust ends at age 21. For larger gifts, worth more than is likely to be used for college,

parents often extend the age from someplace between the late 20s up to age 35.

If the UTMA is applicable in your state (review the list on page 7/8), using a children's trust is sensible if you don't want your gift turned over to your children at the age your state's Act requires. As you know, some states require gifts made under the Act to be turned over to the child when she becomes 18. In these states, a children's trust is often sensible for any gift above $25,000 made to your minor child. If the gift is relatively small—under $50,000—it usually makes sense to specify the trust ends when the child becomes 21. If the UTMA is applicable in your state, and the gift isn't turned over to the child until she becomes 21 or older, a children's trust is generally advisable only for larger, gifts, those in excess of $50,000, where you want the property supervised until the child is at, or near, 35.

Depending on your state, consider making small gifts to your children through the UTMA, or directly to your spouse or co-parent, informally trusting them to use it on the children's behalf. Another good approach for people with small estates is to buy a term life insurance policy so that the children will inherit enough to justify establishing a children's trust. Only as a last resort should you leave small gifts to minors outright in your will, to be supervised by the property guardian (see Section C(1)(c)).

Other Types of Children's Trusts

 In some situations, you might want a different type of children's trust than the ones in the will forms in this book. Consult a lawyer if you want to:

• Create a children's trust that avoids probate. Property left through a children's trust created by a will must go through probate. A children's trust can also be created as part of a revocable living trust, in which case the property avoids probate. For parents who want to engage in full-scale estate planning, creating this type of living trust can result in overall savings for their family (see Chapter 8). My book, *Plan Your Estate With a Living Trust* (Nolo Press), contains complete forms and thorough instructions for creating a children's trust as part of a living trust.

- Place extensive controls over the use of property in the trust (for example, you place real estate in the trust that you want managed in a specific way).

- Provide for special care for a mentally or physically disadvantaged child.

- Place property for different children in one trust (in legalese, called a "family pot" trust), giving the trustee power to use all property in the trust as she decides is best. In the children's trusts in the will forms in this book, one child's trust property, or income from that property, may not be used for the benefit of another child. By contrast, in a "family pot" trust, the trustee could expend twice as much money for one child as for another. A family pot trust lasts until the youngest child reaches the age for termination of the trust. Also, it often involves difficult tax accounting problems and complex personal problems for the trustee (who must choose how to distribute the trust property among the children).

- Create a trust to continue after a child becomes 35, or for a child already over 35.

MINOR CHILDREN AS BENEFICIARIES OF LIFE INSURANCE

If your minor children are beneficiaries (or alternate beneficiaries) of your life insurance, you will want to consider what happens to the proceeds if you die. If your children are under 18, and you simply name them as beneficiaries or alternate beneficiaries, any proceeds they receive will have to be managed by an adult, normally the property guardian named in your will, until they reach 18. As discussed in Section C(1)(c), it's usually not desirable to have a property guardian manage large amounts of money, because of the burdens of court supervision, reporting and legal restrictions on how the money can be spent. Also, if large sums are involved, you probably don't want the remaining property turned over to them at 18.

Unfortunately, the methods you can use to impose age controls over other property you leave for your children—the Uniform Transfers to Minors Act, and, especially, using a children's trust created in a will—don't typically work for insurance proceeds. Most insurance companies are unwilling to allow policy beneficiaries to be named to receive property under the terms of the Uniform Transfers to Minors Act. And most insurance companies will not permit a children's trust created by a will to be a life insurance beneficiary, because that trust isn't (yet) operational (since you're obviously still alive). What you can do is create a revocable living trust, name your children as beneficiaries of it, and name that living trust as beneficiary of your policy. Then, if you die, the policy proceeds will be turned over to the children's trust, free of probate, to be managed by the trustee for them until the age you have determined.

Step-by-step instructions on how to do this is explained in *Plan Your Estate With a Living Trust*, or you can discuss this issue with a lawyer.

c. Method 3: By Outright Gift in Your Will

It's possible to make gifts to your minor child in your will without using either the UTMA or a children's trust. If you do this and die before your child reaches 18, the gift is supervised by the property guardian you name in your will (unless the gift is so small, generally less than $5,000, that no adult supervision is required). In a few states, the property guardian may sometimes be given a technically different name, such as "property custodian." However, using the phrase "property guardian" makes your intent clear, and suffices in all states. Once the child becomes 18, the property must be turned over to her outright by the property guardian.

Unfortunately, there are serious drawbacks to having gifts you make in your will to your minor children be managed by the property guardian. In many states, a property guardian who's supervising a minor's property must make frequent burdensome reports to a court, which usually means paying a lawyer to get the job done. In addition, state law often imposes restrictions and controls on how a property guardian can spend children's property. By contrast, a trustee of a children's trust or a custodian under the Uniform Transfers to Minors Act is generally free of court supervision and reporting requirements, and has considerable power to use money for living expenses, health needs and education. Also, as mentioned, a property guardian must turn property over to the minor when she becomes a legal adult at age 18. Again, in contrast, in some states, as I've discussed, gifts made under the Uniform Transfers to Minors Act can be managed by the custodian until the child is 21, or even 25, and gifts made through a children's trust are turned over to the child at the age you specify up to 35.

Although it's not desirable to plan to rely on a property guardian named in your will to supervise property you leave your minor children, you should nevertheless name one (and an alternate property guardian as well) as a back-up method in case an adult manager is somehow needed for any property your minor children might inherit. If you fail to name a property guardian, and one is needed, a guardian will be selected by a judge, who could be more concerned with insuring a crony a fee than with your children's best interest. If the need for a property guardian arises a substantial time after a parent dies, that parent's nomination of a property guardian may not be binding on a court. Still, it's often persuasive, and at least won't hurt.

2. Choose the Property Management Methods for Property You Leave For Your Children

It's time to finalize your decisions regarding adult supervision for your gifts to your minor, or younger adult, children. Below are summaries of the three methods for providing supervision and age controls over your gifts. After reviewing those summaries and re-reading any material in Section C(1) you need to, you'll list each of your minor children, and each of your younger adult children on whose gifts you want to impose age controls. Then decide how you want each child's gifts managed. Put "UTMA" if you want to use the Act to provide adult supervision for that child's gift. Put "T" if you want to use a children's trust to provide adult supervision, and age controls, for that child's gift.

Important: In the will forms in this book, you cannot leave the same child some property under the UTMA, and other property by a children's trust. You can only use one of these methods for any one child.

In Section C(3), you'll record the actual information for gifts made using the UTMA that you'll later transfer into your will. In Section C(4), you'll record the actual information for gifts made using a children's trust. Finally, in Section C(5), you'll list the name of your children's property guardian.

a. Summary: Making Gifts to Your Minor or Young Adult Children in Your Will

	Gift Under UTMA	Children's Trust	Property Guardian
Legally permitted	Must be authorized by your state's law	Yes, in all states	Yes, in all states
Amount of Property	• If age for release of gift is 18 in your state, use for smaller gifts under $25,000 • If age for release is 21 or older, sensible for gifts for $50,000, or any amount for college expenses	• Good for gifts in excess of $50,000 if UTMA applies in your state and age for release of gift is 21 or older • Good for gifts of any amount if UTMA age for release of gift in your state is 18, or if UTMA isn't applicable in your state	Last resort no matter what the amount
Paperwork	No trust tax returns required, but minor must file a yearly return based on money actually received Custodian must give accounting when property turned over to child	Trustee must file yearly income tax returns for trust Income tax rate higher than individual for most income retained by trust	Usually substantial because reports must be presented to court
Court Supervision	None	None	Guardian must make regular reports to court
Termination	In most states, custodian must turn over property to child at age specified by statute, usually 18-21	You specify the age at which the child gets control of the trust property	Guardian must turn property over to child at age 18
Uses of Property	Custodian has broad statutory power to use property for child's living expenses, health needs, and education	In wills in this book, trustee has power to use any of child's trust property for minor's needs for living expenses, health needs and education	Heavily limited and regulated by state law

b. Summary: Deciding Which Property Management Method(s) You Want to Use

Here's one final aid you can use to decide which property management method you want to use for gifts you've made in your will to your minor, or younger adult, children:

- Review the list of states that have the Uniform Transfers to Minors Act (in Section C(1). If your state is not listed, consider using a children's trust for a any minor who may receive property worth more than $25,000.
- If your state does have the Uniform Transfers to Minors Act, does it require that the property be distributed at age 18? If it does, use a children's trust if you want your child to receive the property at an age later than 18. Otherwise, choose the Uniform Transfers to Minors Act.
- If your state allows distribution under the Uniform Transfers to Minors Act up to age 21 (up to 25 in California), are you willing to have the gift turned over to the child when he reaches that age? If so, use the Uniform Transfers to Minors Act option. If not, use the trust option to extend the age the gift is turned over past age 21 (age 25 in California).

c. Property Management Chart

Now, in the spaces below, list each of your minor children, and each of your younger adult children, for whom you want to impose age controls, over their gifts. Then write UTMA or T in the Property Management Method column.

Child's Name	Property Management Method
_____	_____
_____	_____
_____	_____
_____	_____
_____	_____
_____	_____

3. How to Use the Uniform Transfers to Minors Act When Preparing Your Will

If you've decided to use the UTMA for gifts to one or more of your minor children, here's how you'll accomplish that in your will. If you don't want to use the UTMA at all, skip ahead to Section 4.

Will forms II, IV and VI in Chapter 11, and the assemble-it-yourself will in Chapter 12, contain a clause you can complete to have gifts you've made in your will to a child be managed under your state's Uniform Transfers to Minors Act (again, assuming your state has one; review the list in Section C(1) to be sure). When preparing your will, you'll first list all gifts you make, including all your gifts to your minor, or young adult, children, whether as direct beneficiaries alternate beneficiaries, residuary beneficiaries or alternate residuary beneficiaries. Then to use the Uniform Transfers to Minors Act for gifts made to one or more children, you complete a separate UTMA clause for each child by filling in:

- the minor's name;
- the names of the custodian and successor custodian you appoint to manage that child's property. You can only name one custodian and one successor custodian per clause. You cannot name shared or joint custodians or successor custodians
- your state.

In addition, for a few states, you have the opportunity to control (within limits) the age at which the child takes the property free of supervision.

Example

"I give __$2,000__ to __my son Alex Corbin__ , or if
__Alex Corbin__ fails to survive me by 45 days to
__my brother Sean Corbin__ ."

"All property given in this will to ____Alex Corbin____
                                    minor's name

shall be given to ____Elizabeth Corbin____ as custodian
                          custodian's name

for ____Alex Corbin____ under the Uniform Transfers to
            minor's name

Minors Act of __Ohio__ . If __Elizabeth Corbin__
              your state   custodian's name

cannot serve as custodian,

_____Lynn Cooke_____ Shall serve as custodian."
successor custodian's name

Notice that the UTMA clause in the wills in this book provides that "all property given in this will" to the named minor is given under the Act. As mentioned earlier, this means that in your will you cannot leave that child some property by the Act, and other property by a children's trust.

a. Choosing the Custodian

You can name any adult you want to as custodian. By law, no bond is required, and the custodian is entitled to be paid reasonable compensation from the gift property. Of course, it isn't mandatory that the custodian take compensation, and commonly, when the custodian is a parent or close relative or friend, the custodian chooses not to be paid.

When selecting a custodian for gifts made under the UTMA to your own children, it is normally a good idea to name the same person who will most likely be taking care of the child after your death, assuming the person is competent to manage property. This will usually be the other natural parent, if one is living. The logical choice for successor custodian under this arrangement would be the person you've named as your children's personal guardian. However, if you make gifts to your children as alternate beneficiaries, e.g., only if your spouse doesn't survive you, it obviously makes no sense to name that spouse as the custodian. So, in this case, the sensible choice for custodian would be the children's personal guardian; the successor custodian would then logically be the alternate personal guardian.

You aren't required to name the children's personal guardian or alternate personal guardian as custodian or successor custodian. It's usually sensible to do so, as there is an obvious risk of conflict if you name one person to raise a child and another to handle that child's property. However, there are instances when the personal guardian simply doesn't have sufficient economic or practical experience to manage property prudently. In this situation, it's preferable to choose someone better qualified to serve as custodian, trying to minimize the possibility of conflict between the care provider and the financial supervisor by selecting someone who gets along with your choice for personal guardian.

You don't have to appoint the same custodian and successor custodian for gifts you make under the Act to different children. While normally a parent wants the same adult to serve as custodian for gifts she makes to all her children, sometimes there are sensible reasons to name different custodians for different children. This is often the case when children don't share the same two parents.

Example: Joan, a single parent, has two children, Don, age 14 and Mavis, age 3. She gives each child $50,000 in her will, under the Uniform Transfers to Minors Act of California, and specifies that each child receives his or her property at age 25. Don is close to Joan's brother Bill, who agrees to serve, if necessary, as custodian for the gift to Don. But Bill doesn't want the additional responsibility of supervising Joan's gift to Mavis, should Joan die before Mavis is 25. So Joan names another friend, Ted, who's willing to do the job as Mavis' custodian.

b. Choosing the Age at Which a Minor Child Is to Receive a Gift Made Under the Uniform Transfer to Minors Act

In most states that have adopted the UTMA, the minor must receive what remains of the gift at an age established by state law, either 18 or 21. A few states use a different approach. While they also establish an age the minor is to receive outright, they allow you to change this age to one within a pre-established range. Specifically, in the following states, you can change the age of receipt as described:

STATE	COLUMN 1 Statutory Age Minor Receives Gift Unless You Change It	COLUMN 2 Age Can Be Changed By Will Writer From
Alaska	18	19 to 25
Arkansas	21	20 to 18
California	18	19 to 25
Maine	18	19 to 21
Nevada	18	19 to 25
New Jersey	21	20 to 18
North Carolina	21	20 to 18
Virginia	18	21

If you live in one of these "flexible age" states, want to make a gift to a child using the Uniform Transfers to Minors Act, and also want to vary the age at which the minor will receive the gift from the statutory age for your state, you must prepare a will from Chapter 12. The basic wills in Chapter 11 don't permit you to vary the age at which a minor receives a gift made under the Act, which means that for all flexible age states, the age listed in Column 1 will apply.

c. Completing the UTMA Clause for Gifts to Your Children

In Section C(2)(c), you decided which of your children would have their gifts managed under your state's UTMA. Below, you'll record each of those children's names, and the names of the custodian and successor custodian you've chosen for each child. If you live in a state that allows you to select an age at which the child receives the gift outright, and you want to select an age different from the statutory one, record that decision as well.

Later, when you prepare your will from Chapter 11 or Chapter 12, you'll transfer this information to it.

_____
child

_____
age child is to receive gift (if you can choose that age)

_____
custodian

_____
successor custodian

_____
child

_____
age child is to receive gift (if you can choose that age)

_____
custodian

_____
successor custodian

_____
child

_____
age child is to receive gift (if you can choose that age)

_____
custodian

_____
successor custodian

4. How to Create a Children's Trust When Preparing Your Will

If you've decided to use a children's trust for gifts to one or more of your children, here's how you'll accomplish that in your will. Will forms II, IV and VI in Chapter 11, and the assemble-it-yourself will in Chapter 12, contain a children's trust clause. When preparing your will, you'll first list all gifts you make, including all your gifts to your minor or young adult children, whether as direct beneficiaries, alternate beneficiaries, residuary beneficiaries or alternate residuary beneficiaries. Then, to create a children's trust, in a separate clause you subsequently list each child for whom you want to create a trust. You complete the children's trust clause by listing the age each child is to receive her trust property outright.

Example:

"I give my house equally to my son Dan Klein and my daughter Samantha Klein, or, if either fails to survive me by 45 days, to the other."

All property I give in this will to any of the children listed in Section A below shall be held for each of them in a separate trust, pursuant to the following trust terms, which shall apply to each trust:

A. Trust Beneficiaries and Age Limits

Each trust shall end when the following beneficiaries become 35, except as otherwise specified:

Trust for	Shall end at age
Samantha Klein	30

a. Choose the Trustee

You can name any adults you want to as trustee and successor trustee of your children's trust. The job of a trustee can involve work, of course, especially if she must actually manage a child's trust property for many years. A very large or complicated trust can require a substantial amount of work by the trustee. Normally, though, the trustee's main responsibility is simply to act honestly and manage each child's trust competently. This usually means investing the trust principal conservatively, using the income (and invading the principal, if necessary) to provide for your children's living expenses, health and education, and also keeping good financial records and filing the annual trust income tax return. If you pick someone with integrity and common sense, your children's property will probably be in good hands. If substantial funds are involved, the trustee can pay for help to handle the more technical aspects of financial management. For instance, where large amounts are involved, it's routine for a property manager to turn tax and accounting duties over to an accountant.

If both parents are involved in raising the children, and one or both uses their will to establish a children's trust, the other parent is normally named as trustee. However, one parent isn't legally required to name the other as trustee. Particularly if the parents are separated or divorced, one parent may decide that some other adult, rather than the other parent, is better suited to managing the child's trust property. For example, if a parent names a personal guardian for his or her children who isn't the other parent, that personal guardian is commonly named as trustee.

It's desirable that the trustee, and successor trustee, live in the same state as the children. There are inherent personal and practical problems in managing property for a child who lives far away, and some state courts may require an out-of-state trustee to post a bond. However, it isn't legally required that the trustee live in the same state as your children. if the trustee lives nearby, that may be close enough for practical purposes. For example, a trustee who lived in Manhattan could most likely suitably manage trust property of children who lived in nearby New Jersey or Connecticut, especially if he was in close personal touch with the kids. But do think twice about naming a Manhattan trustee for a minor who lives in Los Angeles. Not only is such a trustee likely to face logistical problems managing trust assets, she will probably not be in close enough personal touch with the minor to do a good job.

If you name the other parent as trustee, it's usually sensible to name the person you've chosen as the children's personal guardian as the alternate trustee. If both parents die and the personal guardian must actually raise the children, it's usually wise to have that person handle the children's money, too, rather than split these functions. But here, too, you can split them if you believe that the person named as the personal guardian simply isn't able to manage money sensibly.

If you choose someone besides the other parent to be the trustee (e.g., the person you've named as the children's personal guardian), it's generally sensible to name the person selected as the alternate personal guardian as successor trustee. Again, though, you can name someone else if there are compelling reasons to do so.

What about naming a bank or other financial institution as trustee? While this is legal, I recommend against it, except as a last resort. Most banks won't act as trustees for accounts they consider too small to be worth the bother; as a rough rule, this means accounts worth less than $250,000. And even for larger estates, they charge hefty fees for every little act. In addition, it's my experience that banks are simply too impersonal to properly meet your own children's needs. Far better, I think, to name a human being you trust than a bureaucracy.

Note on Trustee Compensation: The children's trust forms in the wills in this book provide that a trustee is entitled to "reasonable compensation" for her services. Since a trustee of an operational children's trust will be engaged in ongoing responsibility, some compensation seems fair. However, in practice, many trustees will decline payment, preferring to maximize trust assets for the child. They have the right to do this.

 If you don't want to allow the trustee to have the right to be paid, see a lawyer.

NAMING DIFFERENT TRUSTEES FOR DIFFERENT TRUSTS

It's legally permissible to name different people as trustees, or successor trustees, for trusts for different children. In most cases, parents want the same person acting as trustee for all their children's trusts. But, in some situations, for instance when a parent recommends that different children have different personal guardians, she may also want to name different trustees.

Example: Lori, a single parent, makes a will and names Sid as personal guardian of her sixteen-year-old son, Joe, and Eileen as personal guardian of her four-year-old daughter, Cheri. Sid and Eileen are also both willing and competent to manage the property Lori leaves in trust for her children. So Lori names Sid as trustee of Joe's trust, and Eileen as trustee of Cheri's.

If you want to name different trustees, or successor trustees, for different children's trusts, you'll need to prepare your will from Chapter 12. The basic Chapter 11 wills require all children's trusts to be managed by the same trustee and successor trustee.

b. Completing the Children's Trust Clause for Gifts to Your Children

In Section C(2)(c), you decided which of your children would have their gifts managed by children's trusts. Below you'll record each of those children's names. For each child listed, put down the age between 18 and 35 the child must reach to be entitled to receive his or her trust property outright. To remind you, if you don't specify an age, the trust clause in the will form states that each child listed shall receive property at age 35. Next, you list the trustee and successor trustee for each trust. (If they're the same for all trusts, you need only list these names once.) Again, you'll transfer this information into your will when you prepare your will from Chapter 11 or Chapter 12.

Child _____ Age _____

Trustee _____

Successor Trustee _____

Child _____ Age _____

Trustee _____

Successor Trustee _____

Child _____ Age _____

Trustee _____

Successor Trustee _____

5. Choosing a Property Guardian

It's prudent to name a property guardian and alternate property guardian for your children in your will. The property guardian supervises any gifts you make in your will directly to your minor children, i.e., without using either the Uniform Transfers to Minors Act or a children's trust. As I've already discussed, leaving gifts to children to be managed by the property guardian is generally undesirable. Still, naming a property guardian in your will is important because it provides a supervision mechanism in case:

• you live in a state that hasn't adopted the Uniform Transfers to Minors Act, and you leave a small amount of money for your children, and decide that a children's trust isn't warranted.
• your minor children earn substantial money after you die, or receive a large gift or inheritance from a grandparent, other relative or friend that doesn't, itself, name a property manager.

a. Choosing the Property Guardian

Legally, you can name whomever you want as your children's property guardian and alternate property guardian. Usually, the sensible choices are the persons you named to be the children's personal guardian and alternate personal guardian.

You can also appoint different property guardians for different children if you want to. To accomplish this, you'll need to prepare your will from Chapter 12.

b. List the Property Guardian

In the spaces below, record your choices for property guardian(s) and alternate property guardian(s) for your children.

_____
Property Guardian

_____
Alternate Property Guardian

If you want to name different property guardians for different children, complete the following:

_____
Children

_____
Property Guardian

_____
Alternate Property Guardian

_____
Children

_____
Property Guardian

_____
Alternate Property Guardian

D. Leaving Property to Other's Children

SOME WILL WRITERS WANT TO MAKE GIFTS to minor or young adult children who aren't their own—to grandchildren, nieces or nephews, grand-nieces or grand-nephews, or the child of a close friend. You can, of course, make gifts to any children, including any minors, you choose to. If you make gifts to others' minor or young adult children, you can choose among the several legal methods discussed below to provide adult supervision for those gifts. You can impose age controls over gifts you make to others' adult "children" by use of two methods discussed in Section C, a children's trust or, in the majority of states, by use of the Uniform Transfer to Minors Act. At the risk of being a bit repetitive, this section discusses how to use those methods for gifts to others' children.

1. Making a Gift to a Minor Child While You're Alive

While you're alive, you can give any minor child any gift you want to, under your state's Uniform Gifts, or Transfers, to Minors Act. (Every state has adopted either one or the other of these Acts.)[6] Particularly for those with estates in excess of $600,000, the federal estate tax threshold, making gifts while alive can be a desirable option. As discussed in Chapter 8, gifts of up to $10,000 a year can be given to any person, including a minor child, free of tax. Aside from the estate tax savings that may be obtained by making gifts during your life, you also have the pleasure of seeing the helpful effects of your gift.

If the child is under 14 when the gift is received, any income over $1,000 obtained by the child is taxed at whatever tax rate is higher, the child's or the parents'—which almost invariably means the parent's. This is often called the "kiddie tax." (If the parents are a couple but file separate tax returns, the tax rate—naturally—is the parent's with the higher income. If the parents are separated, it's the custodial parent's rate.) If you're interested in making substantial gifts now to children under 14, investigate the various ways to give property that won't accrue interest or pay income until after the child is 14. Series EE U.S. savings bonds, which are tax-deferred until the bonds are turned in, provide one way to do this; zero-coupon tax-exempt municipal bonds are another. Also, some states sell tax-deferred bonds specifically designed for educational purposes. A competent

---

[6]The primary difference between these two Acts is that the Uniform Transfers Act allows you to make gifts using it in your will, while the Uniform Gifts Act does not. Also, in some states, you cannot make gifts of real estate under the Uniform Gifts Act.

investment advisor should be able to offer other possibilities.

2. Make the Gift in Your Will to a Parent of the Minor Child

Using this method, you rely on the parent to use a gift made in your will for the benefit of the child. The parent is under no legal obligation to do so, only a moral one. The advantage of this method is that no formal supervision of the gift—no record keeping of any kind—is required. This kind of gift can make sense for money intended to be used for college expenses, if you completely trust the parent.

3. Make a Gift to a Minor in Your Will Using the Uniform Transfers to Minors Act (UTMA)

You can use the UTMA, which has been adopted by a majority of states (see list in Section C(1)) for gifts made to minors in your will.

 If your state doesn't appear on this list, don't try to use another state's UTMA for gifts in your will, unless you see a lawyer. As discussed in Section C(1), it is theoretically possible for you to use the UTMA in your will if the minor, or custodian, or gift itself, resides in a UTMA state when you die. The problem is that you don't know, now, where they will be when you die. Committing yourself to this kind of updating is an unnecessary burden, since you can easily use a children's trust to make supervised gifts to minors who live in other states.

Will forms II, IV and VI in Chapter 11, and the assemble-it-yourself will of Chapter 12, each contain a clause you can complete to make a gift to a minor under the Act, if it's permitted in your state. You must complete a separate clause for each child you make a gift to using the UTMA.

To use the UTMA, you appoint a "custodian" and "successor custodian" in your will to supervise gifts you've made in it to a minor. In many states, as the list in Section C(1) shows, the gift must be turned over by the custodian to the child when he becomes 18. In others, the age for release of the gift is 21, or up to 25 in California.

Particularly in states where a gift made under the UTMA isn't released to the child until she becomes 21 (or 25 in California), gifts of roughly up to $50,000 can be sensibly made using the Act. These days, the entire $50,000 (or even more) is likely to be needed for college or other education expenses. There is likely to be little of the gift left after the child becomes 21. By contrast, for very large gifts, a children's trust is usually desirable, because it allows you to choose the age the child must reach to receive her gift outright.

To use the UTMA for a gift in your will to someone else's minor child, you first complete the clause making the gift itself—i.e., naming that child as primary beneficiary, or alternate beneficiary. Then you complete an additional UTMA clause, stating that all property you give in your will to the named minor is given under the Uniform Transfers to Minors Act of your state; in that UTMA clause, you appoint a custodian and alternate custodian to supervise the gift property until it's turned over to the child. You can appoint whomever you want as custodian and successor custodian of the children's gifts. Often it's sensible to appoint the child's parent.

Example: John, an elderly widower, wants to give $15,000 to his 12-year old niece Sally in his will. He decides to name her mother, Mary, as the custodian, and her father, Ben, as successor custodian. In his will, John first writes that he gives $15,000 to Sally Earners. Then he completes a Uniform Transfers to Minors Act clause as follows:

All property given in this will to Sally Earners shall be given to Mary Earners as custodian for Sally Earners under the Uniform Transfers to Minors Act of Minnesota. If Mary Earners cannot serve as custodian, Ben Earners shall serve as custodian.

You don't have to appoint the same custodian and successor custodian for all gifts you make to others' children under the Act. For instance, if you make gifts to three grandchildren, each with different parents, you might sensibly decide to appoint each child's mother as his or her custodian, and each child's father as successor custodian.

If you make gifts using the Act to minors who aren't your own children, the sensible choice for custodian is normally the person who is currently caring for the child, whether it be one of the child's parents or a legal guardian. A sensible choice for alternate custodian would normally be another adult who is close to the child, perhaps the other parent. However, when naming the custodian and successor custodian, you're entitled to choose any other adult who you believe would do the best job in managing the property.

Reminder: Varying the Age at Which a Minor Receives a Gift Under the Act: In Alaska, Arkansas, California, Maine, New Jersey, North Carolina or Virginia, you can vary the age at which a minor receives a gift made under the UTMA from the age set in the Act to any age within 18 to 21, or up to 25 in Alaska or California. See the chart in Section C(3)(b) of this chapter. If you decide you want to vary the age from the statutory one to a permissible one, you must prepare your will from Chapter 12.

4. Make a Gift to a Minor or Young Adult

A children's trust created in your will can be used to impose age controls over gifts you make to others' children, whether they're minors or young adults. (Children's trusts are defined and discussed in Section C(1).) The children's trusts in the will forms in this book allow you to select any age between 18 and 35 each child must reach to receive his or her trust property outright. Since these trusts are primarily designed for minor children, and not for lifelong management of property, they aren't suitable to tie up property after a child becomes 35.

 If you want a trust to last after a child has reached age 35, see a lawyer.

In all states, a children's trust is generally the best method to impose adult supervision over substantial gifts made to children, roughly those in excess of $50,000. Also, if you live in a state that has not adopted the Uniform Transfers to Minors Act, or one that has adopted it, but requires property to be turned over to them at age

18 (see list, Section C(2)), a children's trust is sensible for any gift worth more than $25,000.

When you create a children's trust, you name a trustee and successor trustee to manage each child's trust property. You can name whomever you want for this job. Often it's sensible to name a child's parents to serve. It's preferable to name a trustee, and successor trustee, who reside in the same state, or at least the same part of the country, as the child.

Will forms II, IV and VI in Chapter 11, and the assemble-it-yourself will of Chapter 12, each contain a children's trust clause. If you prepare a basic will from Chapter 11, the same persons must serve as trustee and successor trustee for all children's trusts you create in your will. If you want to name different trustees for different children, you'll need to prepare your will from Chapter 12.

5. Make the Gift Outright to the Child in Your Will

Simply leaving property to a minor will almost surely require court proceedings to appoint a property guardian to supervise the gift, if it's worth more than $2,500-$5,000 (depending on the state) and it is a generally undesirable transfer method. This is doubly so because, unlike a parent, you can't even appoint a property guardian for him or her in your will to guide the court in making this appointment.

6. Make the Gift Through a Living Trust

It's also possible to make a gift to a minor or young adult through a revocable living trust. The advantage of making a gift to a child through a living trust is that the gift avoids probate. You can establish a children's trust as part of a living trust, and so extend the age at which the child receives her property. Probate and living trusts are discussed in Chapter 8, and explained thoroughly in *Plan Your Estate With a Living Trust,* which contains all the information and forms you need to create your own living trust.

7. Determine the Property Management Method You Want to Use for Gifts to Others' Children Made in Your Will

Now, in the spaces below, record your decisions regarding the method or methods you want to use to impose adult management or age controls over gifts you make in your will to others' children. For purposes of completing your will, you're only concerned here with options 3 (making the gift under your state's Uniform Transfers to Minors Act) or 4 (using a children's trust), as discussed above. The other options discussed don't require, indeed don't allow, you to create a property management method for the gifts made in your will.

a. Gifts to Others' Children Under the Uniform Transfers to Minors Act

In the spaces below, record the name of each minor to whom you want to make a gift using the UTMA, and the name of the custodian and successor custodian for that minor. You'll transfer this information to your will when you prepare it from Chapter 11 or 12. If you don't want to use the UTMA for any child, go on to Section b, below.

If your state allows you to vary the statutory age when the minor must receive the gift to another age, and you want to vary that age to a permissible one, also record the age you've selected. If you do this, you must prepare your will from Chapter 12.

_____

Child

_____

Age child is to receive gifts (if you can choose that)

_____

Custodian

_____

Successor Custodian

_____

Child

_____

Age child is to receive gifts (if you can choose that)

_____

Custodian

_____

Successor Custodian

_____

Child

_____

Age child is to receive gifts (if you can choose that)

_____

Custodian

_____

Successor Custodian

_____

Child

_____

Age child is to receive gifts (if you can choose that)

_____

Custodian

_____

Successor Custodian

_____   _____

Child   Age

_____

Trustee

_____

Successor Trustee

_____   _____

Child   Age

_____

Trustee

_____

Successor Trustee

_____   _____

Child   Age

_____

Trustee

_____

Successor Trustee

b. Gifts to Others' Children Through a Children's Trust

In the space below, list each child for whom you want to create a trust. For each child listed, put down any age, between 18 and 35, the child must reach to be entitled to his or her trust property. (If you don't specify an age, the trust form states that the child shall receive property at 35.) Next, you list the trustee and successor trustee for each trust. If you choose different trustees for different trusts, you'll need to prepare your will from Chapter 12. In a Chapter 11 will, you must name the same trustee and successor trustee for all children's trusts.

E. Your Children of Any Age

IN MOST INSTANCES, FOR WILL PURPOSES your adult children can be treated just like any other adult. Of course, as discussed in Sections C and D, you can leave children between the ages of 18 to 35 property in a children's trust, but this certainly isn't mandatory; some parents do leave gifts outright to their children if they're over 18. And generally, adult children over 35 do receive their gifts outright.

There are two areas where special will-making rules apply to one's own children no matter what their age:

1. Disinheritance of children and
2. Concerns about adopted children or children born outside marriage.

These will-making rules are discussed below.

Other special problems involving children of any age are discussed in Chapter 8, including:

- A child with a physical or mental disadvantage who may need ongoing care for life;
- Children from a former marriage. Commonly, people who remarry want to provide for their spouse and also protect the right of their own children to ultimately inherit.

These concerns are addressed in more depth in *Plan Your Estate With a Living Trust* (Nolo Press).

1. Disinheriting Children

To an outsider, it may seem sad that a parent would want to disinherit a child, but nevertheless, it's surely been known to happen. It's legal to disinherit a child unless you run afoul of laws that give minor children certain rights or laws that protect children from being accidentally disinherited.

State law may give your minor children (less than 18 years old) the right to inherit the family residence. The Florida constitution, for example, prohibits the head of a family from leaving his residence in his will (except to his spouse) if he is survived by a spouse or minor child.[7]

Legal rules also protect children, and children of a deceased child, from being accidentally disinherited. The legalese for accidentally overlooked children is "pretermitted heirs." Grandchildren don't have any statutory right to inherit if their parent (your child) is still alive, so there's no need to expressly disinherit such grandchildren if you don't want them to inherit any of your property. But in many states, children of a deceased child do have a statutory right to inherit from a grandparent, if they or their parent (the grandparents' deceased child) aren't mentioned in a grandparent's will.

If you want to expressly disinherit a child, you must state this in your will. If you don't explicitly disinherit a child or leave her something in your will, the general rule is that the omitted child, or the children of a child who has died before you, are entitled to some of your property anyway. How much she gets depends on whether you leave a spouse and how many other children you have. In addition, the laws of most states protect your children who are born after the will is made ("afterborn children") by entitling them to a similar share of your estate.

There are two ways to disinherit a child in a will. One is to expressly disinherit the child in the will, by naming him and stating that you aren't leaving him anything. The other is to leave the child a minimal amount which ensures the child cannot successfully claim to have been accidentally omitted.

To help you make sure your will won't become enmeshed in an overlooked heir problem, all wills prepared from this book ask you to name all your living children, whether natural, adopted or born out of wedlock, and all living children of any child who has died. All children and grandchildren listed should either be provided for in your will (any amount will do) or specifically disinherited. If you do want to specifically disinherit any of your children (or children of a deceased child), you must say so in clear language. For example, "I disinherit my son, Arthur Jones, and direct that he receive nothing from my estate."

If you wish to explicitly disinherit a child, prepare a will from Chapter 12. You can leave a child a token amount in either a Chapter 11 or Chapter 12 will.

REVISE YOUR ESTATE PLAN WHEN A CHILD IS BORN OR DIES

If, after preparing your will, you have an additional child or children, you must revise the will by providing for, or disinheriting, the new child.

If a child dies, leaving children (your grandchildren), you should revise your will to provide for or disinherit these grandchildren. You should also, of course, make sure that all property given to the deceased child is redirected to other beneficiaries.

---

2. Adopted and Out-of-Wedlock Children

For centuries, courts have been confronted with the issue of whether a gift to "my children" includes adopted children and children born out of wedlock. To avoid such confusion, when you make a will, simply name all your children, including any born while you weren't married and any you have adopted. Then, as discussed, leave each child some property or disinherit him or her by name.

If, despite this advice, you make a gift to "my children," and there's a dispute over what you meant, a court will attempt to determine what you intended. Most states consider adopted persons, whether they were minors or adults when adopted, as "children" for the purpose of a gift to "my children."

The rule for out-of-wedlock children isn't nearly so clear. Basically, for inheritance purposes, states

---

[7]Fla. Const. Art. 10, § 4.

recognize an out-of-wedlock child as a child of the mother unless the child was formally released by the mother for adoption. However, an out-of-wedlock child isn't a child of the father for inheritance purposes unless the father has legally acknowledged the child as his. However, there are a number of special circumstances and exceptions that can easily have the effect of changing this rule.

Happily, if you're a parent of an adopted or out-of-wedlock child, you don't need to worry about legal technicalities of what a court would do if you haven't mentioned the child. *Nolo's Simple Will Book* allows you to make sure the child receives exactly what you desire, no more and no less. Again, when you're asked to name each of your children in your will, simply name them all, whether they were born when you were married to your current spouse, a previous spouse, or no spouse at all. Then, leave them what you wish. If you don't want a child you've listed to inherit anything at all, list that child's name and then expressly disinherit him or her (using a Chapter 12 will).

CHAPTER 8

ESTATE PLANNING BASICS

A.	Probate	8/2
B.	Do You Need To Avoid Probate?	8/3
C.	Why Wills Are Necessary	8/3
D.	Probate Avoidance Methods	8/4
E.	Estate Planning to Reduce Taxes	8/6
F.	Estate Planning Designed to Place Controls on Property	8/9
G.	Planning for Incapacity: The Durable Power of Attorney	8/10
H.	Estate Planning—Summing Up	8/11

WHEN PREPARING YOUR WILL, you should also consider whether you want to engage in more extensive estate planning. Basically, estate planning is concerned with avoiding probate and reducing death taxes. Also, it can involve personal concerns, such as providing for a disadvantaged child, establishing a scholarship fund for grandchildren, handling the potential inheritance conflicts arising from a second or subsequent marriage when one has children from a first marriage, or making charitable gifts.

This chapter gives you an overview of the basic estate planning methods so you can decide if you want to investigate the matter further. If you're sure that, for now, all you want is a will, you can skip this chapter and get on with preparing it. Experience has taught me that many people are in exactly this position—a will that achieves their goals of distributing their property to the people or organizations they want to have it, and providing for the care and support of their minor children, if they have any, is all they want. For example, many younger people rely on a will to dispose of their property and name a guardian for their children should they die unexpectedly, and put off worrying about estate planning until they're older. Others, no matter what their age, conclude that they don't have enough property to warrant more planning than writing a will. In sum, whether you want to consider estate planning now is a personal decision; it certainly isn't mandatory for every sensible person.

In the next several pages I summarize the common techniques used for probate avoidance and estate tax reduction and discuss how trusts can be used to handle personal problems. Please realize, however, that in one chapter, I can only provide an overview. A good source of more sophisticated information (I say modestly) is my book, *Plan Your Estate with a Living Trust* (Nolo Press). This book treats these questions thoroughly and I believe that anyone with even a moderate-sized estate will benefit by reading it.

A. Probate

AS HAS BEEN MENTIONED, PROPERTY LEFT BY A WILL must go through probate, with the exceptions noted in Section B(2) of this chapter, which primarily involve very small estates. "Probate" is the legal process that includes filing a deceased person's will with a court, locating and gathering his assets, paying off his debts and death taxes, and (eventually) distributing what's left as the will directs. If the deceased didn't leave a will, or if his will isn't valid, the estate will undergo probate through similar "intestacy" proceedings. The major difference between the probate of a will and the probate of an estate under "intestate succession" laws is that, in the former instance, the property is left as you direct, and in the latter, it goes to relatives, as mandated by the law of your state.

1. Drawbacks of Probate

Probate certainly has its drawbacks. The probate process often takes six to nine months, commonly a year, and sometimes even longer. Further, probate normally requires lawyers, which automatically means that the cost goes up. The fees of the attorney and executor are paid from the estate property. Either by law or custom, in many states the fees of the attorney who guides your estate through the probate court are based on a percentage of the probate estate's value. Moreover, in some states the fees are computed from the estate's total market value.

Let's take an example from California. If Harry dies with a gross estate—that is, the total value of everything he owns, without subtracting debts owed on the property—of $500,000, the attorney's fee under the state statute would be $11,150. The fee is based on the $500,000 figure, even if Harry's house has a $100,000 mortgage on it.[1]

2. Reducing Probate Fees

Clearly, where probate fees are based on the size of the probate estate, you can reduce the fees by reducing the probate estate's worth. It is both legal and safe to avoid probate. One approach to reducing probate fees is to transfer the big ticket items of your property—for example, your house, and stock portfolio—outside of probate, and only transfer the less valuable items by your will. Remember, most property transferred by a will (or by intestacy proceedings) is subject to probate while property transferred by probate avoidance devices is not.

Probate fees can also be reduced if the attorney who handles the work agrees to take less than the conventional fee. State statutory or court fee schedules aren't mandatory—no matter what a lawyer may indicate. There's one glitch here. The executor of the will is the person legally responsible for selecting the probate attorney. The will writer cannot legally hire the probate attorney because the attorney must be responsible to a living person, not a deceased one. However, since the will writer and the executor are, presumably, close and trusting, in reality, the will writer can usually negotiate a reasonable fee agreement with a particular attorney and request the executor and attorney to abide by it. Assuming the agreement provides good values for the money, the executor (who is commonly a beneficiary of the estate) will very likely do so. Presumably, the attorney will too, since the executor is free to hire someone else if he doesn't.

---

[1]This example comes from the California edition of *How To Probate an Estate,* by Julia Nissley (Nolo Press). The author estimates that if Harry's will left everything to his children and one of them acts as executor and probated the estate without an attorney, the process could be accomplished through the mail for approximately $650.

B. Do You Need To Avoid Probate?

BASIC ESTATE PLANNING METHODS, SUCH AS LIVING TRUSTS and joint tenancy (see Section D), are used to avoid probate. But before investigating these devices, the initial issue is whether you need to worry about avoiding probate. If only a small amount of your property will be subject to probate, arranging to avoid it usually isn't worth the bother.

1. How Much Is In Your Probate Estate?

It's simple to calculate the value of your property that will pass through probate (called your "probate estate"), to determine how much effort it's worth expending to transfer it outside of probate. Turn to the chart listing your property in Chapter 5, Section B and follow these steps (assuming you used the Chapter 5 Inventory Chart):

Step One: Exclude all property that will be transferred by means other than your will. This includes property in joint tenancy, or informal bank account trusts (pay-on-death accounts), or living trusts and the proceeds of life insurance policies (unless your estate has been made the beneficiary).

Step Two: Calculate the value of your probate estate by computing the market value for all items of property remaining. In other words, value your house, car, land in the country, boat, etc., as if you owned them free and clear. This number will be larger than the net value of these items, unless you don't owe any money on any of them, in which case it will be the same.

If the result of your calculation indicates that property of substantial value is still included in your estate, consider what additional property, if any, can easily be removed from your probate estate and transferred by probate avoidance devices so that your probate fees will be minimized.

2. Special State Law Exemptions from Probate

Many states have laws that allow a certain amount of property, usually in the $5,000 to $60,000 range, to be left by will (or by intestate succession) either free of probate or subject only to a simple, informal, do-it-yourself probate process. The details of these laws vary significantly from state to state. If this is of concern to you, a 50-state chart of these laws is set out in *Plan Your Estate With a Living Trust* as part of its more comprehensive treatment of estate planning.

Some states also simplify or eliminate probate for property left by one spouse to the other.

 If you're interested in exploring whether your state exempts property left to a surviving spouse from probate, see a lawyer or research the question yourself (see Chapter 9, Section C).

C. Why Wills Are Necessary

BEFORE DISCUSSING THE PRINCIPAL PROBATE AVOIDANCE DEVICES, let's deal with an obvious question: "If a will puts property into the probate system and this results in delays and substantial attorney fees, why have one at all if there are good alternatives?" As I indicated earlier, there are a number of good reasons. Among them are:

• A will is an easy way to make a quick estate plan that can be refined later on, as you get more property. Probate avoidance techniques pay dividends in the form of saving on probate fees, but obviously they only do this at your death. In the meantime, unfortunately, some of them involve at least some paperwork (e.g., living trusts), and others actually require you to give up control over some or all of your property (e.g., making gifts and transferring property into joint tenancy). Accordingly, many younger people decide to rely primarily on a will to dispose of their property should they die unexpectedly and wait to make a probate avoiding estate plan until they're older and more settled.

• In a will you can achieve the vital goal of naming a personal guardian for your minor children.

- A will enables you to appoint a property guardian for any property of your minor children that doesn't come with a built-in adult supervisor. Also, in a will you can leave property to your minor children, either by a children's trust or (in a majority of states) the Uniform Transfers to Minors Act, or directly, to be supervised by the property guardian.
- Even if you've provided for your property by some other means than a will, you may end up acquiring valuable property at or shortly before death, such as winning a lottery or receiving back your share of a joint tenancy because of a simultaneous death. So, for this reason alone, a will is extremely valuable to back up other estate planning devices.
- As mentioned, if your estate is modest (in the $5,000-$60,000 range, depending on state law), many states don't require probate or provide simplified and cheap probate procedures. If you're in this category, there is little need to transfer property outside of your will.
- In some states, no probate is required to pass property from one spouse to another, so if this is your plan, it may not be necessary to plan to avoid probate.

D. Probate Avoidance Methods

HERE NOW IS A BRIEF REVIEW of the principal probate avoidance methods.

1. Living or Inter Vivos Trusts

A revocable living trust is justifiably the most popular probate avoidance device. Under a living trust (inter vivos in Latin, for "among the living"), title to property is transferred by its living owner (called a "trustor" or "settlor") to a trust created by a written document (in legalese, a "trust instrument"). A "trustee," who is normally the same person who created the trust, manages the trust property. A trusted person is named as "successor trustee" to take over trust management when the settlor trustee dies. The trust "beneficiaries" are named by the person who sets up the trust (the settlor). Normally, when the settlor-trustee dies, the trust

property is almost immediately passed by the successor trustee to these beneficiaries free of probate.

The attraction of a revocable living trust as a probate avoidance device is that it allows you (the settlor) to retain full control over your property before you die. You do this by naming yourself as the initial trustee, so you fully control management of the trust property. You retain full rights to use of and income from all trust property in any name you want until you die. You also retain full rights to sell or give away all trust property. And the trust is revocable by you (the settlor) at any time, for any (or no) reason.

> **Example:** James wants to leave his valuable painting collection to his son Bill, but wants total control over it until he dies. He doesn't want the value of his collection, $800,000, included in his probate estate. So he establishes a revocable living trust for the paintings, naming himself as trustee while he lives, and his younger brother Ed to be successor trustee, to act after James' death. James names his son as the trust beneficiary. When James dies, the successor trustee, Ed, will transfer the paintings to Bill outside of probate. However, should James want to sell a painting, or all the paintings, and end the trust before he dies, he can do so at any time. Similarly, if James subsequently decides he wants to leave the paintings to a museum, he can readily change the trust's beneficiary to provide for that.

The only real drawback of a living trust as an estate planning device is that certain formalities are required. A formal trust document must be prepared. If property has formal legal title (e.g., a house, car, stock), it must be actually transferred to the trust's name. Thus, if you put your house in a living trust, you must properly execute and record a deed transferring ownership to the trust. However, as long as you (the settlor) are also the trustee until you die, no trust income tax returns are required, and separate trust records don't have to be maintained.

Living trusts are explained in depth in *Plan Your Estate With a Living Trust,* which contains basic living trust forms and thorough instructions for how to prepare one.

USING A "POUR-OVER" WILL

A "pour-over" will is one which directs that the property subject to it go to (be "poured over" into) another legal entity, often a trust. For example, sometimes people make their living trust the beneficiary of their will. After the will property is "poured-over" into the trust, it is then distributed as the trust directs.

In my opinion, there's rarely a sensible reason to use a "pour-over" will.

If you're using a will to transfer some or all of your property, it's simpler to name the real beneficiaries for that property in the will itself, rather than in another document, such as a living trust.

Likewise, there's rarely a good reason to use a "pour-over" will with a living trust. The purpose of using a living trust is to avoid probate. Using a "pour-over" will simply ensures that some property that will eventually wind up in the trust must go through probate anyway.

Candidly, it's my impression that some lawyers push "pour-over" wills because they not only sound sophisticated, they also ensure that some probate attorney fees can be collected.

2. Informal Bank Trusts (also called Totten Trusts or "Pay-on-Death" Accounts)

These are a very simple type of living trust. A person (the "trustor") opens a bank account (e.g., checking, savings, certificate, or bank money market) in her name but adds a designation stating that the account is in trust for a named beneficiary. The original depositor retains complete and exclusive control over the money in the account until her death, at which point any money left in the account belongs to the named beneficiary without any necessity for probate. If all the money has been withdrawn prior to death, the beneficiary gets nothing. If you want to establish this type of trust, simply visit your bank and complete the appropriate forms. They're simple.

3. Joint Tenancy and Tenancy by the Entirety

As discussed in Chapter 4, joint tenancy is a form of shared property ownership where, legally, the surv-iving owner(s) automatically inherit the interest of a deceased owner through a "right of survivorship." In many states, marital joint tenancy is called tenancy by the entirety. All joint tenancy property is transferred to the survivor(s) outside of probate when the first joint tenant dies.

Joint tenancy can be a useful probate-avoidance device for people who buy property together, in circumstances where each is sure they want their share of the property to go to the other owner(s) when they die. If any owner wants to leave his share to anyone other than the other owner(s), joint tenancy isn't desirable. Transferring solely-owned property into joint tenancy, with the intention that the property will be transferred outside of probate when the original owner dies, is generally a bad idea. Unlike a revocable living trust, the new owner gains a present interest in the property. This interest can be sold by the joint tenant, or foreclosed against by her creditors. Also, gift taxes will be assessed in one year if you transfer property worth more than $10,000 into joint tenancy with another person. Finally, complicated federal tax basis rules make transfers of property that has appreciated in value into joint tenancy undesirable. (*Plan Your Estate With a Living Trust* contains a thorough discussion of how federal basis rules work and why they mitigate against transferring appreciated property into joint tenancy.)

By contrast, a revocable living trust is a far better probate-avoidance method for solely-owned property than transfer into joint tenancy. As I've emphasized, the beneficiaries of a living trust have no rights to any of your property while you live, and you can change the beneficiary or end the trust at any time. In addition, the federal basis rules have no negative impact on appreciated property transferred to inheritors by a living trust.

Okay, now that you know what joint tenancy is, and a little bit about its advantages and disadvantages, the question is do you already own property in joint tenancy? If you're concerned with real estate, look at the deed. If it says: "To John and Sarah Jones, in joint tenancy," or "Joint Tenant WROS (with right of survivorship)," or "As tenants by the entirety," it's clear that you do. If the deed says, "To John and Arthur Jones as tenants in common," then it's just as clear that you aren't joint tenants. Tenancy in common, another traditional form of co-ownership, doesn't carry with it rights of survivorship.[2] In this situation, each co-owner is free to give their share of the property to anyone they want to have it at death.

What if your deed says, "To John and Arthur Jones"? Is this a joint tenancy or tenancy in common? The answer is that most states presume it is a tenancy in common, reasoning that if the co-owners wanted to create a right of survivorship, they would have explicitly said so in the deed. Similarly, if the persons whose names are listed on the deed are married, community property states will generally treat the property as community property, which means you and your spouse are each free to dispose of one-half of it.[3]

Can personal property (all property that isn't real estate) be held in joint tenancy? Generally yes, so long as there is a written document to that effect. Joint tenancy bank accounts, for example, require a written form that is signed by the joint tenants and specifies the account as a joint tenancy. If you don't know whether your shared account fits this description, ask your bank. Likewise, automobiles, securities and business interests can be held in joint tenancy by appropriate registration on the ownership documents with the Motor Vehicles Department.

4. Gifts

As you know by now, the phrase "gifts" as used so far in this book means property left by a will. However, as you also know, the word "gifts" has another meaning, which is any property transferred freely, without commercial intent, from one living person to another (or to an organization). It's this meaning of the word "gifts" that is discussed here.

Property given away at any time before death isn't part of the probate estate upon death. For property to be considered a gift, the person giving it needs to actually surrender ownership and control of the prop-

erty while he is living. (Tax consequences of gifts are discussed in Section E(2).)

5. Life Insurance

Assuming that you designate a specific beneficiary in your life insurance policy, the proceeds of the policy pass under the terms of the policy rather than under the terms of your will and therefore don't go through probate. Accordingly, the purchase of life insurance policies is a popular way to avoid probate. However, if for some reason a person designates her estate (as opposed to a person or institution), as the beneficiary of the policy, which is rarely done, the proceeds would be part of the probate estate.

6. IRAs, Keoghs and Other Retirement Plans

Many retirement plans—including IRAs and Keoghs—allow you to name a beneficiary to receive any funds remaining in the plan when you die. The beneficiary you name receives any such funds directly, outside of probate.

7. Debts and Taxes

Transferring some, or all, of your property outside of probate can raise questions about how any debts and death taxes are to be paid. For many people, this isn't a problem. Their estate is under the $600,000 federal estate tax threshold, so they aren't liable for federal estate taxes. And they have no substantial debts; their regular debts can be handily paid from their checking accounts or other bank or money market funds. However, if your estate is likely to be liable for death taxes, or if you have serious debts, you should do some planning to see what assets you want to use to pay those debts and taxes.

E. Estate Planning to Reduce Taxes

AT DEATH, ALL PROPERTY OWNED BY YOU is subject to a federal estate tax (and state death taxes, if your

---

[2]A tenant in common can, and should, use a will or other estate planning device, such as a living trust, to dispose of her share of such property, since it won't pass automatically to the other owner(s) upon her death.

[3]California and some other states have a simplified probate procedure for property one spouse leaves to the other by will.

state has them) unless it is exempt under the statutes. This is true not only for property passed by your will, but also for property passed at death outside of probate, such as property placed in joint tenancy or in a living trust or bank account trust. Only if you've actually given the property away prior to death will the taxing authorities consider it outside your estate. However, since gifts made during your lifetime are subject to gift taxes, which are basically the same as estate taxes, giving property away doesn't work to reduce your tax liability, with one major exception: You may give away $10,000 per person per year free of gift tax.

One primary goal of sophisticated estate planning is either to reduce the amount of death taxes by giving property away before you die or leaving property in a way that results in the minimum possible taxation. For those with small, or moderate, estates—roughly anyone with property worth less than $1,000,000—there are only a few possible means to reduce taxes, which are discussed here. If your estate is in the $1,000,000 class or above, you'll be wise to invest a few of those dollars in a consultation with a tax attorney, accountant, or both.

1. Many Estates Are Exempt from Taxation

Before worrying about reducing death taxes, be sure you need to bother with the matter at all.

Federal estate law exempts from tax estates of less than $600,000.[4] Further, all property left to a surviving spouse is exempt except property left to a non-citizen spouse [see *Plan Your Estate With a Living Trust,* Chapter 14, Section A(2)]. So, in general, if your anticipated net estate is less than $600,000, and you haven't given away large amounts of property (above $10,000 per person per year) while living, you don't need to worry about how to reduce federal taxes and

should proceed directly to Section F. If, on the other hand, either your estate alone, or the combined value of your own and your spouse's estate, if you're leaving most of your property to her, is expected to be larger than $600,000, then thought as to how to reduce your taxes is warranted. This is because the federal estate tax rates are stiff. They start at 37% for non-exempt property.

What about state death taxes? A number of states, including the most populous, California, don't have any. Many that do exempt substantial dollar amounts of property.[5] Perhaps most importantly, state death tax rates are much lower than the federal rates. So even if your estate is subject to state death taxes, the bite taken is relatively small. In general, this means it's not worth the bother and cost to try to reduce only state death taxes. (State death tax rules are contained in *Plan Your Estate With a Living Trust* (Nolo Press).

Let's now turn to some of the methods commonly used to reduce federal estate taxes.

2. Gifts

One way to reduce the size of your estate and save on estate taxes is to transfer some of your property while you're still alive. As mentioned, you may give $10,000 per year, per person, free of gift taxes. Your spouse may do the same. Thus, if a couple has three children, they could each give $10,000 to each child each year, thus transferring $20,000 free of federal gift tax per child; they could remove a total of $60,000 per year from their estate. In ten years, $600,000 could be transferred in this way, tax-free. This would probably result in saving an even larger sum, because of the interest and dividends this money earns, which would, absent the gifts, have ended up in the parents' estate. With a gift, the interest and dividends are instead earned by the people to whom you give the money, who may well be in a lower income tax bracket.[6]

Another kind of property suitable for gifts is ownership of a life insurance policy. The value of the proceeds from life insurance is included in the taxable

---

[4]Certain types of property do not have to be valued at their "best use" market value for federal estate tax purposes. These include family farmland and wooded land. Also, an estate can have up to 14 years to pay off estate taxes on a closely held business if the value of your interest in it exceeds 35% of the value of your estate.If you have any of these kinds of property, consult a lawyer before completing your will.

[5]Thus New York and some other states exempt all property transferred to a surviving spouse.
[6]Income from gifts by adults to children under 14 is taxed at the adult's tax rate.

estate of the deceased (i.e., the person insured) if he was the legal owner of the policy at his death. If the policy has a large death benefit—say proceeds in the range of hundreds of thousands of dollars—inclusion of that sum in the taxable estate can result in federal estate taxes, or additional taxes. The taxes attributable to the insurance proceeds can be eliminated if the owner (the insured) gives the policy to someone else. Under IRS regulations, this gift must be given at least three years prior to the insured's death. (The beneficiary isn't necessarily the owner of the policy. The owner is the person who pays for the policy, has the right to name the beneficiary, etc.)

3. Irrevocable Trusts to Save on Estate Taxes

There are a number of ways that irrevocable trusts can be used to save on estate taxes. An irrevocable trust is one that cannot be revoked or altered (except in very narrow circumstances defined by the terms of the trust). A living trust, in contrast, can be revoked as long as the person who set it up is alive. Only when he dies does that trust becomes irrevocable and the property pass to the beneficiary. Here are some examples of uses of irrevocable trusts for tax savings.

a. The Marital Life Estate Trust

All property transferred from one spouse to another at death is exempt from federal estate tax. (This is called the "marital deduction.") This is true even if you leave far more than the $600,000 amount that is automatically exempt from federal tax. Even so, it may not be wise for one spouse to transfer a large estate to a surviving spouse. Why? Because if the survivor has property of his own, and that property, combined with what the other spouse leaves him, is worth more than $600,000, a large and unnecessary estate tax will have to be paid when the second spouse dies. This is why estate planners refer to this as the "second tax" problem. The larger the estate, the steeper the tax rate.

A marital life estate trust can be used to lower the couple's overall estate taxes. With this type of trust, each spouse leaves use and income of his or her

property to the other spouse only for that spouse's life. When that spouse dies, the trust property goes to whomever was named as the ultimate trust beneficiary. The spouse who received the life estate has only the power to use the trust property, and receive its income, during her life; she cannot consume the principle of the trust, or dispose of it as part of her own estate.

Example: Suppose Calvin and Phyllis, husband and wife, each have an estate worth $550,000, i.e., their total combined worth is $1,100,000. Calvin dies in 1990, leaving all his property to Phyllis. Because of the marital deduction, no estate tax is assessed. Phyllis dies in 1991. Her estate is the entire $1,100,000, which she leaves to the children. Since $600,000 can be left to anyone free of estate tax, $500,000 of the money left to the children is subject to tax. The tax assessed is $155,800.

Now suppose Calvin hadn't left his property outright to Phyllis, but had established a trust, with Phyllis having a "life estate" in the trust property and Calvin's children being the trust's ultimate beneficiaries. As discussed, Phyllis has the right to the income and use of the trust property.[7] And, if Phyllis is named as trustee, she can manage the trust property. Except as noted below, Phyllis cannot spend the trust principal. She is never the legal owner of the trust property. The trust property is subject to estate tax when Calvin dies, but isn't included in Phyllis' taxable estate.

In this situation there would be no tax liability at all. When Calvin dies (in 1990) he can transfer his $550,000 to anyone, including the trust, free of estate tax. Likewise, when Phyllis dies in 1991, she can transfer her $550,000 to the children free of estate tax.

Marital life estate trusts can be particularly desirable for elderly prosperous couples. If it's unlikely that one spouse will outlive the other by many years, it's probable that the surviving spouse won't need to

---

[7] Phyllis can be given additional rights, such as the right to receive 5% of the principal annually and the right to use any amount of the principal necessary for her health, welfare, or support.

consume the trust principal. By contrast, younger spouses are often understandably reluctant to risk imposing these types of restrictions on property one spouse leaves for the other's benefit.

b. Generation-Skipping Trusts

You can establish a "generation-skipping" trust for the benefit of your grandchildren (with the income to go to your children during their lives) instead of leaving the money directly to the children and hope they pass the money along when they die. Under a special Internal Revenue Code provision, your estate pays an estate tax when you die, but no additional tax is owed when the children die and the grandchildren get the money. A total of $1,000,000 can be passed in this way. Obviously, establishing this sort of trust only makes sense if your children have enough money so they can get along with only the interest, not the principal of this million dollars.

c. Preparation of an Irrevocable Estate Tax-Saving Trust

 Irrevocable estate tax-saving trusts are discussed in more detail in *Plan Your Estate With a Living Trust*. However, that book doesn't show you how to draft one yourself. An attorney's help is necessary to draft any irrevocable estate tax-saving trust. IRS regulations applicable to irrevocable trusts are complicated. A mistake can cost you all the tax savings you'd planned for. Also, irrevocable trusts are designed to last for quite a while, which means there must be a thorough consideration of contingencies over time. And, many complexities and options can be involved (e.g., use of a "QTip" marital life estate trust to postpone payment of estate taxes due when the first spouse dies). It simply isn't safe to prepare any irrevocable trust yourself, unaided.

4. Charities

All property left to bona-fide tax-exempt charities is exempt from federal estate tax. Technically, the amount given to charity is deducted from the net

estate, before determining its size for federal estate tax purposes.

F. Estate Planning Designed to Place Controls on Property

FOR ANY NUMBER OF REASONS, A PERSON MAY WANT to impose controls over property given to beneficiaries. The usual solution is to create a trust imposing the desired controls. Except for a simple children's trust, all require preparation by a lawyer.

1. The Children's Trust

As discussed in detail in Chapter 7, Section C(2), many people leaving property to minors want to delay the age at which the minors receive the property outright, and a children's trust is routinely used to achieve this. As you know, you can establish a children's trust in wills prepared from this book and choose any age you wish for the property to be turned over to the children.

2. Second Marriages

Another common use of a trust to impose controls over property occurs in second or subsequent marriages. If either spouse has children from a prior marriage, the spouse may want to leave property for use of the other spouse, but be sure her property eventually goes to her children. The standard way to achieve this is by use of a marital life estate trust, with the surviving spouse receiving the deceased spouse's property only for use during his or her life.

Example: Sherry and Raymond marry. Each has children from a prior marriage. They buy an expensive house together. Each contributes 50% of the purchase price and mortgage payments. If they die, each wants the other to be able to continue to live in the house for his or her life. But on the second spouse's death, each wants his or her share of the house to go to their own children. So Sherry and Raymond each create a marital life estate trust for their share of the house, the surviving spouse receiving only the rights to lifetime use of the other spouse's share of the house. When both spouses are dead, each spouse's children receive a total of half the value of the house.

3. 'Spendthrift' Trusts

If you want to leave property to an adult, but worry that the adult cannot sensibly handle that property, you can create a "spendthrift trust," which restricts the ability of that adult to consume the trust property.

Example: Bill wants to leave a significant amount of money to 35 year old Tim, but worries that Tim is improvident and easily influenced. So Bill leaves the money in a "spendthrift" trust that ends when Tim becomes 50. Until then, the trustee controls distribution of the trust funds to Tim, who cannot legally pledge them or use them before actual receipt. (This is a different and more complex trust than the children's trust contained in this book's will forms.)

4. A Trust for a Disadvantaged Person

A person with a physical or mental disability may not be able to handle property left to them. So a trust, often called a "special needs" trust, is established, with a competent adult as trustee, to manage the disadvantaged person's trust property.

Example: Elizabeth's daughter is hospitalized with a grave physical disability. Elizabeth leaves all her property in trust for her daughter, with her best friend, Mona, as trustee. The trust is carefully prepared by an expert, so that the trust money available to the daughter won't jeopardize her eligibility for government benefits.

5. Flexible Trusts

For one of a variety of reasons, someone may want the determination of how their property is spent after their death to be decided in the future, not before they die. The usual way to accomplish this is to create a trust authorizing the trustee discretion in deciding how to spend trust money.

Example: Vivian leaves money for her six grandchildren. She wants the money used where it is most needed, which she realizes she can't determine in advance. So she leaves the money in a "sprinkling" trust, with the trustee having the power to distribute trust monies as she determines the beneficiaries need.

G. Planning for Incapacity: The Durable Power of Attorney

ALTHOUGH NOT STRICTLY SPEAKING ESTATE PLANNING, it is obviously sensible to prepare for the contingency that you become incapacitated and can no longer handle your own financial affairs or make medical decisions.

The wisest way to plan for incapacity is to prepare what's called a "Durable" Power of Attorney, a document in which you appoint someone else (called your "attorney in fact") to manage your financial and business affairs, and make health care decisions for you, should you become incapacitated. Normally, a durable power of attorney doesn't take effect unless and until you do become incapacitated. So it functions as a kind of legal insurance, making sure you're protected, without court proceedings, if you ever need it.

In your durable power of attorney you can make provision for your medical treatment if you're incapacitated and hospitalized. Of paramount concern to many people is the issue of life sustaining procedures. If they are ever in a terminal condition or have a fatal illness, many people want to die a natural death, rather than having their life artificially prolonged by life support equipment. You can make your desires regarding life sustaining procedures, including life support equipment, binding by use of a durable power of attorney for health care.

H. Estate Planning—Summing Up

FOR MOST PEOPLE WITH MODEST AMOUNTS OF PROPERTY (say less than $60,000), a will adequately solves all their estate planning problems because their estate will probably neither be subjected to federal estate tax nor substantial probate fees. For estates of moderate size ($100,000-$600,000), consideration should be given to the pros and cons of probate avoidance. Are the savings to your inheritors worth the time, effort, and costs involved in probate avoidance? Is a will sufficient for your needs now, with probate avoidance to be considered (much) later?

People with large estates (over $600,000) will find that estate planning involves both making a will and trying to reduce death taxes. The more an estate is worth, the more important estate planning becomes. As noted above, even though you might want to limit the property you pass by your will, you still need one.

Finally, it's sensible to prepare a durable power of attorney to prepare in advance for what happens if you ever become incapacitated.

CHAPTER 9

LAWYERS, TYPING SERVICES AND DOING YOUR OWN LEGAL RESEARCH

A. Do You Need a Lawyer?   9/1

B. Working With a Lawyer   9/1

C. Do You Need a Will Typing Service?   9/4

D. Doing Your Own Research   9/4

AS ALREADY DISCUSSED, I BELIEVE MOST PEOPLE can safely prepare their own will by using *Nolo's Simple Will Book* without any help from a lawyer. However, the decision of whether you want, or need, legal assistance is one only you can make. For a variety of reasons, you may need more information than is presented in this book. Or you may want review of your work by a lawyer to reassure yourself that your will is proper and legal.

A. Do You Need a Lawyer?

HERE'S A SUMMARY OF THE MAIN REASONS the services of a lawyer are usually warranted:

- You want to learn more about a specific area of your state's laws;
- Your estate is in the $600,00 range or more and will be subject to a substantial federal estate tax unless you engage in tax planning;
- You want to establish a trust, other than a simple trust for your children;
- You want to give a gift with complex shared ownership, such as a marital life estate;
- You own a part of a small business and have questions as to the rights of surviving owners, your ownership share, etc.;

- You must make arrangements for long-term care of a beneficiary (for example, to create a trust for a disadvantaged child);
- You fear someone will contest your will (on grounds of fraud, undue influence or incompetence);
- You wish to disinherit, or substantially disinherit, your spouse.

B. Working With a Lawyer

FOR INTELLIGENT CONSUMERS, CONSULTING WITH A LAWYER should most definitely not mean that you hire one and say, "I want a will, so please prepare one for me." At a minimum, you should take the time to understand your needs, and prepare a rough draft of your own will. Indeed, most readers of this book who do hire a lawyer will probably want their attorney to do little more than resolve specific questions and insure that the finished product achieves their goals. If you decide you want a lawyer to review your draft will, be clear with yourself and the lawyer, on what you expect the lawyer to do. You obviously don't want to let any lawyer cast you in the role of a passive "client" (interestingly, the Latin root of the word client translates as "to obey," or "to hear"). If he tries to do this, it's wise to hire someone else.

1. Paying Your Lawyer

As you already know, lawyers are expensive. They charge by the hour at fees ranging from $75 to $250 per hour. While fancy office trappings, three-piece suits and solemn faces are no guarantee (or even any indication) that a lawyer is one you'll like, this conventional style will almost always insure that you'll be charged a fee towards the upper end of this range. Interestingly, at Nolo our experience tells us that high fees and quality service don't necessarily go hand in hand. Indeed, the attorneys I think most highly of tend to charge moderate fees (for lawyers, that is).

Be sure you've settled your fee arrangement at the start of your relationship. Generally, I feel that fees in the range of $75-$150 per hour are fair (given a lawyer's overhead) depending on the area of the country and what you want the lawyer to do. In addition to the amount charged per hour, you also want a clear commitment from the lawyer concerning how many hours he expects to put in on your problem. Often, one office consultation is all you need. If a lawyer tells you wills are complex and it will take him many hours to handle your problems, go somewhere else.

2. Finding a Lawyer

All this sounds good, you may think, but how do you find a lawyer? Believe me, this isn't difficult. Indeed, ours is such a lawyer-ridden society that it's something of a miracle if one hasn't already found you. The trick, of course, isn't just finding (or being found by) any lawyer, but retaining one who is trustworthy, competent, and charges fairly. A few words of advice may be helpful.

First, decide what type of lawyer you need. This depends on what your problem is. If you want to engage in sophisticated estate planning, especially the creation of an irrevocable trust to save on estate taxes (discussed in Chapter 8), see someone who specializes in the field. Irrevocable trusts are quite technical. Most general practice lawyers are simply not sufficiently educated in this field to hire them to do this type of

work. An expert may charge relatively high fees ($150 or more per hour), but if she's good, she's worth it. And if you need this sort of estate planning help, you (or you and your spouse together) presumably have more than $600,000 and can afford it.

On the other hand, if you want a lawyer to review a will created with this book, or check a particular provision of your state's laws, a competent attorney in general practice is adequate.

Next, it's important that you feel a personal rapport with your lawyer. You want one who treats you as an equal. When talking with a lawyer on the phone, or at the first conference, ask some specific questions. If the lawyer answers them clearly and concisely—explaining, but not talking down to you—fine. If he acts wise, but says little except to ask that the problem be placed in his hands (with the appropriate fee, of course), watch out. You're either talking with someone who doesn't know the answer and won't admit it (common), or someone who finds it impossible to let go of the "me expert, you peasant" way of looking at the world (even more common).

To find a lawyer you'll like (and who will do a good job), the best route is the traditional one—ask your friends. If you've got a close friend who found a lawyer he liked, chances are you'll like her too. Otherwise you've got work to do. Here are some suggestions on how you can find a lawyer you'll be pleased with:

- Check with people you know who own their own businesses. Almost anyone running a small business has a relationship with a lawyer. Chances are they've found one they like. If this lawyer doesn't handle wills, he'll know someone who does. And, best of all, because he has a continuing relationship with your friend, he has an incentive to recommend someone who's good, not just his brother-in-law who owes him money.
- Check with people you know in any political or social organization you're involved with. They may well know of a competent lawyer whose attitudes are similar to yours. Groups that advise and assist older people are particularly likely to have a list of local lawyers who specialize in wills and estate planning and are generally regarded as competent and caring.

- Join a prepaid legal insurance plan[1] that offers extensive advice, and preferably a will, at no extra charge. Your initial membership fee may be worth the consultation you receive, even if you use it only once. Most plans have renewal fees; it's common to join a plan for a specific service and then not renew. The plans are sold by companies such as Bank of America, Montgomery Ward and Amway, and are often offered to credit card holders, or sold door to door. Of course, there's no guarantee that the lawyers available through these plans are of the best caliber; sometimes they aren't. As with any consumer transaction, check out the plan, and the lawyer you're referred to, carefully before signing up. Whenever you avail yourself of any service offered by these prepaid insurance plans, be forewarned: The lawyer is probably getting only $2 or $3 per month from the plan for dealing with you, and may have agreed to this minimal amount in the hope of snaring people into paying for extra legal services not covered by the monthly premium. So, if the lawyer recommends an expensive legal procedure rather than a simple will or probate avoidance device such as a living trust, get a second opinion before you agree. For example, some plans that offer a will for no charge beyond the original membership fee charge hundreds of dollars extra if you want to include a simple children's trust such as the one included in many of the wills in this book.

- Some unions, employers and consumer action organizations offer group legal plans to their members or employees, who can obtain comprehensive legal assistance free or for low rates. If you're a member of such a plan, check with it first for a lawyer referral if your problem is covered free of charge. However, if the plan only gives you a slight reduction in a lawyer's fee, as many do, keep in mind that you may be referred to a lawyer whose main virtue is the willingness to reduce his price in exchange for a high volume of referrals. As noted throughout this chapter, we believe there are better criteria for picking a good lawyer.

- Law clinics such as Hyatt Legal Services and Jacoby and Meyers loudly advertise their low initial consultation fees. This generally means that a basic consultation is cheap (often about $20); anything beyond that isn't so cheap. If you consult a law clinic, the trick (for you) often is to quickly extract what information you need and resist any attempt to convince you that you need further services. If the lawyer you talk to is experienced with wills, however, and you're comfortable with the person and the representation, it may be worth it to pay for a full consultation in exchange for more thorough information and advice. Generally, you will find that rates charged are about the same as those charged by the average lawyer in general practice. Perhaps the worst problem with these clinics is lawyer turnover. It's extremely high and, as a result, it's often not possible to form a long-term relationship with a lawyer.

- Most county bar associations maintain referral services that will give you the names of some attorneys who practice in your area. Usually you can get a referral to an attorney who specializes in wills, and an initial consultation, for a low fee. A problem with the panel is that they usually provide minimal screening for the attorneys listed, which means those who participate may not be the most experienced or competent. It may be possible to find a skilled attorney willing to work for a reasonable fee following this approach, but take the time to check out the credentials and experience of the person to whom you're referred.

- Check the classified ads under "Attorneys." There are quite a few attorneys around who are no longer interested in handling court-contested matters but do provide consultations and will-drafting at relatively low rates. This could be just what you need.

---

[1]It's a misnomer to refer to these programs as legal insurance. The programs provide an initial level of service for a low fee (usually $75-$100), and then charge specific fees for additional or different work. Thus, most prepaid plans are more a marketing device for the participating lawyers than they are an insurance plan.

C. Do You Need a Will Typing Service?

ALTHOUGH YOU SHOULD BE ABLE to draft your own will without a lawyer's assistance, you may want to consult with someone who is familiar with this book and knows how it should be used. A will typing service can:

- supply a questionnaire to help you prepare an Assemble-the-Clauses will;
- guide you through relevant portions of this book;
- review your draft will and suggest additional reading where necessary;
- help you over any rough spots;
- type or print your will on high quality paper and provide a blue back for the outer cover.

For routine will preparation and help with this book, will typing services normally charge from $25 - $50.

When using a will typing service, it is important to understand that they are very different from lawyers. They can't give legal advice or represent you in court—only lawyers are allowed to do those things. When you use a will typing service, you remain responsible for the decision making in your case. You must decide what information to put in your will and who to leave it to. You cannot, legally, pass this responsibility on to a will typing service.Referrals to will typing services near you may be obtained from the National Association for Independent Paralegals at (800) 542-0034.

D. Doing Your Own Research

THERE'S OFTEN A VIABLE ALTERNATIVE to hiring a lawyer to resolve legal questions that affect your will— you can do your own legal research. This can provide some real benefits for those willing to learn how to do it. Not only will you save some money, you'll gain a sense of mastery over an area of law, generating a confidence that will stand you in good stead should you have other legal problems.

Fortunately, researching wills and related issues is an area generally well suited to doing your own legal research. Most problems don't involve massive or abstruse legal questions. Often you need only check the statutes of your state to find one particular provision. Or you can learn how to use legal form books, the very books lawyers often refer to in order to solve a problem.

If you decide you want to do your own research, how do you go about it? First, it surely helps to have a research aid. If you can't hire your own law librarian, the best book explaining how to do your own legal work is Elias, *Legal Research: How To Find and Understand the Law* (Nolo Press). It tells you all you need to know to do effective research.

Next, locate a law library (or a public library with a good law collection). There's usually one in your principal county courthouse. These law libraries are normally supported by your tax dollars or by the fees paid to file legal papers, and are open to the public. The librarians in county law libraries are generally most helpful and courteous to nonlawyers who wish to learn to do their own legal research. Ask them how you can locate the state's statutes (these are called "codes," "laws," "statutes," depending on the state). Usually what you want is called the "annotated version," which contains both your state's statutes and excerpts from any relevant judicial decisions and cross references to related articles and commentaries.

Once you've found your state's statutes, check the index for provisions dealing with wills or a specific subject that concerns you. Generally, you'll find what you want in the volume of statutes dealing with your state's basic civil or probate laws. These are usually called a name such as "Civil Code" or "Probate Laws." These codes are numbered sequentially, and once you get the correct number in the index, it's easy to find the statute you need. If you have trouble, the law librarian will usually be happy to help.

Once you've looked at the basic statutes contained in the hardcover volume, and checked the pocket part at the back of the book for any amendments, you'll probably want to skim the summaries of recent court decisions contained in the "Annotation" section immediately following the statute itself. If a summary looks like it might help answer your question, you'll want to read the full court opinion that the summary was taken from.

CHAPTER 10

AN OVERVIEW OF THE WILLS YOU
CAN DRAFT USING THIS BOOK

A.	How to Proceed	10/1
B.	Basic Form Wills	10/1
C.	Assemble-It-Yourself Wills	10/2
D.	Formalities	10/3

A. How to Proceed

NOW THAT YOU'VE ASSEMBLED all the personal information you need to prepare your will, it's time to focus on actually preparing it. Unfortunately, no one generic will form suits all needs. Recognizing this, the Will Book offers two basic formats for you to draft your will:

1. Six basic fill-in-the-blank will forms for use in many common situations. These are set out and explained in Chapter 11; and

2. A set of will clauses from which you select the appropriate ones to be included in your will. This assemble-it-yourself will format, set out in Chapter 12, allows more flexibility in choosing what to include in your will.

To help you decide which format is best for you, let's briefly examine these two approaches to will drafting.

B. Basic Form Wills

IF YOUR DESIRES ARE STRAIGHTFORWARD, one of the six basic wills set out in Chapter 11 will probably meet your needs. These are specifically designed for the following personal situations:

I.   Will for a single person with no minor children.

This form is also appropriate for a single person with no children or with adult children only.

II.   Will for a single person with minor children

(or for a person who wants to leave gifts in trust to any minor children).

III. Will for a husband or wife with no minor children.

This form is also appropriate for a married person with no children or with adult children only.

IV. Will for a husband or wife with minor children

(or for a person who wants to leave gifts in trust to any minor children).

V.   Will for a person who lives with a lover/mate and who has no minor children.

This form is also appropriate for a person who lives with a mate/lover and who has no children, or who has adult children only.

VI. Will for a person who lives with a lover/mate and who has minor children

(or for a person who wants to leave gifts in trust to any minor children).

You can use a Chapter 11 will to achieve such fundamental purposes of will writing as:

- Making gifts of all your personal and real property to named beneficiaries;
- Naming an alternate beneficiary for each gift in case the first beneficiary you name fails to survive you by 45 days;
- Naming a residuary beneficiary (and an alternate residuary beneficiary) to receive any property not specifically given to named beneficiaries;
- Establishing a 45-day survivorship period for beneficiaries;
- Appointing an adult as personal guardian of your minor children;
- Setting up a trust for your minor children;
- Making gifts to your minor children, grandchildren or other minors under The Uniform Transfers to Minors Act;
- Appointing an adult to serve as property guardian for your minor children, in case one is needed;
- Appointing your executor (personal representative).

As I indicate in Chapter 11, you can alter the printed text of a fill-in-the-blanks will to make minor technical changes, but the text of the will shouldn't be revised or changed in major ways. If after you review the wills in Chapter 11 you find that one or more of your basic desires cannot be accommodated, check to see whether a will in Chapter 12 will meet your needs.

C. Assemble-It-Yourself Wills

IN CHAPTER 12 YOU HAVE THE OPPORTUNITY to assemble your will clause by clause. Where there are sensible alternatives to handling a particular legal need, I provide you with a choice of different clauses, with accompanying explanations. This approach allows you to address all the concerns covered in Chapter 11 wills, plus the following matters that aren't covered in a Chapter 11 basic will:

- Specifying how your probate costs and death taxes are to be paid by identifying particular assets to pay them. This subject isn't covered explicitly in the Chapter 11 wills. In many states, this means that all probate costs and death taxes are pro-rated

between beneficiaries according to the percentage of the total worth of your property they receive. But if you want to be more definite about this, use a clause from Chapter 12;
- Appointing co-executors;
- Imposing a survivorship period of your choosing on all your beneficiaries. Chapter 11 wills contain a standard 45-day clause. In Chapter 12, you have the opportunity to lengthen or shorten this period;
- Stating why it's in your children's best interest for the person you named as their personal guardian to be legally appointed. This isn't necessary, but is a good idea if you expect your nomination to be contested after your death;
- Giving particular items of property (especially real estate) free of liens or encumbrances, such as mortgages. Normally, if you make a gift of any property you owe money on, that debt goes with the property, For example, if you give your kids your house, they get the mortgage you owe on it, too. Occasionally, someone wants to give property free of debt. For instance, a parent wants to give her children a house free and clear, so they aren't burdened with mortgage payments. You can provide for this in your will. Of course, you also need to provide in your will for how the mortgage, or debt, is to be paid, and be sure the assets you specify for payment are sufficient to cover the debt;
- Forgiving debts;
- Expressly disinheriting a child or child of a deceased child (i.e., your grandchild);
- Varying the normal statutory age at which a minor is entitled to receive a gift under The Uniform Transfer to Minors Act in those few states that permit this (see Chapter 7, Section C(2));
- Including a no-contest clause in your will. This states that if a person to whom you leave property contests your will, he is automatically disinherited;
- Including provisions in your will regarding body part donations, your funeral, and your burial; and
- Providing for your pets.

Chapter 12 doesn't attempt to present every conceivable will clause relevant to every possible issue. To do so would result in a book of encyclopedic length. Chances are, though, that your intentions and goals can be met using the clauses in Chapter 12. If you're the exception to this rule and you need to modify or add to the material presented, you'll have to do your own research or see a lawyer.

D. Formalities

ONCE YOU'VE DRAFTED YOUR WILL in Chapter 11 or Chapter 12, you need to accurately and neatly type (or have typed) a final copy. This final copy must then be signed by you in front of three witnesses, who must then in turn sign the will. In Chapter 13 I tell you in detail how to go about each of these tasks. Pay particular attention to the requirements for witnesses explained in Sec. C (2) Chapter 13.

Once your will is made following the instructions in this book and is properly signed and witnessed, it's valid. This means it will be implemented after your death. In some instances, especially those involving small estates, this can often be done by the person you name as executor (personal representative) with no need for formal probate. More typically, your will will be presented to a probate court that will supervise its implementation. To get your will admitted to probate, your executor will have to convince the judge that the will is genuine (i.e., that it's really your will). This is generally accomplished by having one or two of your witnesses testify to that effect, either in person or through a written sworn statement.

In most states, the need for this type of proof can usually be avoided if you and your witnesses appear before a notary public and all sign an affidavit to the effect that your will was properly signed and witnessed. This procedure is aptly called "self proving" your will. If you want to take this additional step, Chapter 13 also provides the proper form and detailed accompanying instructions.

To summarize, your job will be easiest if you can fit your desires within one of the basic wills in Chapter 11. If not, Chapter 12 should do the trick. Whether you use Chapter 11 or Chapter 12, however, you will need to have your will typed, signed and witnessed as I instruct in Chapter 13. If you wish you may choose to make your will "self proving," also discussed in Chapter 13.

CHAPTER 11

B A S I C   W I L L S

A. Introduction   11/1

B. To Complete Your Basic Will   11/1

C. What Is Included In a Basic Will Form   11/3

D. Sample Completed Basic Will   11/10

E. Basic Will Forms   11/21

A. Introduction

THIS CHAPTER EXPLAINS HOW to complete a basic fill-in-the-blanks will. Six different basic will forms are provided in Section E. The form right for you depends on your marital or mate's status and whether you have children. These no-frills, no-fuss wills allow you to:

1. Leave your property to the people and organizations you choose to; this includes your spouse, children, grandchildren, other relatives, friends, charitable institutions, or anyone else;

2. Name alternate beneficiaries for gifts you make, in case any beneficiary fails to survive you by 45 days;

3. Name a personal guardian and alternate personal guardian to care for your minor children if you die before they reach 18 and a guardian becomes needed;

4. Leave property to your minor children, grandchildren, or other minors under the terms of the Uniform Transfers to Minors Act (if it's applicable in your state);

5. Leave property to one or more children in a simple children's trust, so that each gets the property at an age designated by you;

6. Name a property guardian and alternate property guardian for your minor children, to manage any of their property that isn't supervised under the Uniform Transfers to Minors Act or a children's trust;

7. Appoint your executor; and

8. If you're married or part of an unmarried couple, provide for the contingency of simultaneous death.

   Note on Traditional But Unnecessary Will Language: The wills in this chapter are both legal and practical. Because they use a minimum of legalese, some traditional, but legally unnecessary, phrases have been omitted.

B. To Complete Your Basic Will

TO COMPLETE ONE OF THE WILLS in this chapter, follow these steps:

   Step 1. Read this section and sections C and D of this chapter to gain an understanding of how the basic will format works.

   Step 2. Select the one will form from the six in Section E that best fits your situation.

   Step 3. Fill in the form.

   Step 4. Prepare your final will from the completed form by following the directions in Chapter 13.

MAKING GIFTS TO MINOR CHILDREN OR YOUNG ADULTS

Chapter 7, Sections C and D explain the different ways you can leave property to minors or young adult children. If you plan to make gifts to minors or young adult children in your will, and haven't read those sections, do so now. Gifts to minor children under the Uniform Transfers to Minors Act can only be made in wills II, IV or VI. Similarly, you can only leave property for minors or young adults in a children's trust in wills II, IV or VI. And you can only appoint a personal or property guardian for your minor children in wills II, IV and VI. Again, to sensibly choose which device to use for gifts to minors and young adults, you must read Chapter 7.

The will forms are perforated so you can remove the one which fits your situation and conveniently use it as a worksheet to prepare your draft will. The captions of the six forms are:

I. Will for a single person with no minor children

This is normally the form people in this group will choose. However, if you're a single person without your own minor children, but decided, in Chapter 7, to make gifts to any children using either your state's Uniform Transfers to Minors Act, or a children's trust, use form II.

II. Will for a single person with minor children

III. Will for a husband or wife with no minor children

This is normally the form people in this group will choose. However, if you're a married person without your own minor children, but decided, in Chapter 7, to make gifts to any children using either your state's Uniform Transfers to Minors Act, or a children's trust, use form IV.

Reminder: Each spouse must complete his or her own will.

IV. Will for a husband or wife with minor children

V. Will for a person who lives with a lover/mate and who has no minor children

This is normally the form people in this group will choose. However, if you're living with a lover/mate and have no minor children of your own, but decided, in Chapter 7, to make gifts to any children using either your state's Uniform Transfers to Minors Act, or a children's trust, use form VI.

VI. Will for a person who lives with a lover/mate and who has minor children

Step 3. Complete the appropriate blanks in the will form you've chosen. Here's how to proceed:
- Use a pencil, since you may need to erase mistakes, or make changes (this is your first draft).
- If you need more space than the form provides to complete a particular blank, here's what to do:
a. Put "continued on Attachment 1" at the end of the too short space on the form. Then title a piece of blank typing paper by marking it "Attachment 1, continuation of Clause _____ ," filling in the number of the clause that's being continued (e.g., "Attachment 1, continuation of Clause 3").
b. Complete the Attachment by providing all information needed. Finally, attach the continuation page or pages to your draft.
c. If you need another attachment for another clause, repeat the process, numbering this Attachment 2.

Step 4. If a portion of a will clause doesn't apply to you, simply draw a line through it so you, or your typist, will know to leave it out of the final draft. For example, each basic will form contains a clause for you to list your children. The clause contains space for listing five children. If you have two children, delete the last three spaces for listing children. And, of course, if you have no children, delete the entire clause.

If you eliminate an entire clause, be sure you renumber the rest of the clauses. For example, clause 10 of Will IV, for a husband or wife with minor children, is for making gifts using the Uniform

Transfers to Minors Act. If you're using Form IV, but don't make gifts using the Act, delete this clause 10 from your draft will. The next clause in will Form IV, creating a children's trust, is numbered 11. In your draft will, renumber this children's trust clause as 10, and so on.

MAKING CHANGES IN A BASIC WILL FORM

As has been emphasized, making any changes in a basic will form other than simple common sense ones, such as adjusting pronouns or renumbering clauses after one has been deleted, is discouraged. The purpose of a basic will is to provide clarity and simplicity. Making changes risks creating a confusing and possibly even an ineffective document.

Step 5. After you've filled in the blanks on the will form of your choice, review your draft until you're confident your will does what you want it to. Also use this opportunity to make sure that all personal pronouns (his, hers, theirs, etc.) and references to the singular and plural are correct.

Step 6. Have your will typed, following the instructions in Chapter 13. If you type your will yourself, you should have little trouble understanding exactly what to include. However, if someone else will type your will, be sure your typist:

- Receives a neatly prepared draft so he or she won't make a mistake as a result of being confused.
- Understands exactly where any attachments are to be inserted in the will;
- Knows to insert the standard language for executor powers at the appropriate place and, if you establish a trust for one or more of your children, also knows where to insert the minor's trust provisions.
- Knows that the instructional words printed on the form below the blank lines and any clauses you've drawn lines through aren't to be typed in the final will.
- Understands the rules for format and neatness. Generally, I recommend that your will be typed double-spaced, although this isn't a legal requirement. After the will has been typed, carefully proof read it.

Step 7. Depending on the degree of your uncertainty and/or confusion about any of these matters, and the amount of property you have, you may want to have your will checked by an attorney. Do remember, though, that if you can use one of the forms in this chapter and follow all the instructions in this book, your will is probably already in good shape and fully legal.

Step 8. Comply with the signing and witnessing requirements outlined in Chapter 13.

C. What Is Included In a Basic Will Form

NOW LET'S EXAMINE THE BASIC WILLS included in this chapter by studying each clause separately. Remember, as you do this, the places where you are to insert information have blank lines. Don't enter information now. These clauses are presented here only for the purpose of introducing you to the will form. The actual drafting of your will starts in Section E.

1. Will Identification Provision

Your will should identify you by the name you customarily use when you sign legal documents and other important papers. If, for any reason, you've used different names—e.g., you changed your name to Jerry Adams, but still own some property in the name of Jerry Adananossos, identify yourself with both names, as "Jerry Adams 'aka' [also known as] Jerry Adananossos," and sign your will that way. Providing your city, county and state can help eliminate any doubt about the state in which you reside. It also helps establish which county the will is to be probated in.[1]

WILL OF ___Denis Clifford___
    your name

I, ___Denis Clifford___, a
    your name

resident of ___Berkeley___,
    city

___Alameda County___,
    county

___California___ declare that this
    state

is my will.

Clause 1.   Revoke All Previous Wills

This is a standard clause which revokes all previous wills, including any handwritten ones. A revocation clause helps prevent any possible confusion or litigation regarding the validity of prior wills. To be safe, a revocation clause is used whether or not you have in fact made another will. All wills in this chapter contain a revocation clause; you don't have to add anything.

1. I revoke all wills and codicils I have previously made.

Clause 2.   Name Your Spouse and Children (if any)

If currently married, you should select either Will III (will for a husband or wife with no minor children) or Will IV (will for a husband or wife with minor children). Either way, insert your spouse's name. The clause where you do this states that whenever you

refer to your "husband" or "wife" elsewhere in the will, you're referring to the person named in this clause.

Whether or not you're currently married, each of the six wills in this chapter provides space for you to list the names of former spouses and how the marriage ended (i.e., death, annulment, or divorce).

If you use one of the six wills in this chapter, your will should both name and provide for (give something to) all of your children and all children of a deceased child. If you wish to completely disinherit a child, you must use Chapter 12 to make your will. It is not enough to name a child in a Chapter 11 will and then omit to provide for him. However, if you give a child $1.00, you accomplish the same purpose. This includes children of previous marriages, children born out of wedlock, and legally adopted children. The Chapter 11 wills do not contain a clause allowing you to expressly disinherit a child.

2. I am married to ___Patti Jones___,
    name

and all references in this will to my ___wife___
    wife/husband

are to ___her___.
    him/her

[If appropriate, complete:

I was previously married to ___Carol Riordan___.

That marriage was terminated by ___divorce___.]

[Repeat if you were married more than once.]

I am the ___father___ of the following
    mother/father

children, whose names and dates of birth are:

___Michael Jones___   ___2/19/81___
Name   Date of Birth

_____   _____
Name   Date of Birth

_____   _____
Name   Date of Birth

Add more lines to the simple will form as needed to list additional former spouses, children and children

---

[1]If you move to another state, your will remains valid. See Chapter 14 for a discussion of when you need to revise your will if you move.

of deceased children. If there are no deceased children, or no living children of a deceased child, cross out that provision so it's not included in your final will.

Living Together Note: If you're living with a lover or mate and select Will V (will for a person who lives with a lover/mate and who has no minor children) or Will VI (will for a person who lives with a lover/mate and who has minor children), those forms provide a space for you to list and identify your lover or mate, and state that all references to your lover or mate are to that person.

Clauses 3, 4, & 5. Making Specific Gifts

You'll recall that in Chapter 5 you were asked to provide a thorough description of all your property. If your situation was simple, with most or all of your property going to one or a few beneficiaries, you probably didn't need to go into much detail describing your property. Then, in Chapter 6, you selected the beneficiary or beneficiaries you want to inherit your property. In addition, you probably selected alternate beneficiaries to take your gifts in case your primary beneficiaries fail to survive you by the period specified in your will, which is 45 days in all Chapter 11 basic wills.

Now you need to transfer the information you recorded in Chapters 5 and 6 to the appropriate location in the basic will you have selected by completing Clauses 3, 4, 5 and 6 to make all your gifts. This includes all gifts you want to make to minor children, and to young adults using either a children's trust or the Uniform Transfer to Minors Act. You list those gifts here, naming the child or children as the beneficiary, or alternate beneficiary. If you're leaving all your

property to the same beneficiary or beneficiaries—your spouse, children, or a charity—you don't need to make special gifts. You can simply leave all your property through clause 6, the residuary clause.

Later, in wills II, IV or VI, there's a clause for naming which minor beneficiaries receive their gifts under the Uniform Transfers to Minors Act (assuming it's applicable in your state) and another clause to establish a children's trust.

To Complete Clause 3: Transfer each cash gift from the Beneficiary Chart in Chapter 6 to Clause 3. Then, fill in the names of the primary and alternate beneficiaries who you designated in Chapter 6 to receive these cash gifts. Here is what Clause 3 looks like:

3. I make the following cash gifts:

I give _____ *$ 10,000* _____ to
_____ *Rudolph Phelps* _____ or, if
_____ *he* _____ doesn't survive me by
45 days, to _____ *Andrew Phelps* _____ .

To Complete Clause 4: Transfer each personal property gift (other than cash) listed in Chapter 6 to Clause 4. For your description of each gift, use the one you prepared in the chart in Chapter 5.[2]

Then, fill in the names of the primary and alternate beneficiaries who you designated in Chapter 6 to receive these personal property items. Here is an example of Clause 4:

4. I make the following specific gifts of personal property:

I give _____ *all my stocks* _____ to
_____ *my mate Ellen Zywansky* _____ or, if
_____ *she* _____ doesn't survive me
by 45 days, to _____ *my brother Ted O'Connor* .

_____

[2]If you skipped the property inventory chart in Chapter 5 because of the simple way you plan to leave your property, review the instructions in that chapter for making property descriptions before filling out the will clauses in this chapter.

Note: It is perfectly okay to give a number of personal property items in one blank (e.g., "I give my gold watch, skis, and coin collection to ___Wilfred Brown...___ ").

To Complete Clause 5: Transfer each real property gift listed in Chapter 6 to Clause 5. Use the description for this property which you prepared in Chapter 5.[3]

Here is what Clause 5 looks like.

5. I make the following specific gifts of real property:

I give the property commonly known as _my condominium_ _apartment at 2 Park Ave., New York, New York_ to _my wife Rose Elliott_____ or, if _____ _she_ _____ doesn't survive me by 45 days, to _my best friend Michael L. Smith_.

That's all there is to it. If you run out of room in Clauses 3, 4 or 5, prepare an attachment following the instructions at the beginning of this chapter.

Clause 6.   The 'Residue' of Your Estate

As you know by now, the "residue" of your estate is exactly what it sounds like—all that remains after all specific gifts have been distributed. You named your residuary beneficiary and alternate residuary beneficiary in the chart in Chapter 6. Now you enter this information here, in the residuary clause:

6. I give my residuary estate, i.e., the rest of my property not otherwise specifically and validly disposed of by this will or in any other manner, to _my husband Tom Harras_ or if _____he_____ fails to survive me by 45 days, to _my child Linda Harras Smith_.

                   alternate beneficiary

Note: In addition to naming your primary and alternate residuary beneficiaries, the residuary clause in these will forms also provides that:

---

[3]See the previous footnote.

- Specific gifts become part of your residuary estate if all the primary and alternate beneficiaries you named to receive that gift fail to survive you by 45 days; and
- Alternate beneficiaries of shared gifts of all types (including shared residuary gifts) only take the gift if all the primary beneficiaries fail to survive you by 45 days. Thus, if you name two residuary beneficiaries—Edgar and Cory—and one alternate residuary beneficiary—Sidney—and Edgar dies before you, Cory would receive all your residue. Only if Edgar and Cory both die before you would Sidney receive your residue.

 If you want to create a different provision for alternate beneficiaries of shared gifts, see a lawyer.

Important: The form wills provide that all your debts and taxes are paid from your residuary estate, assuming it is large enough to do the job. This is a common way to deal with this problem. If you want a different arrangement, however, use Chapter 12 to construct your will.

Clause 7.   Name Your Executor

Here you name your executor and successor executor, the people you chose in Chapter 3 to be responsible for supervising the distribution of your property. Here is what the clause looks like:

7. I nominate _Mary O'Railley_____ as executor to serve without bond. If _Mary O'Railley_ shall for any reason fail to qualify or cease to act as executor, I nominate _Tom O'Railley_____, also to serve without bond.

Clause 8. Simultaneous Death Clause (for those with a spouse or mate)

NOTE: The sample clause below assumes a married woman is making a will. A husband would obviously complete this clause by filling in his wife's name, or simply by using the word "wife" in the appropriate blank.

8. If my _____*husband*_____ and I
       wife/husband

should die simultaneously, or under such circumstances as to render it difficult or impossible to determine by clear and convincing evidence who predeceased the other, I

shall be conclusively presumed to have survived

_____*my husband*_____ for purposes of this will.
       wife/husband

Clause 9. Name a Personal Guardian for Your Minor Children

If you have minor children, you should be using basic will form II, IV or VI, depending upon your marital/ mate status. Each of these will forms contains a clause for you to name a personal guardian for your minor children to serve if there is no living person entitled to custody and available to assume it at your death.

Please review the discussion of choosing a personal guardian for your minor children in Chapter 7, Section B. In that section, you listed the names of the persons you've chosen as personal guardian and alternate personal guardian for your children. To complete the personal guardian clause of your will, simply transfer these names to the appropriate blanks below.

Naming Different Personal Guardians for Different Children, or Explaining the Reasons for Your Choices

Using a basic Chapter 11 will, you must name one personal and one alternate guardian for all your children. If you want to name different personal guardians for different children, or if you want to explain why you named the personal guardian you did, you'll need to prepare your will from Chapter 12.

Following is a sample completed personal guardian clause from a Chapter 11 will.

9. If at my death any of my children are minors and a

personal guardian is needed, I recommend that

_____*Ruby Johnson*_____, be appointed
              name

guardian of the person(s) of my   minor children. If

_____*Ruby Johnson*_____ cannot serve as personal
              name

guardian, I recommend that _____*Fran Johnson*_____
                                        name

be appointed personal guardian.

I direct that no bond be required of any personal

guardian.

Clause 10. Make Gifts Using the Uniform Transfers to Minors Act (Wills II, IV and VI)

Will forms II, IV and VI contain a clause allowing gifts you make to minors to be managed under the terms of the Uniform Transfers to Minors Act, if it's applicable in your state. You can only use the Act if you live in one of the following states:

Alabama, Alaska, Arizona, Arkansas, California, Colorado, District of Columbia, Florida, Georgia, Hawaii, Idaho, Illinois, Indiana, Iowa, Kansas, Kentucky, Maine, Maryland, Massachusetts, Minnesota, Missouri, Montana, Nevada, New Hampshire, New Jersey, New Mexico, North Carolina, North Dakota, Ohio, Oklahoma, Oregon, Rhode Island South Dakota, Utah, Virginia, Washington, West Virginia, Wisconsin, Wyoming.

As explained in Chapter 7, Sections C and D, you can use the Act to establish a simple, effective way to manage gifts made to a minor. If you decided to use the Act for gifts to one or more beneficiaries, or alternate beneficiaries, you listed each one's name, and the adult custodian and successor custodian for that gift, in Chapter 7, Sections C(3) or D(7). Now, to actually use the Act for gifts made in your will to minors, you'll simply transfer this information into the Uniform Transfers to Minors Act clause.

Reminder: If you live in one of the states listed below, and you decided to change the age at which a minor is to receive a gift you make from the age set by statute to another permissible one, you'll need to prepare your will from Chapter 12. The basic wills in this chapter don't allow you to change the basic statutory age at which a minor receives a gift made under the Act.

STATE	STATUTORY AGE FOR RECEIVING GIFT	CAN BE CHANGED BY WILL WRITER TO AN AGE
Alaska	18	up to 25
Arkansas	21	down to 18
California	18	up to 25
Maine	18	up to 21
New Hampshire	21	down to 18
North Carolina	21	down to 18
Virginia	18	to 21

To complete a Uniform Transfers to Minors Act clause of a Chapter 11 will, you:

- list the name of the minor, and the name of the custodian and successor custodian in the clause, as you recorded them in Chapter 7, Sections C(3) and D(7). Remember, you can appoint only one custodian and one successor custodian per child. You cannot appoint joint or shared custodians.
- complete the clause by filling in the name of your state.
- complete a separate Uniform Act clause for each minor to whom you want to make a gift to using the Act.

The Minors Act clause itself states that "All property given in this will …" to the named minor is given under the Act. In other words, there's no need for you to itemize the property here. To remind you, you've already made your gifts, including all gifts to minors, in clauses 3 through 6. Here you're just plugging in the Act into your will for those minors for whom you want to use the Act.

Following is a sample completed Minors Act clause from a Chapter 11 will.

10. All property given in this will to _Jeremy Schneider_ shall be given
minor's name
to _Caroline Chambers_ as
custodian's name
custodian for _Jeremy Schneider_
minor's name
under the Uniform Transfers to Minors Act of
California. If
your state
Caroline Chambers cannot serve as custodian,
custodians name
Karen Chambers shall serve as custodian.
successor guardian

Clause 11.   Establish Trusts for Property Left to Children

Will forms II, IV, and VI contain a clause you can complete to create simple children's trusts. You can use this clause to create separate trusts for one or more of:

- your own minor children;
- your own adult children under age 35;
- others' children to any age under 35.

The reasons for creating a children's trust in your will was explained in Chapter 7, Sections C(2) and D(4). If you decided to create a children trust for one or more beneficiaries, or alternate beneficiaries, you listed each such child's name, the age each child must reach to receive his or her trust property outright, and the trustee and successor trustee for each child's trust, in Section C(4) or D(7). To create a children's trust in your will, you transfer this information in the children's trust clause. A separate trust is created for each child. The trust clause itself states that "All property given in this will …" to each listed child is held in trust. In other words, you don't need to itemize the property you give each child listed in this children's trust clause. You've already made your gifts, including all gifts to children, in clauses 3 through 6. Here you're simply defining which children will receive their property in trust.

Naming Different Trustees for Different Children's Trusts

In a basic Chapter 11 will, you must appoint one trustee and one successor trustee for all children's trusts. If you want to name different trustees or different successor trustees for different children's trusts, you'll need to use one of the wills from Chapter 12.

Following is a sample completed children's trust clause from a Chapter 11 will.

11. All property I give in this will to any of the children listed in Section A below shall be held for each of them in a separate trust, pursuant to the following trust terms, which shall apply to each trust:

A.   Trust Beneficiaries and Age Limits

Each trust shall end when the following beneficiaries become 35, except as otherwise specified:

Trust for	Shall end at age
my son Jaime	28
my daughter Juanita	24

After you've completed the children's name and age provision for the trusts, you next complete the provision appointing the trustee to manage the trust or trusts, and the successor trustee to serve if your first choice isn't able to. Here is what the trustee provision looks like:

The trustee shall be _Ruby Johnson_ ,

name

or, if _Ruby Johnson_ cannot serve as

name

trustee, the trustee shall be _Fran Johnson_ .

name

No bond shall be required of any named trustee.

Clause 12.   Appoint a Property Guardian for Your Minor Children

If you have minor children, it's prudent to name a property guardian for them in your will, in case one is needed to manage any of the children's property that doesn't come with a built-in adult supervisor. Since most people leave property to their own minor children through either the Uniform Transfers to Minors Act or a children's trust, the property guardian named in a will normally serves only as a backup, in case an adult is needed to manage some other property of the children.

Naming a property guardian for your minor children was discussed in Chapter 7, Section C. And in Section C(5) of that chapter, you listed the names of the adults you'd chosen to serve as property guardian and alternate property guardian. To complete the property guardian clause of your will, you simply transfer those names into the appropriate blanks.

Following is a sample complete property guardian clause from a Chapter 11 will:

12. If any of my children are minors and a property guardian is needed, I appoint _Allen Muir_

name

as the property guardian of my minor children. If _Allen Muir_ cannot serve as

name

property guardian, I appoint _Suzanne Manning_

name

as property guardian.

I direct that no bond be required of any property guardian.

Signature Clause

I show you how to sign your will and have it witnessed in Chapter 13. In addition, if you decide to make your will self-proving, follow the instructions in Chapter 13, Section D.

D. Sample Completed Basic Will

BEFORE FILLING IN YOUR BASIC WILL, it can be helpful to see what a filled-in one looks like. For this reason I provide the following example. Examining it with care should reassure you that it really isn't hard to do your own will.

Mark and Linda are married, in their 40s, with two minor children. Mark is employed as an accountant. Linda works part-time as a proofreader for a publisher. They live in a community property state and own their house (heavily mortgaged) "as community property." (In a common law state, they would also each own one-half of the house, since they listed both names on the deed.) The house is their major asset. They also own, as community property, two cars, an old Ford convertible and a Toyota station wagon, the furnishings of their home, personal possessions like clothing, tools stereos, etc., $6,000 in a savings account in Mark's name, and $8,000 each in IRAs.

Mark and Linda each want to leave their entire estate to the other, except that Mark wants to give his tools to his brother, his Ford convertible to a friend, and $5,000 to his sister.[4] In determining their estate plan, they decide they need to purchase substantial amounts of insurance on both their lives to protect their children. They each purchase $100,000 worth of term life insurance. Each names the other as beneficiary of their IRA. Then each prepares a will, using form IV (will for a husband or wife with minor children).

Here is Mark's will after he's drafted it. Note that Mark doesn't sign his will yet, as it hasn't been typed, and isn't in its final form.

THE CHOOSE YOUR WILL FASHION SHOW

---

[4]These items are community property, so Mark legally can only give his one-half interest in them by his will unless Mark's wife agrees, in writing, to allow him to give away her half interest. In a common law state, Mark could give $6,000 from the savings account (since it's in his name) and the tools if he purchased them.

IV. WILL FOR A HUSBAND OR WIFE WITH MINOR CHILDREN

WILL OF ___Mark P. Creery_____
your name

I, _____Mark P. Creery_____, a resident of
your name

___Hayward_____, ___Alameda County_____, ___California_____
city   county   state

declare that this is my will.

1. I revoke all wills and codicils that I have previously made.

2. I am married to ___Linda F. Creery_____,
spouse's name

and all references in this will to my ___wife___ are to ___her_____.
husband/wife   him/her

[If appropriate, complete and repeat as needed]:

I was previously married to _____.
name of former spouse

That marriage was terminated by _____.
death/annulment/divorce

I am the ___father_____ of the following children whose names and dates of birth are:
mother/father

Anthony A. Creery	10/12/83
name	date of birth
Jennifer S. Creery	11/7/85
name	date of birth
name	date of birth
name	date of birth
name	date of birth

[repeat as needed]

There are _____ living children of my deceased child _____:
number   name

name of grandchild	date of birth
name of grandchild	date of birth

[repeat as needed]

3. I make the following cash gifts:

I give _____ $ 5000 _____ to _my sister Mary Creery Noonan_ ____ or, if
<u>amount</u>   <u>beneficiary</u>

_____ she _____ doesn't survive me by 45 days, to _her children in equal shares_
<u>beneficiary</u>   <u>alternate beneficiary</u>

I give _____ to _____ or, if
amount   beneficiary

_____ doesn't survive me by 45 days, to _____
beneficiary   alternate beneficiary

I give _____ to _____ or, if
amount   beneficiary

_____ doesn't survive me by 45 days, to _____
beneficiary   alternate beneficiary

I give _____ to _____ or, if
amount   beneficiary

_____ doesn't survive me by 45 days, to _____
beneficiary   alternate beneficiary

I give _____ to _____ or, if
amount   beneficiary

_____ doesn't survive me by 45 days, to _____
beneficiary   alternate beneficiary

I give _____ to _____ or, if
amount   beneficiary

_____ doesn't survive me by 45 days, to _____
beneficiary   alternate beneficiary

[repeat as needed]

4. I make the following specific gifts of personal property:

I give _my power tools_ _____
<u>description of gift</u>

to _my brother John Creery_ ____ or, if _____ he _____
<u>beneficiary</u>   <u>beneficiary</u>

doesn't survive me by 45 days, to _my wife_ _____.
<u>alternate beneficiary</u>

I give _my 1950 Ford convertible_ _____
<u>description of gift</u>

to _my best friend Ray Ellington_ ____ or, if _____ he _____
<u>beneficiary</u>   <u>beneficiary</u>

doesn't survive me by 45 days, to _my wife_ _____.
<u>alternate beneficiary</u>

I give _____
description of gift

to _____ or, if _____
beneficiary   beneficiary

doesn't survive me by 45 days, to _____
alternate beneficiary

BASIC WILLS   1 1 / 13

I give _____
                          description of gift

to _____ or, if _____
              beneficiary   beneficiary

doesn't survive me by 45 days, to _____.
                                          alternate beneficiary

I give _____
                          description of gift

to _____ or, if _____
              beneficiary   beneficiary

doesn't survive me by 45 days, to _____.
                                          alternate beneficiary

I give _____
                          description of gift

to _____ or, if _____
              beneficiary   beneficiary

doesn't survive me by 45 days, to _____.
                                          alternate beneficiary

[repeat as needed]

5. I make the following specific gifts of real property:

I give the property commonly known as _my share of 107 Dream Ave., Hayward_
                                         address or description of property

_____

to _my wife_____ or, if ___she_____
              beneficiary   beneficiary

doesn't survive me by 45 days, to _my children in equal shares__.
                                          alternate beneficiary

I give the property commonly known as _____
                                         address or description of property

_____

to _____ or, if _____
              beneficiary   beneficiary

doesn't survive me by 45 days, to _____.
                                          alternate beneficiary

I give the property commonly known as _____
                                         address or description of property

_____

to _____ or, if _____
              beneficiary   beneficiary

doesn't survive me by 45 days, to _____.
                                          alternate beneficiary

[repeat as needed]

6. I give my residuary estate, i.e., the rest of my property not otherwise specifically and validly disposed

of by this will or in any other manner, to ___my wife Linda_____,

~~beneficiary~~

or, if _____She_____ fails to survive me by 45 days, to

~~beneficiary~~

___my children in equal shares_____ If any primary beneficiary of a shared residuary or specific

~~alternate beneficiary~~

gift made in this will fails to survive me by 45 days, the surviving beneficiaries of that gift shall equally

divide the deceased beneficiary's share. If all primary beneficiaries of a shared residuary or specific gift fail

to survive me by 45 days, that gift shall pass in equal shares to the alternate beneficiaries named to receive

that gift. If the alternate beneficiaries named by this will to receive a specific gift don't survive me by 45

days, or there are no such named alternate beneficiaries, that gift shall become part of my residuary estate.

7. I nominate ___Linda F. Creery_____ as executor, to serve

~~executor~~

without bond. If _____She_____ shall for any reason fail to

~~executor~~

qualify or cease to act as executor, I nominate___John Creery._____ as

~~alternate executor~~

executor, also to serve without bond. I direct that my executor take all actions legally permissible to have

the probate of my estate done as simply as possible, including filing a petition in the appropriate court for

the independent administration of my estate.

I hereby grant to my executor the following powers, to be exercised as he or she deems to be in the

best interests of my estate:

(a) To retain property without liability for loss or depreciation resulting from such retention.

(b) To dispose of property by public or private sale, or exchange, or otherwise, and receive or

administer the proceeds as a part of my estate.

(c) To vote stock, to exercise any option or privilege to convert bonds, notes, stocks or other securities

belonging to my estate into other bonds, notes, stocks or other securities, and to exercise all other rights

and privileges of a person owning similar property in his own right.

(d) To lease any real property that may at any time form part of my estate.

(e) To abandon, adjust, arbitrate, compromise, sue on or defend and otherwise deal with and settle

claims in favor of or against my estate.

(f) To continue, maintain, operate or participate in any business which is a part of my estate, and to effect incorporation, dissolution or other change in the form of organization of the business.

(g) To pay all my debts, and all taxes that may, by reason of my death, be assessed against my estate or any portion of it, whether passing by probate or not, provided that such debts and taxes shall be first satisfied out of my residuary estate.

(h) To do all other acts, which in his or her judgment may be necessary or appropriate for the proper and advantageous management, investment and distribution of my estate.

The foregoing powers, authority and discretion granted to my executor are intended to be in addition to the powers, authority and discretion vested in him or her by operation of law by virtue of his or her office, and may be exercised as often as is deemed necessary or advisable, without application to or approval by any court in any jurisdiction.

8. If my _____*wife*_____ and I should die simultaneously or under such circumstances as to render it
          wife/husband
difficult or impossible to determine by clear and convincing evidence who predeceased the other, I shall be conclusively presumed to have survived my _____*wife*_____ for purposes of this will.
                                          wife/husband

9. If at my death any of my children are minors, and a personal guardian is needed, I nominate
_____*my wife's sister Joan Roy*_____ be appointed guardian of the person(s) of my
                    name
minor children. If _____*Joan Roy*_____ cannot serve as personal
                            name
guardian, I nominate _____*Mary Roy*_____ be appointed
                            name
guardian.

I direct that no bond be required of any personal guardian.

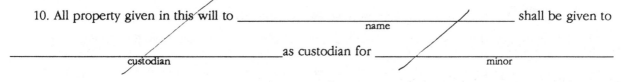

10. All property given in this will to _____ shall be given to
                                          name
_____ as custodian for _____
          custodian   minor

under the Uniform Transfers to Minors Act of _____. If _____

your state   custodian's name

cannot serve as custodian, _____ shall serve as custodian.

successor custodian's name

[repeat as needed]

11. All property I give in this will to any of the children listed in Section A below shall be held for each of them in a separate trust, pursuant to the following trust terms, which shall apply to each trust:

A. Trust Beneficiaries and Age Limits

Each trust shall end when the following beneficiaries become 35, except as otherwise specified in this section:

Trust for	Shall end at age
anthony A Creery	25
Jennifer S. Creery	25

B. Trustees

The trustee shall be _____Joan Roy_____, or, if _____Joan Roy_____

name   name

cannot serve as trustee, the trustee shall be _____Mary Roy_____

successor trustee

No bond shall be required of any trustee.

C. Beneficiary Provisions

(1) As long as a child is a beneficiary of this trust, the trustee may distribute from time to time to or for the benefit of the beneficiary as much, or all, of the net income or principal of the trust, or both, as the trustee deems necessary for the beneficiary's health, support, maintenance, and education.

Education includes, but isn't limited to, college, graduate, postgraduate, and vocational studies, and reasonably related living expenses.

(2) In deciding whether to make a distribution to the beneficiary, the trustee may take into account the beneficiary's other income, resources, and sources of support.

(3) Any trust income which isn't distributed to a beneficiary by the trustee shall be accumulated and added to the principal of the trust administered for that beneficiary.

D. Termination of Trust

The trust shall terminate when any of the following events occur:

(1) The beneficiary becomes the age specified in Paragraph A of this trust;

(2) The beneficiary dies before becoming the age specified in Paragraph A of this trust;

(3) The trust is exhausted through distributions allowed under these provisions.

If the trust terminates for reason (1), the remaining principal and accumulated net income of the trust shall pass to the beneficiary. If the trust terminates for reason (2), the remaining principal and accumulated net income of the trust shall pass to the trust beneficiary's heirs.

E. Powers of Trustee

In addition to other powers granted the trustee in this will, the trustee shall have:

(1) All the powers generally conferred on trustees by the laws of the state having jurisdiction over this trust;

(2) In respect to property in the trust, the powers conferred by this will on the executor; and

(3) The authority to hire and pay from the trust assets the reasonable fees of investment advisors, accountants, tax advisors, agents, attorneys, and other assistants for the administration of the trust and for the management of any trust asset and for any litigation affecting the trust.

F. Trust Administrative Provisions

(1) It is my intent that this trust be administered independent of court supervision to the maximum extent possible under the laws of the state having jurisdiction over this trust.

(2) The interests of trust beneficiaries shall not be transferable by voluntary or involuntary assignment or by operation of law and shall be free from the claims of creditors and from attachment, execution,

bankruptcy, or other legal process to the fullest extent permissible by law.

(3) Any trustee serving hereunder shall be entitled to reasonable compensation out of the trust assets for ordinary and extraordinary services, and for all services in connection with the complete or partial termination of any trust created by this will.

(4) The invalidity of any provision of this trust instrument shall not affect the validity of the remaining provisions.

12. If any of my children are minors and a property guardian is needed, I appoint _____
                                                                                        name

_____*Joan Roy*_____ as the property guardian of my minor children. If

_____*Joan Roy*_____ cannot serve as property guardian, I
                        name

appoint _____*Mary Roy*_____as property guardian.
                                        name

I direct that no bond be required of any property guardian.

I subscribe my name to this will this _____ day of _____, 19_____, at

_____,_____,_____,
        city   county   state

and do hereby declare that I sign and execute this instrument as my last will and that I sign it willingly, that I execute it as my free and voluntary act for the purposes therein expressed, and that I'm of the age of majority or otherwise legally empowered to make a will, and under no constraint or undue influence.

_____
                        your signed name

On this _____ day of _____, 19___, _____*Mark P. Creery*_____
                                                                        your name

declared to us, the undersigned, that this instrument was __*his*__ will and requested us to act as witnesses
                                                                        his/her

to it. __*He*__ thereupon signed this will in our presence, all of us being present at the same time. We now, at
        He/She

__*his*__ request, in __*his*__ presence, and in the presence of each other, subscribe our names as
    his/her   his/her

witnesses and declare we understand this to be __*his*__ will, and that to the best of our knowledge the
                                                                his/her

testator is of the age of majority, or is otherwise legally empowered to make a will, and under no constraint or undue influence.

We declare under penalty of perjury that the foregoing is true and correct, this _____ day of

_____ at _____.

_____
witness' signature

_____ residing at _____,
witness' typed name   street address

_____, _____, _____
city   county   state

_____
witness' signature

_____ residing at _____,
witness' typed name   street address

_____, _____, _____
city   county   state

_____
witness' signature

_____ residing at _____,
witness' typed name   street address

_____, _____, _____.
city   county   state

E. Basic Will Forms

NOW IT'S TIME TO ACTUALLY PREPARE the draft of your will. After reviewing Section B of this chapter, select the form that applies to you and complete it following the instructions set out above.

After reviewing Section B of this chapter, select the one that applies to you and prepare it following the instructions set out above.

I.   Will for a single person with no minor children.

II.   Will for a single person with minor children

III. Will for a husband or wife with no minor children.

IV. Will for a husband or wife with minor children

V.   Will for a person who lives with a lover/mate and who has no minor children.

VI. Will for a person who lives with a lover/mate and who has minor children

II. WILL FOR A SINGLE PERSON WITH MINOR CHILDREN

WILL OF _____
your name

I, _____, a resident of
your name

_____, _____, _____
city   county   state

declare that this is my will.

1. I revoke all wills and codicils that I have previously made.

2. I am not married.

[If appropriate, complete and repeat as needed]:

I was previously married to _____.
name of former spouse

That marriage was terminated by _____.
death/annulment/divorce

I am the _____ of the following children whose names and dates of birth are:
mother/father

_____   _____
name   date of birth

_____   _____
name   date of birth

_____   _____
name   date of birth

_____   _____
name   date of birth

_____   _____
name   date of birth

[repeat as needed]

There are _____ living children of my deceased child _____:
number   name

_____   _____
name of grandchild   date of birth

_____   _____
name of grandchild   date of birth

_____   _____
name of grandchild   date of birth

[repeat as needed]

3. I make the following cash gifts:

I give _____ to _____ or, if
　　　　　　amount　　　　　　　　　　　　　　　　beneficiary

_____ doesn't survive me by 45 days, to _____
　　beneficiary　　　　　　　　　　　　　　　　　　　　　　　alternate beneficiary

I give _____ to _____ or, if
　　　　　　amount　　　　　　　　　　　　　　　　beneficiary

_____ doesn't survive me by 45 days, to _____
　　beneficiary　　　　　　　　　　　　　　　　　　　　　　　alternate beneficiary

I give _____ to _____ or, if
　　　　　　amount　　　　　　　　　　　　　　　　beneficiary

_____ doesn't survive me by 45 days, to _____
　　beneficiary　　　　　　　　　　　　　　　　　　　　　　　alternate beneficiary

I give _____ to _____ or, if
　　　　　　amount　　　　　　　　　　　　　　　　beneficiary

_____ doesn't survive me by 45 days, to _____
　　beneficiary　　　　　　　　　　　　　　　　　　　　　　　alternate beneficiary

I give _____ to _____ or, if
　　　　　　amount　　　　　　　　　　　　　　　　beneficiary

_____ doesn't survive me by 45 days, to _____
　　beneficiary　　　　　　　　　　　　　　　　　　　　　　　alternate beneficiary

I give _____ to _____ or, if
　　　　　　amount　　　　　　　　　　　　　　　　beneficiary

_____ doesn't survive me by 45 days, to _____
　　beneficiary　　　　　　　　　　　　　　　　　　　　　　　alternate beneficiary

[repeat as needed]

4. I make the following specific gifts of personal property:

I give _____
　　　　　　　　　　　　　　　　description of gift

to _____ or, if _____
　　　　　　beneficiary　　　　　　　　　　　　　　　　beneficiary

doesn't survive me by 45 days, to _____.
　　　　　　　　　　　　　　　　　　　　alternate beneficiary

I give _____
　　　　　　　　　　　　　　　　description of gift

to _____ or, if _____
　　　　　　beneficiary　　　　　　　　　　　　　　　　beneficiary

doesn't survive me by 45 days, to _____.
　　　　　　　　　　　　　　　　　　　　alternate beneficiary

I give _____
　　　　　　　　　　　　　　　　description of gift

to _____ or, if _____
　　　　　　beneficiary　　　　　　　　　　　　　　　　beneficiary

doesn't survive me by 45 days, to _____.
　　　　　　　　　　　　　　　　　　　　alternate beneficiary

I give _____
                              description of gift

to _____ or, if _____
              beneficiary   beneficiary

doesn't survive me by 45 days, to _____.
                                          alternate beneficiary

I give _____
                              description of gift

to _____ or, if _____
              beneficiary   beneficiary

doesn't survive me by 45 days, to _____.
                                          alternate beneficiary

I give _____
                              description of gift

to _____ or, if _____
              beneficiary   beneficiary

doesn't survive me by 45 days, to _____.
                                          alternate beneficiary

[repeat as needed]

5. I make the following specific gifts of real property:

I give the property commonly known as _____
                                            address or description of property

_____

to _____ or, if _____
              beneficiary   beneficiary

doesn't survive me by 45 days, to _____.
                                          alternate beneficiary

I give the property commonly known as _____
                                            address or description of property

_____

to _____ or, if _____
              beneficiary   beneficiary

doesn't survive me by 45 days, to _____.
                                          alternate beneficiary

I give the property commonly known as _____
                                            address or description of property

_____

to _____ or, if _____
              beneficiary   beneficiary

doesn't survive me by 45 days, to _____.
                                          alternate beneficiary

[repeat as needed]

6. I give my residuary estate, i.e., the rest of my property not otherwise specifically and validly disposed

of by this will or in any other manner, to _____,
beneficiary

or, if _____ fails to survive me by 45 days, to
beneficiary

_____ If any primary beneficiary of a shared residuary or specific
alternate beneficiary

gift made in this will fails to survive me by 45 days, the surviving beneficiaries of that gift shall equally

divide the deceased beneficiary's share. If all primary beneficiaries of a shared residuary or specific gift fail

to survive me by 45 days, that gift shall pass in equal shares to the alternate beneficiaries named to receive

that gift. If the alternate beneficiaries named by this will to receive a specific gift don't survive me by 45

days, or there are no such named alternate beneficiaries, that gift shall become part of my residuary estate.

7. I nominate _____ as executor, to serve
executor

without bond. If _____ shall for any reason fail to
executor

qualify or cease to act as executor, I nominate_____ as
alternate executor

executor, also to serve without bond. I direct that my executor take all actions legally permissible to have

the probate of my estate done as simply as possible, including filing a petition in the appropriate court for

the independent administration of my estate.

I hereby grant to my executor the following powers, to be exercised as he or she deems to be in the

best interests of my estate:

(a) To retain property without liability for loss or depreciation resulting from such retention.

(b) To dispose of property by public or private sale, or exchange, or otherwise, and receive or

administer the proceeds as a part of my estate.

(c) To vote stock, to exercise any option or privilege to convert bonds, notes, stocks or other securities

belonging to my estate into other bonds, notes, stocks or other securities, and to exercise all other rights

and privileges of a person owning similar property in his own right.

(d) To lease any real property that may at any time form part of my estate.

(e) To abandon, adjust, arbitrate, compromise, sue on or defend and otherwise deal with and settle

claims in favor of or against my estate.

(f) To continue, maintain, operate or participate in any business which is a part of my estate, and to effect incorporation, dissolution or other change in the form of organization of the business.

(g) To pay all my debts, and all taxes that may, by reason of my death, be assessed against my estate or any portion of it, whether passing by probate or not, provided that such debts and taxes shall be first satisfied out of my residuary estate.

(h) To do all other acts, which in his or her judgment may be necessary or appropriate for the proper and advantageous management, investment and distribution of my estate.

The foregoing powers, authority and discretion granted to my executor are intended to be in addition to the powers, authority and discretion vested in him or her by operation of law by virtue of his or her office, and may be exercised as often as is deemed necessary or advisable, without application to or approval by any court in any jurisdiction.

8. If at my death any of my children are minors, and a personal guardian is needed, I nominate

_____ as guardian of the person(s) of my
                name

minor children. If _____ cannot serve as personal
                 name

guardian, I nominate _____ as
                  name

personal guardian.

I direct that no bond be required of any personal guardian.

9. All property given in this will to _____ shall be given to
                 name

_____ as custodian for _____
      custodian   minor

under the Uniform Transfers to Minors Act of _____ . If _____
                        your state   custodian's name

cannot serve as custodian, _____ shall serve as custodian.
                 successor custodian's name

[repeat as needed]

10. All property I give in this will to any of the children listed in Section A below shall be held for each of them in a separate trust, pursuant to the following trust terms, which shall apply to each trust:

A. Trust Beneficiaries and Age Limits

Each trust shall end when the following beneficiaries become 35, except as otherwise specified in this section:

Trust for   Shall end at age

_____   _____

_____   _____

_____   _____

_____   _____

_____   _____

_____   _____

_____   _____

B. Trustees

The trustee shall be _____, or, if _____
                                    name   name
cannot serve as trustee, the trustee shall be _____
                                                                    successor trustee
No bond shall be required of any trustee.

C. Beneficiary Provisions

(1) As long as a child is a beneficiary of this trust, the trustee may distribute from time to time to or for the benefit of the beneficiary as much, or all, of the net income or principal of the trust, or both, as the trustee deems necessary for the beneficiary's health, support, maintenance, and education.

Education includes, but isn't limited to, college, graduate, postgraduate, and vocational studies, and reasonably related living expenses.

(2) In deciding whether to make a distribution to the beneficiary, the trustee may take into account the beneficiary's other income, resources, and sources of support.

(3) Any trust income which isn't distributed to a beneficiary by the trustee shall be accumulated and added to the principal of the trust administered for that beneficiary.

D. Termination of Trust

The trust shall terminate when any of the following events occur:

(1) The beneficiary becomes the age specified in Paragraph A of this trust;

(2) The beneficiary dies before becoming the age specified in Paragraph A of this trust;

(3) The trust is exhausted through distributions allowed under these provisions.

If the trust terminates for reason (1), the remaining principal and accumulated net income of the trust shall pass to the beneficiary. If the trust terminates for reason (2), the remaining principal and accumulated net income of the trust shall pass to the trust beneficiary's heirs.

E. Powers of Trustee

In addition to other powers granted the trustee in this will, the trustee shall have:

(1) All the powers generally conferred on trustees by the laws of the state having jurisdiction over this trust;

(2) In respect to property in the trust, the powers conferred by this will on the executor; and

(3) The authority to hire and pay from the trust assets the reasonable fees of investment advisors, accountants, tax advisors, agents, attorneys, and other assistants for the administration of the trust and for the management of any trust asset and for any litigation affecting the trust.

F. Trust Administrative Provisions

(1) It is my intent that this trust be administered independent of court supervision to the maximum extent possible under the laws of the state having jurisdiction over this trust.

(2) The interests of trust beneficiaries shall not be transferable by voluntary or involuntary assignment or by operation of law and shall be free from the claims of creditors and from attachment, execution, bankruptcy, or other legal process to the fullest extent permissible by law.

(3) Any trustee serving hereunder shall be entitled to reasonable compensation out of the trust assets for ordinary and extraordinary services, and for all services in connection with the complete or partial termination of any trust created by this will.

(4) The invalidity of any provision of this trust instrument shall not affect the validity of the remaining provisions.

11. If any of my children are minors and a property guardian is needed, I appoint _____

name

_____ as the property guardian of my minor children. If

_____ cannot serve as property guardian, I

name

appoint _____as property guardian.

name

I direct that no bond be required of any property guardian.

I subscribe my name to this will this _____ day of _____, 19_____, at

_____,_____, _____,

city   county   state

and do hereby declare that I sign and execute this instrument as my last will and that I sign it willingly, that I execute it as my free and voluntary act for the purposes therein expressed, and that I'm of the age of majority or otherwise legally empowered to make a will, and under no constraint or undue influence.

_____

your signed name

On this _____ day of _____, 19____, _____

your name

declared to us, the undersigned, that this instrument was _____ will and requested us to act as witnesses

his/her

to it. _____thereupon signed this will in our presence, all of us being present at the same time. We now, at

He/She

_____ request, in _____ presence, and in the presence of each other, subscribe our names as

his/her   his/her

witnesses and declare we understand this to be _____will, and that to the best of our knowledge the

his/her

testator is of the age of majority, or is otherwise legally empowered to make a will, and under no constraint or undue influence.

We declare under penalty of perjury that the foregoing is true and correct, this _____ day of

_____ at _____.

_____
witness' signature

_____ residing at _____,
witness' typed name   street address

_____, _____, _____
city   county   state

_____
witness' signature

_____ residing at _____,
witness' typed name   street address

_____, _____, _____
city   county   state

_____
witness' signature

_____ residing at _____,
witness' typed name   street address

_____, _____, _____.
city   county   state

III. WILL FOR A HUSBAND OR WIFE WITH NO MINOR CHILDREN

WILL OF _____
                                    your name

I, _____, a resident of
                                    your name

_____, _____, _____
         city   county   state

declare that this is my will.

    1. I revoke all wills and codicils that I have previously made.

    2. I am married to _____,
                                    spouse's name

and all references in this will to my _____ are to _____.
                                              husband/wife   him/her

[If appropriate, complete and repeat as needed]:

    I was previously married to _____.
                                              name of former spouse

That marriage was terminated by _____.
                                              death/annulment/divorce

    I am the _____ of the following children whose names and dates of birth are:
                         mother/father

_____   _____
                    name   date of birth

_____   _____
                    name   date of birth

_____   _____
                    name   date of birth

_____   _____
                    name   date of birth

_____   _____
                    name   date of birth

[repeat as needed]

    There are _____ living children of my deceased child _____:
                         number   name

_____   _____
              name of grandchild   date of birth

_____   _____
              name of grandchild   date of birth

[repeat as needed]

3. I make the following cash gifts:

I give _____ to _____ or, if
                    amount   beneficiary

_____ doesn't survive me by 45 days, to _____
           beneficiary   alternate beneficiary

I give _____ to _____ or, if
                    amount   beneficiary

_____ doesn't survive me by 45 days, to _____
           beneficiary   alternate beneficiary

I give _____ to _____ or, if
                    amount   beneficiary

_____ doesn't survive me by 45 days, to _____
           beneficiary   alternate beneficiary

I give _____ to _____ or, if
                    amount   beneficiary

_____ doesn't survive me by 45 days, to _____
           beneficiary   alternate beneficiary

I give _____ to _____ or, if
                    amount   beneficiary

_____ doesn't survive me by 45 days, to _____
           beneficiary   alternate beneficiary

I give _____ to _____ or, if
                    amount   beneficiary

_____ doesn't survive me by 45 days, to _____
           beneficiary   alternate beneficiary

[repeat as needed]

4. I make the following specific gifts of personal property:

I give _____
                                    description of gift

to _____ or, if _____
                beneficiary   beneficiary

doesn't survive me by 45 days, to _____.
                                            alternate beneficiary

I give _____
                                    description of gift

to _____ or, if _____
                beneficiary   beneficiary

doesn't survive me by 45 days, to _____.
                                            alternate beneficiary

I give _____
                                    description of gift

to _____ or, if _____
                beneficiary   beneficiary

doesn't survive me by 45 days, to _____.
                                            alternate beneficiary

I give _____
                              description of gift

to _____ or, if _____
          beneficiary   beneficiary

doesn't survive me by 45 days, to _____.
                                              alternate beneficiary

I give _____
                              description of gift

to _____ or, if _____
          beneficiary   beneficiary

doesn't survive me by 45 days, to _____.
                                              alternate beneficiary

I give _____
                              description of gift

to _____ or, if _____
          beneficiary   beneficiary

doesn't survive me by 45 days, to _____.
                                              alternate beneficiary

[repeat as needed]

5. I make the following specific gifts of real property:

I give the property commonly known as _____
                                              address or description of property

_____

to _____ or, if _____
          beneficiary   beneficiary

doesn't survive me by 45 days, to _____.
                                              alternate beneficiary

I give the property commonly known as _____
                                              address or description of property

_____

to _____ or, if _____
          beneficiary   beneficiary

doesn't survive me by 45 days, to _____.
                                              alternate beneficiary

I give the property commonly known as _____
                                              address or description of property

_____

to _____ or, if _____
          beneficiary   beneficiary

doesn't survive me by 45 days, to _____.
                                              alternate beneficiary

[repeat as needed]

6. I give my residuary estate, i.e., the rest of my property not otherwise specifically and validly disposed

of by this will or in any other manner, to _____,
 beneficiary

or, if _____ fails to survive me by 45 days, to
 beneficiary

_____ If any primary beneficiary of a shared residuary or specific
 alternate beneficiary

gift made in this will fails to survive me by 45 days, the surviving beneficiaries of that gift shall equally

divide the deceased beneficiary's share. If all primary beneficiaries of a shared residuary or specific gift fail

to survive me by 45 days, that gift shall pass in equal shares to the alternate beneficiaries named to receive

that gift. If the alternate beneficiaries named by this will to receive a specific gift don't survive me by 45

days, or there are no such named alternate beneficiaries, that gift shall become part of my residuary estate.

7. I nominate _____ as executor, to serve
 executor

without bond. If _____ shall for any reason fail to
 executor

qualify or cease to act as executor, I nominate_____ as
 alternate executor

executor, also to serve without bond. I direct that my executor take all actions legally permissible to have

the probate of my estate done as simply as possible, including filing a petition in the appropriate court for

the independent administration of my estate.

I hereby grant to my executor the following powers, to be exercised as he or she deems to be in the

best interests of my estate:

(a) To retain property without liability for loss or depreciation resulting from such retention.

(b) To dispose of property by public or private sale, or exchange, or otherwise, and receive or

administer the proceeds as a part of my estate.

(c) To vote stock, to exercise any option or privilege to convert bonds, notes, stocks or other securities

belonging to my estate into other bonds, notes, stocks or other securities, and to exercise all other rights

and privileges of a person owning similar property in his own right.

(d) To lease any real property that may at any time form part of my estate.

(e) To abandon, adjust, arbitrate, compromise, sue on or defend and otherwise deal with and settle

claims in favor of or against my estate.

(f) To continue, maintain, operate or participate in any business which is a part of my estate, and to effect incorporation, dissolution or other change in the form of organization of the business.

(g) To pay all my debts, and all taxes that may, by reason of my death, be assessed against my estate or any portion of it, whether passing by probate or not, provided that such debts and taxes shall be first satisfied out of my residuary estate.

(h) To do all other acts, which in his or her judgment may be necessary or appropriate for the proper and advantageous management, investment and distribution of my estate.

The foregoing powers, authority and discretion granted to my executor are intended to be in addition to the powers, authority and discretion vested in him or her by operation of law by virtue of his or her office, and may be exercised as often as is deemed necessary or advisable, without application to or approval by any court in any jurisdiction.

8. If my _____ and I should die simultaneously or under such circumstances as to render it
            wife/husband
difficult or impossible to determine by clear and convincing evidence who predeceased the other, I shall be conclusively presumed to have survived my _____ for purposes of this will.
                                                                              wife/husband

I subscribe my name to this will this _____ day of _____, 19_____, at

_____, _____, _____,
             city   county   state
and do hereby declare that I sign and execute this instrument as my last will and that I sign it willingly, that I execute it as my free and voluntary act for the purposes therein expressed, and that I'm of the age of majority or otherwise legally empowered to make a will, and under no constraint or undue influence.

_____
          your signed name

On this _____ day of _____, 19_____, _____
                                                                                              your name

declared to us, the undersigned, that this instrument was _____ will and requested us to act as witnesses
                                                                                his/her

to it. _____thereupon signed this will in our presence, all of us being present at the same time. We now, at
          He/She

_____ request, in _____ presence, and in the presence of each other, subscribe our names as
   his/her   his/her

witnesses and declare we understand this to be _____will, and that to the best of our knowledge the
                                                                             his/her

testator is of the age of majority, or is otherwise legally empowered to make a will, and under no constraint

or undue influence.

    We declare under penalty of perjury that the foregoing is true and correct. This _____ day of

_____ at _____.

_____
                  witness' signature

_____ residing at _____,
           witness' typed name   street address

_____, _____, _____
                city   county   state

_____
                  witness' signature

_____ residing at _____,
           witness' typed name   street address

_____, _____, _____
                city   county   state

_____
                  witness' signature

_____ residing at _____,
           witness' typed name   street address

_____, _____, _____.
                city   county   state

IV. WILL FOR A HUSBAND OR WIFE WITH MINOR CHILDREN

WILL OF _____
your name

I, _____, a resident of
your name

_____, _____, _____
city   county   state

declare that this is my will.

    1. I revoke all wills and codicils that I have previously made.

    2. I am married to _____,
spouse's name

and all references in this will to my _____ are to _____.
husband/wife   him/her

[If appropriate, complete and repeat as needed]:

    I was previously married to _____.
name of former spouse

That marriage was terminated by _____.
death/annulment/divorce

    I am the _____ of the following children whose names and dates of birth are:
mother/father

_____   _____
name   date of birth

_____   _____
name   date of birth

_____   _____
name   date of birth

_____   _____
name   date of birth

_____   _____
name   date of birth

[repeat as needed]

    There are _____ living children of my deceased child _____:
number   name

_____   _____
name of grandchild   date of birth

_____   _____
name of grandchild   date of birth

[repeat as needed]

3. I make the following cash gifts:

I give _____ to _____ or, if
                amount   beneficiary

_____ doesn't survive me by 45 days, to _____
        beneficiary   alternate beneficiary

I give _____ to _____ or, if
                amount   beneficiary

_____ doesn't survive me by 45 days, to _____
        beneficiary   alternate beneficiary

I give _____ to _____ or, if
                amount   beneficiary

_____ doesn't survive me by 45 days, to _____
        beneficiary   alternate beneficiary

I give _____ to _____ or, if
                amount   beneficiary

_____ doesn't survive me by 45 days, to _____
        beneficiary   alternate beneficiary

I give _____ to _____ or, if
                amount   beneficiary

_____ doesn't survive me by 45 days, to _____
        beneficiary   alternate beneficiary

I give _____ to _____ or, if
                amount   beneficiary

_____ doesn't survive me by 45 days, to _____
        beneficiary   alternate beneficiary

[repeat as needed]

4. I make the following specific gifts of personal property:

I give _____
                          description of gift

to _____ or, if _____
        beneficiary   beneficiary

doesn't survive me by 45 days, to _____.
                                        alternate beneficiary

I give _____
                          description of gift

to _____ or, if _____
        beneficiary   beneficiary

doesn't survive me by 45 days, to _____.
                                        alternate beneficiary

I give _____
                          description of gift

to _____ or, if _____
        beneficiary   beneficiary

doesn't survive me by 45 days, to _____.
                                        alternate beneficiary

I give _____
description of gift

to _____ or, if _____
beneficiary   beneficiary

doesn't survive me by 45 days, to _____.
alternate beneficiary

I give _____
description of gift

to _____ or, if _____
beneficiary   beneficiary

doesn't survive me by 45 days, to _____.
alternate beneficiary

I give _____
description of gift

to _____ or, if _____
beneficiary   beneficiary

doesn't survive me by 45 days, to _____.
alternate beneficiary

[repeat as needed]

5. I make the following specific gifts of real property:

I give the property commonly known as _____
address or description of property

_____

to _____ or, if _____
beneficiary   beneficiary

doesn't survive me by 45 days, to _____.
alternate beneficiary

I give the property commonly known as _____
address or description of property

_____

to _____ or, if _____
beneficiary   beneficiary

doesn't survive me by 45 days, to _____.
alternate beneficiary

I give the property commonly known as _____
address or description of property

_____

to _____ or, if _____
beneficiary   beneficiary

doesn't survive me by 45 days, to _____.
alternate beneficiary

[repeat as needed]

6. I give my residuary estate, i.e., the rest of my property not otherwise specifically and validly disposed

of by this will or in any other manner, to _____,
beneficiary

or, if _____ fails to survive me by 45 days, to
beneficiary

_____ If any primary beneficiary of a shared residuary or specific
alternate beneficiary

gift made in this will fails to survive me by 45 days, the surviving beneficiaries of that gift shall equally

divide the deceased beneficiary's share. If all primary beneficiaries of a shared residuary or specific gift fail

to survive me by 45 days, that gift shall pass in equal shares to the alternate beneficiaries named to receive

that gift. If the alternate beneficiaries named by this will to receive a specific gift don't survive me by 45

days, or there are no such named alternate beneficiaries, that gift shall become part of my residuary estate.

7. I nominate _____ as executor, to serve
executor

without bond. If _____ shall for any reason fail to
executor

qualify or cease to act as executor, I nominate_____ as
alternate executor

executor, also to serve without bond. I direct that my executor take all actions legally permissible to have

the probate of my estate done as simply as possible, including filing a petition in the appropriate court for

the independent administration of my estate.

I hereby grant to my executor the following powers, to be exercised as he or she deems to be in the

best interests of my estate:

(a) To retain property without liability for loss or depreciation resulting from such retention.

(b) To dispose of property by public or private sale, or exchange, or otherwise, and receive or

administer the proceeds as a part of my estate.

(c) To vote stock, to exercise any option or privilege to convert bonds, notes, stocks or other securities

belonging to my estate into other bonds, notes, stocks or other securities, and to exercise all other rights

and privileges of a person owning similar property in his own right.

(d) To lease any real property that may at any time form part of my estate.

(e) To abandon, adjust, arbitrate, compromise, sue on or defend and otherwise deal with and settle

claims in favor of or against my estate.

(f) To continue, maintain, operate or participate in any business which is a part of my estate, and to effect incorporation, dissolution or other change in the form of organization of the business.

(g) To pay all my debts, and all taxes that may, by reason of my death, be assessed against my estate or any portion of it, whether passing by probate or not, provided that such debts and taxes shall be first satisfied out of my residuary estate.

(h) To do all other acts, which in his or her judgment may be necessary or appropriate for the proper and advantageous management, investment and distribution of my estate.

The foregoing powers, authority and discretion granted to my executor are intended to be in addition to the powers, authority and discretion vested in him or her by operation of law by virtue of his or her office, and may be exercised as often as is deemed necessary or advisable, without application to or approval by any court in any jurisdiction.

8. If my _____ and I should die simultaneously or under such circumstances as to render it
        wife/husband

difficult or impossible to determine by clear and convincing evidence who predeceased the other, I shall be

conclusively presumed to have survived my _____ for purposes of this will.
                                                    wife/husband

9. If at my death any of my children are minors, and a personal guardian is needed, I nominate

_____ as guardian of the person(s) of my
                            name

minor children. If _____ cannot serve as personal
                                          name

guardian, I nominate _____ as personal
                                          name

guardian.

I direct that no bond be required of any personal guardian.

10. All property given in this will to _____ shall be given to
                                                    name

_____ as custodian for _____
            custodian   minor

under the Uniform Transfers to Minors Act of _____. If _____
                                              your state   custodian's name

cannot serve as custodian, _____ shall serve as custodian.
                                  successor custodian's name

[repeat as needed]

11. All property I give in this will to any of the children listed in Section A below shall be held for each

of them in a separate trust, pursuant to the following trust terms, which shall apply to each trust:

A. Trust Beneficiaries and Age Limits

Each trust shall end when the following beneficiaries become 35, except as otherwise specified in this

section:

Trust for   Shall end at age

_____   _____

_____   _____

_____   _____

_____   _____

_____   _____

_____   _____

_____   _____

B. Trustees

The trustee shall be _____, or, if _____
                              name   name

cannot serve as trustee, the trustee shall be _____
                                                          successor trustee

No bond shall be required of any trustee.

C. Beneficiary Provisions

(1) As long as a child is a beneficiary of this trust, the trustee may distribute from time to time to or for

the benefit of the beneficiary as much, or all, of the net income or principal of the trust, or both, as the

trustee deems necessary for the beneficiary's health, support, maintenance, and education.

Education includes, but isn't limited to, college, graduate, postgraduate, and vocational studies, and

reasonably related living expenses.

(2) In deciding whether to make a distribution to the beneficiary, the trustee may take into account the beneficiary's other income, resources, and sources of support.

(3) Any trust income which isn't distributed to a beneficiary by the trustee shall be accumulated and added to the principal of the trust administered for that beneficiary.

D. Termination of Trust

The trust shall terminate when any of the following events occur:

(1) The beneficiary becomes the age specified in Paragraph A of this trust;

(2) The beneficiary dies before becoming the age specified in Paragraph A of this trust;

(3) The trust is exhausted through distributions allowed under these provisions.

If the trust terminates for reason (1), the remaining principal and accumulated net income of the trust shall pass to the beneficiary. If the trust terminates for reason (2), the remaining principal and accumulated net income of the trust shall pass to the trust beneficiary's heirs.

E. Powers of Trustee

In addition to other powers granted the trustee in this will, the trustee shall have:

(1) All the powers generally conferred on trustees by the laws of the state having jurisdiction over this trust;

(2) In respect to property in the trust, the powers conferred by this will on the executor; and

(3) The authority to hire and pay from the trust assets the reasonable fees of investment advisors, accountants, tax advisors, agents, attorneys, and other assistants for the administration of the trust and for the management of any trust asset and for any litigation affecting the trust.

F. Trust Administrative Provisions

(1) It is my intent that this trust be administered independent of court supervision to the maximum extent possible under the laws of the state having jurisdiction over this trust.

(2) The interests of trust beneficiaries shall not be transferable by voluntary or involuntary assignment or by operation of law and shall be free from the claims of creditors and from attachment, execution,

bankruptcy, or other legal process to the fullest extent permissible by law.

(3) Any trustee serving hereunder shall be entitled to reasonable compensation out of the trust assets for ordinary and extraordinary services, and for all services in connection with the complete or partial termination of any trust created by this will.

(4) The invalidity of any provision of this trust instrument shall not affect the validity of the remaining provisions.

12. If any of my children are minors and a property guardian is needed, I appoint _____

name

_____ as the property guardian of my minor children. If

_____ cannot serve as property guardian, I

name

appoint _____ as property guardian.

name

I direct that no bond be required of any property guardian.

I subscribe my name to this will this _____ day of _____, 19_____, at

_____, _____, _____,

city   county   state

and do hereby declare that I sign and execute this instrument as my last will and that I sign it willingly, that I execute it as my free and voluntary act for the purposes therein expressed, and that I'm of the age of majority or otherwise legally empowered to make a will, and under no constraint or undue influence.

_____

your signed name

On this _____ day of _____, 19____, _____

your name

declared to us, the undersigned, that this instrument was _____ will and requested us to act as witnesses

his/her

to it. _____ thereupon signed this will in our presence, all of us being present at the same time. We now, at

He/She

_____ request, in _____ presence, and in the presence of each other, subscribe our names as

his/her   his/her

witnesses and declare we understand this to be _____ will, and that to the best of our knowledge the

his/her

testator is of the age of majority, or is otherwise legally empowered to make a will, and under no constraint or undue influence.

We declare under penalty of perjury that the foregoing is true and correct, this _____ day of

_____ at _____.

_____

witness' signature

_____ residing at _____,

witness' typed name   street address

_____, _____, _____

city   county   state

_____

witness' signature

_____ residing at _____,

witness' typed name   street address

_____, _____, _____

city   county   state

_____

witness' signature

_____ residing at _____,

witness' typed name   street address

_____, _____, _____.

city   county   state

V. WILL FOR A PERSON WHO LIVES WITH A LOVER/MATE AND WHO HAS NO MINOR CHILDREN

WILL OF _____
your name

I, _____, a resident of
your name

_____, _____, _____
city   county   state

declare that this is my will.

1. I revoke all wills and codicils that I have previously made.

2. My _____ name is _____
lover/mate's   name

and all references in this will to my _____ are to _____
lover/mate   him/her

[If appropriate, complete and repeat as needed]:

I was previously married to _____.
name of former spouse

That marriage was terminated by _____.
death/annulment/divorce

I am the _____ of the following children whose names and dates of birth are:
mother/father

_____   _____
name   date of birth

_____   _____
name   date of birth

_____   _____
name   date of birth

_____   _____
name   date of birth

_____   _____
name   date of birth

[repeat as needed]

There are _____ living children of my deceased child _____:
number   name

_____   _____
name of grandchild   date of birth

_____   _____
name of grandchild   date of birth

[repeat as needed]

3. I make the following cash gifts:

I give _____ to _____ or, if
                amount   beneficiary

_____ doesn't survive me by 45 days, to _____
         beneficiary   alternate beneficiary

I give _____ to _____ or, if
                amount   beneficiary

_____ doesn't survive me by 45 days, to _____
         beneficiary   alternate beneficiary

I give _____ to _____ or, if
                amount   beneficiary

_____ doesn't survive me by 45 days, to _____
         beneficiary   alternate beneficiary

I give _____ to _____ or, if
                amount   beneficiary

_____ doesn't survive me by 45 days, to _____
         beneficiary   alternate beneficiary

I give _____ to _____ or, if
                amount   beneficiary

_____ doesn't survive me by 45 days, to _____
         beneficiary   alternate beneficiary

I give _____ to _____ or, if
                amount   beneficiary

_____ doesn't survive me by 45 days, to _____
         beneficiary   alternate beneficiary

[repeat as needed]

4. I make the following specific gifts of personal property:

I give _____
                                    description of gift

to _____ or, if _____
              beneficiary   beneficiary

doesn't survive me by 45 days, to _____.
                                          alternate beneficiary

I give _____
                                    description of gift

to _____ or, if _____
              beneficiary   beneficiary

doesn't survive me by 45 days, to _____.
                                          alternate beneficiary

I give _____
                                    description of gift

to _____ or, if _____
              beneficiary   beneficiary

doesn't survive me by 45 days, to _____.
                                          alternate beneficiary

I give _____
description of gift

to _____ or, if _____
beneficiary   beneficiary

doesn't survive me by 45 days, to _____.
alternate beneficiary

I give _____
description of gift

to _____ or, if _____
beneficiary   beneficiary

doesn't survive me by 45 days, to _____.
alternate beneficiary

I give _____
description of gift

to _____ or, if _____
beneficiary   beneficiary

doesn't survive me by 45 days, to _____.
alternate beneficiary

[repeat as needed]

5. I make the following specific gifts of real property:

I give the property commonly known as _____
address or description of property

_____

to _____ or, if _____
beneficiary   beneficiary

doesn't survive me by 45 days, to _____.
alternate beneficiary

I give the property commonly known as _____
address or description of property

_____

to _____ or, if _____
beneficiary   beneficiary

doesn't survive me by 45 days, to _____.
alternate beneficiary

I give the property commonly known as _____
address or description of property

_____

to _____ or, if _____
beneficiary   beneficiary

doesn't survive me by 45 days, to _____.
alternate beneficiary

[repeat as needed]

6. I give my residuary estate, i.e., the rest of my property not otherwise specifically and validly disposed

of by this will or in any other manner, to _____,
beneficiary

or, if _____ fails to survive me by 45 days, to
beneficiary

_____ If any primary beneficiary of a shared residuary or specific
alternate beneficiary

gift made in this will fails to survive me by 45 days, the surviving beneficiaries of that gift shall equally

divide the deceased beneficiary's share. If all primary beneficiaries of a shared residuary or specific gift fail

to survive me by 45 days, that gift shall pass in equal shares to the alternate beneficiaries named to receive

that gift. If the alternate beneficiaries named by this will to receive a specific gift don't survive me by 45

days, or there are no such named alternate beneficiaries, that gift shall become part of my residuary estate.

7. I nominate _____ as executor, to serve
executor

without bond. If _____ shall for any reason fail to
executor

qualify or cease to act as executor, I nominate_____ as
alternate executor

executor, also to serve without bond. I direct that my executor take all actions legally permissible to have

the probate of my estate done as simply as possible, including filing a petition in the appropriate court for

the independent administration of my estate.

I hereby grant to my executor the following powers, to be exercised as he or she deems to be in the

best interests of my estate:

(a) To retain property without liability for loss or depreciation resulting from such retention.

(b) To dispose of property by public or private sale, or exchange, or otherwise, and receive or

administer the proceeds as a part of my estate.

(c) To vote stock, to exercise any option or privilege to convert bonds, notes, stocks or other securities

belonging to my estate into other bonds, notes, stocks or other securities, and to exercise all other rights

and privileges of a person owning similar property in his own right.

(d) To lease any real property that may at any time form part of my estate.

(e) To abandon, adjust, arbitrate, compromise, sue on or defend and otherwise deal with and settle

claims in favor of or against my estate.

(f) To continue, maintain, operate or participate in any business which is a part of my estate, and to effect incorporation, dissolution or other change in the form of organization of the business.

(g) To pay all my debts, and all taxes that may, by reason of my death, be assessed against my estate or any portion of it, whether passing by probate or not, provided that such debts and taxes shall be first satisfied out of my residuary estate.

(h) To do all other acts, which in his or her judgment may be necessary or appropriate for the proper and advantageous management, investment and distribution of my estate.

The foregoing powers, authority and discretion granted to my executor are intended to be in addition to the powers, authority and discretion vested in him or her by operation of law by virtue of his or her office, and may be exercised as often as is deemed necessary or advisable, without application to or approval by any court in any jurisdiction.

8. If my _____ and I should die simultaneously or under such circumstances as to render it
              lover/mate

difficult or impossible to determine by clear and convincing evidence who predeceased the other, I shall be conclusively presumed to have survived my _____ for purposes of this will.
                                                                    lover/mate

I subscribe my name to this will this _____ day of _____, 19_____, at

_____,_____, _____,
          city   county   state

and do hereby declare that I sign and execute this instrument as my last will and that I sign it willingly, that I execute it as my free and voluntary act for the purposes therein expressed, and that I'm of the age of majority or otherwise legally empowered to make a will, and under no constraint or undue influence.

_____
              your signed name

On this _____ day of _____, 19____, _____
                                                                                                                              your name

declared to us, the undersigned, that this instrument was _____ will and requested us to act as witnesses
                                                                                                    his/her

to it. _____thereupon signed this will in our presence, all of us being present at the same time. We now, at
          He/She

_____ request, in _____ presence, and in the presence of each other, subscribe our names as
       his/her   his/her

witnesses and declare we understand this to be _____will, and that to the best of our knowledge the
                                                                               his/her

testator is of the age of majority, or is otherwise legally empowered to make a will, and under no constraint

or undue influence.

   We declare under penalty of perjury that the foregoing is true and correct. This _____ day of

_____ at _____.

_____
                    witness' signature

_____ residing at _____,
            witness' typed name   street address

_____, _____, _____
                 city   county   state

_____
                    witness' signature

_____ residing at _____,
            witness' typed name   street address

_____, _____, _____
                 city   county   state

_____
                    witness' signature

_____ residing at _____,
            witness' typed name   street address

_____, _____, _____
                 city   county   state

VI. WILL FOR A PERSON WHO LIVES WITH A LOVER/MATE AND WHO HAS MINOR CHILDREN

WILL OF _____
your name

I, _____, a resident of
your name

_____, _____, _____
city   county   state

declare that this is my will.

1. I revoke all wills and codicils that I have previously made.

2. My _____ name is _____
lover/mate's   name

and all references in this will to my _____ are to _____
lover/mate   him/her

[If appropriate, complete and repeat as needed]:

I was previously married to _____.
name of former spouse

That marriage was terminated by _____.
death/annulment/divorce

I am the _____ of the following children whose names and dates of birth are:
mother/father

_____   _____
name   date of birth

_____   _____
name   date of birth

_____   _____
name   date of birth

_____   _____
name   date of birth

_____   _____
name   date of birth

[repeat as needed]

There are _____ living children of my deceased child _____:
number   name

_____   _____
name of grandchild   date of birth

_____   _____
name of grandchild   date of birth

[repeat as needed]

3. I make the following cash gifts:

I give _____ to _____ or, if
_____ amount _____   _____ beneficiary _____

_____ doesn't survive me by 45 days, to _____
_____ beneficiary _____   _____ alternate beneficiary _____

I give _____ to _____ or, if
_____ amount _____   _____ beneficiary _____

_____ doesn't survive me by 45 days, to _____
_____ beneficiary _____   _____ alternate beneficiary. _____

I give _____ to _____ or, if
_____ amount _____   _____ beneficiary _____

_____ doesn't survive me by 45 days, to _____
_____ beneficiary _____   _____ alternate beneficiary _____

I give _____ to _____ or, if
_____ amount _____   _____ beneficiary _____

_____ doesn't survive me by 45 days, to _____
_____ beneficiary _____   _____ alternate beneficiary _____

I give _____ to _____ or, if
_____ amount _____   _____ beneficiary _____

_____ doesn't survive me by 45 days, to _____
_____ beneficiary _____   _____ alternate beneficiary _____

[repeat as needed]

4. I make the following specific gifts of personal property:

I give _____
_____ description of gift _____

to _____ or, if _____
_____ beneficiary _____   _____ beneficiary _____

doesn't survive me by 45 days, to _____.
_____ alternate beneficiary _____

I give _____
_____ description of gift _____

to _____ or, if _____
_____ beneficiary _____   _____ beneficiary _____

doesn't survive me by 45 days, to _____.
_____ alternate beneficiary _____

I give _____
_____ description of gift _____

to _____ or, if _____
_____ beneficiary _____   _____ beneficiary _____

doesn't survive me by 45 days, to _____.
_____ alternate beneficiary _____

I give _____
                                    description of gift

to _____ or, if _____
                beneficiary   beneficiary

doesn't survive me by 45 days, to _____.
                                                    alternate beneficiary

I give _____
                                    description of gift

to _____ or, if _____
                beneficiary   beneficiary

doesn't survive me by 45 days, to _____.
                                                    alternate beneficiary

I give _____
                                    description of gift

to _____ or, if _____
                beneficiary   beneficiary

doesn't survive me by 45 days, to _____.
                                                    alternate beneficiary

[repeat as needed]

5. I make the following specific gifts of real property:

I give the property commonly known as _____
                                                    address or description of property

_____

to _____ or, if _____
                beneficiary   beneficiary

doesn't survive me by 45 days, to _____.
                                                    alternate beneficiary

I give the property commonly known as _____
                                                    address or description of property

_____

to _____ or, if _____
                beneficiary   beneficiary

doesn't survive me by 45 days, to _____.
                                                    alternate beneficiary

I give the property commonly known as _____
                                                    address or description of property

_____

to _____ or, if _____
                beneficiary   beneficiary

doesn't survive me by 45 days, to _____.
                                                    alternate beneficiary

[repeat as needed]

6. I give my residuary estate, i.e., the rest of my property not otherwise specifically and validly disposed

of by this will or in any other manner, to _____ ,

beneficiary

or, if _____ fails to survive me by 45 days, to

beneficiary

_____ If any primary beneficiary of a shared residuary or specific

alternate beneficiary

gift made in this will fails to survive me by 45 days, the surviving beneficiaries of that gift shall equally

divide the deceased beneficiary's share. If all primary beneficiaries of a shared residuary or specific gift fail

to survive me by 45 days, that gift shall pass in equal shares to the alternate beneficiaries named to receive

that gift. If the alternate beneficiaries named by this will to receive a specific gift don't survive me by 45

days, or there are no such named alternate beneficiaries, that gift shall become part of my residuary estate.

7. I nominate _____ as executor, to serve

executor

without bond. If _____ shall for any reason fail to

executor

qualify or cease to act as executor, I nominate_____ as

alternate executor

executor, also to serve without bond. I direct that my executor take all actions legally permissible to have

the probate of my estate done as simply as possible, including filing a petition in the appropriate court for

the independent administration of my estate.

I hereby grant to my executor the following powers, to be exercised as he or she deems to be in the

best interests of my estate:

(a) To retain property without liability for loss or depreciation resulting from such retention.

(b) To dispose of property by public or private sale, or exchange, or otherwise, and receive or

administer the proceeds as a part of my estate.

(c) To vote stock, to exercise any option or privilege to convert bonds, notes, stocks or other securities

belonging to my estate into other bonds, notes, stocks or other securities, and to exercise all other rights

and privileges of a person owning similar property in his own right.

(d) To lease any real property that may at any time form part of my estate.

(e) To abandon, adjust, arbitrate, compromise, sue on or defend and otherwise deal with and settle

claims in favor of or against my estate.

(f) To continue, maintain, operate or participate in any business which is a part of my estate, and to effect incorporation, dissolution or other change in the form of organization of the business.

(g) To pay all my debts, and all taxes that may, by reason of my death, be assessed against my estate or any portion of it, whether passing by probate or not, provided that such debts and taxes shall be first satisfied out of my residuary estate.

(h) To do all other acts, which in his or her judgment may be necessary or appropriate for the proper and advantageous management, investment and distribution of my estate.

The foregoing powers, authority and discretion granted to my executor are intended to be in addition to the powers, authority and discretion vested in him or her by operation of law by virtue of his or her office, and may be exercised as often as is deemed necessary or advisable, without application to or approval by any court in any jurisdiction.

8. If my _____ and I should die simultaneously or under such circumstances as to render it
       lover/mate
difficult or impossible to determine by clear and convincing evidence who predeceased the other, I shall be conclusively presumed to have survived my _____ for purposes of this will.
                                                                lover/mate

9. If at my death any of my children are minors, and a personal guardian is needed, I nominate

_____ as guardian of the person(s) of my
                          name
minor children. If _____ cannot serve as personal
                                        name
guardian, I nominate _____ as personal
                                          name
guardian.

I direct that no bond be required of any personal guardian.

10. All property given in this will to _____ shall be given to
                                                          name
_____as custodian for _____
              custodian   minor

under the Uniform Transfers to Minors Act of _____. If _____

                                                               your state   custodian's name

cannot serve as custodian, _____ shall serve as custodian.

                                           successor custodian's name

[repeat as needed]

11. All property I give in this will to any of the children listed in Section A below shall be held for each of them in a separate trust, pursuant to the following trust terms, which shall apply to each trust:

A. Trust Beneficiaries and Age Limits

Each trust shall end when the following beneficiaries become 35, except as otherwise specified in this section:

Trust for   Shall end at age

_____   _____

_____   _____

_____   _____

_____   _____

_____   _____

_____   _____

_____   _____

_____   _____

B. Trustees

The trustee shall be _____, or, if _____

                            name   name

cannot serve as trustee, the trustee shall be _____

                                                 successor trustee

No bond shall be required of any trustee.

C. Beneficiary Provisions

(1) As long as a child is a beneficiary of this trust, the trustee may distribute from time to time to or for the benefit of the beneficiary as much, or all, of the net income or principal of the trust, or both, as the trustee deems necessary for the beneficiary's health, support, maintenance, and education.

Education includes, but isn't limited to, college, graduate, postgraduate, and vocational studies, and reasonably related living expenses.

(2) In deciding whether to make a distribution to the beneficiary, the trustee may take into account the beneficiary's other income, resources, and sources of support.

(3) Any trust income which isn't distributed to a beneficiary by the trustee shall be accumulated and added to the principal of the trust administered for that beneficiary.

D. Termination of Trust

The trust shall terminate when any of the following events occur:

(1) The beneficiary becomes the age specified in Paragraph A of this trust;

(2) The beneficiary dies before becoming the age specified in Paragraph A of this trust;

(3) The trust is exhausted through distributions allowed under these provisions.

If the trust terminates for reason (1), the remaining principal and accumulated net income of the trust shall pass to the beneficiary. If the trust terminates for reason (2), the remaining principal and accumulated net income of the trust shall pass to the trust beneficiary's heirs.

E. Powers of Trustee

In addition to other powers granted the trustee in this will, the trustee shall have:

(1) All the powers generally conferred on trustees by the laws of the state having jurisdiction over this trust;

(2) In respect to property in the trust, the powers conferred by this will on the executor; and

(3) The authority to hire and pay from the trust assets the reasonable fees of investment advisors, accountants, tax advisors, agents, attorneys, and other assistants for the administration of the trust and for the management of any trust asset and for any litigation affecting the trust.

F. Trust Administrative Provisions

(1) It is my intent that this trust be administered independent of court supervision to the maximum extent possible under the laws of the state having jurisdiction over this trust.

(2) The interests of trust beneficiaries shall not be transferable by voluntary or involuntary assignment

or by operation of law and shall be free from the claims of creditors and from attachment, execution, bankruptcy, or other legal process to the fullest extent permissible by law.

(3) Any trustee serving hereunder shall be entitled to reasonable compensation out of the trust assets for ordinary and extraordinary services, and for all services in connection with the complete or partial termination of any trust created by this will.

(4) The invalidity of any provision of this trust instrument shall not affect the validity of the remaining provisions.

12. If any of my children are minors and a property guardian is needed, I appoint _____
name

_____ as the property guardian of my minor children. If

_____ cannot serve as property guardian, I
name

appoint _____as property guardian.
name

I direct that no bond be required of any property guardian.

I subscribe my name to this will this _____ day of _____, 19_____, at

_____, _____, _____,
city   county   state

and do hereby declare that I sign and execute this instrument as my last will and that I sign it willingly, that I execute it as my free and voluntary act for the purposes therein expressed, and that I'm of the age of majority or otherwise legally empowered to make a will, and under no constraint or undue influence.

_____
your signed name

On this _____ day of _____, 19____, _____
your name

declared to us, the undersigned, that this instrument was _____ will and requested us to act as witnesses
his/her

to it. _____thereupon signed this will in our presence, all of us being present at the same time. We now, at
He/She

_____ request, in _____ presence, and in the presence of each other, subscribe our names as
his/her   his/her

witnesses and declare we understand this to be _____will, and that to the best of our knowledge the
his/her

testator is of the age of majority, or is otherwise legally empowered to make a will, and under no constraint or undue influence.

We declare under penalty of perjury that the foregoing is true and correct, this _____ day of
_____ at _____.

_____
witness' signature

_____ residing at _____,
witness' typed name   street address

_____, _____, _____
city   county   state

_____
witness' signature

_____ residing at _____,
witness' typed name   street address

_____, _____, _____
city   county   state

_____
witness' signature

_____ residing at _____,
witness' typed name   street address

_____, _____, _____.
city   county   state

CHAPTER 12

ASSEMBLE THE CLAUSES WILL

A. How to Prepare Your Own Will   12/1
B. Making Substantive Changes in Sample Clauses   12/3
C. Prepare Your Will—Clause By Clause   12/4
D. Checklist   12/33
E. Next Steps   12/33

A. How to Prepare Your Own Will

THIS CHAPTER PRESENTS YOU WITH A SERIES of will clauses identified by small letters "a" through "z." Each lettered clause covers a basic component of a will and is accompanied, where appropriate, by:

• A brief discussion of the reasons for its inclusion;

• A cross-reference to the section of the book where the particular legal issue covered in the clause is discussed in more detail; and

• An indication of whether that clause or its equivalent must be included in your will. I do this by making some clauses "mandatory" while others are "optional," to be included or not, depending on your family situation and personal desires.

For several will clauses I present two or more alternates. In this situation, it's up to you to choose the one that best meets your needs. Again, there are accompanying explanations to help you do this.

Example: Clause "o" is entitled "Executor(s) Clause - Mandatory." Alternative Executor's Clause 1 provides you with a clause to appoint a single executor. Alternative Executor's Clause 2 presents a clause for the appointment of dual executors. After referring back to Chapter 3, where you already tentatively decided on your executor(s), your job is to select the clause that best fits your needs, and write in the appropriate name or names.

To use this chapter to prepare your will, read it through at least once. Then, with pencil in hand, go through it section-by-section, clause-by-clause, following these steps:

Step 1. Identify all mandatory will clauses. This is easy, as they're labelled **"Mandatory."** In addition, all mandatory clauses are pre-marked with a large check mark in the box in the margin like this: ☑ If there's more than one alternative to a mandatory clause, be sure you select the one that best meets your needs.

Step 2. Identify the optional will clauses (marked **"Optional"**) you want to include in your will. Any clause which doesn't apply to all people is labelled "Optional," even if it's vital for those who do need it. For example, clause "q" provides 3 alternate choices for naming personal guardian(s) for minor children. This clause is labelled "Optional" because many readers don't have minor children. However, if you do have minor children, you definitely should complete one of the choices in clause "q."

When you decide to use an optional clause, place a check mark in the empty box ☐ in the margin next to the selected clause. These checkmarks will be a big help when it comes time for you to type (or have typed) the final version of your will.

Step 3. Number all the checked clauses sequentially, starting with number 1.[1] These same numbers will be typed on your final will, to identify each clause. To make this process easy, I place a circle ◯ in the margin next to every clause and each alternate. For each clause you've included in your will, simply fill in the next available number. This may seem a little complex now, but rest assured you will find it to be easy enough when it comes time to do it.

Example: The Revocation Clause (clause "c") that appears at the beginning of your will (after the unnumbered identification provisions) is a mandatory clause and therefore is always numbered ①. For many people, the next clause is the Marriage and Children Clause (clause "d"), which, if included, is given the number ②. However, if you've never been married and have no children, you will obviously want to skip this clause. In this situation, the next clause you would normally use would be the Specific Gifts of Personal Property Clause (clause "f"), so you'd number this clause ② in your will. Then continue through all clauses you've included in your will, putting the next number in the circle in the margin.

Step 4. Fill in all necessary information in the blanks in each will clause you've selected. The clauses have adequate space to do this for most situations. However, it's possible that you will require more space. If so, you will need to use an additional sheet of paper. For example, Clause "g," which deals with specific gifts of personal property, contains space for making sixteen separate gifts. If you give gifts to more than sixteen separate persons or organizations, you'll need to create more blanks. Here's how to do it:

- Put "continued on Attachment 1" at the end of the too short space;
- Either photocopy the particular blank or blanks you need more of or write the additional clauses on a piece of typing paper. Title this sheet "Attachment 1,

---

[1]The identification provisions which come at the top of your will do not carry a number.

continuation of [clause which is being continued]," (e.g., "Attachment 1, continuation of Clause 3");

- Complete the attachment by providing all the additional information needed;
- When it's time to actually assemble your draft will, attach this page, or pages, to it;
- If you need more blanks than this book provides for a second will clause, repeat this process, numbering this Attachment 2.

Step 5. When you've completed filling in all the necessary blanks and numbered the clauses you wish to include, you're ready to have your will typed. If someone else is going to type your will, be sure he knows exactly what's to be typed. The best way to achieve this is as follows:

- Tear out the pages containing the clauses with checked boxes. Each of these should be filled out (where appropriate) and numbered sequentially as we indicate earlier. Remember to include all attachment pages. If you prefer, you can photocopy all these pages instead of removing them from the book.
- Draw an "X" through clauses you don't wish to be included.
- Draw a line through titles of clauses, explanatory language, and printed words which appear under the blank lines of the clauses so the typist doesn't mistakenly type these words. For example, in the identification clause at the beginning of your will you should pencil in your name and then delete the words "your name" below the line:

Will of _____
                        your name

- Finally, adapt pronouns (he, she, they, etc.) and tenses to fit your situation. For instance, Clause "g," Specific Gifts of Personal Property, provides "I give _____ to _____, or, if _____ doesn't survive me, to _____ ." This is drafted for a gift to one person. If you make a shared gift, "doesn't" should be changed to "don't." These precautions allow you to present your typist with only and precisely what you want typed in your will. Complete typing instructions are contained in Chapter 13.

B. Making Substantive Changes in Sample Clauses

IF YOU MAKE SUBSTANTIVE CHANGES in the language of a will clause printed in this chapter, you're running a risk that:

1. You won't accomplish what you wish to, and
2. You will cause ambiguities which interfere with your will's effectiveness.

For these reasons, I urge you not to change the meaning of any of these clauses without checking the result with an attorney.

C. Prepare Your Will—Clause By Clause

NOW IT'S TIME TO COMPLETE THE CLAUSES for inclusion in your will.

✔ Clause a. Will Caption Clause—Mandatory

This unnumbered caption is typed at the top of your will. Use the name you commonly use for signing legal papers and other important documents. If for any reason you've used different names—e.g., you changed your name to Sara Burns but still own some property in the name of Sara Burnstein, identify yourself with both names, as "Sara Burns A/K/A/ Sara Burnstein," and sign your will that way.

Will of _____
                           your name

✔ Clause b. Personal Identification Provision Clause—Mandatory

This unnumbered provision identifies you. Use the same form of your name set out in clause a and your permanent address. If there's any question about where you reside, see Chapter 2, Section A.

I, _____ , a resident of
                           your name

_____ , _____ , _____
          city   county   state

declare that this is my will.

✔ Clause c. Revocation Clause—Mandatory

This clause revokes all previous wills and codicils (formal amendments to a will) which you've made. If you know the date of your most recent will (if you have one), it's helpful to both specify that date and destroy that will and all copies, but this isn't required. This is the first numbered clause of your will.

○   I revoke all wills and codicils I've previously made (including the will dated

_____, 19__).

☐   **Clause d.   Marriages and Children Clause—Optional unless you have a
current spouse, former spouse, children or grandchildren who
are children of a deceased child**

If you've never been married nor had any children, skip this clause. Otherwise,
place a check in the box in the margin to indicate that this clause is to be included
in your will and place number ② in the circle to indicate that this is the second
clause in your will. Then fill in the blanks by listing your current spouse, if you
have one, all former marriages and how they ended (e.g., by divorce, annulment,
death, arsenic, etc.)., all your children, and any grandchild of yours who's the son
or daughter of a child who died. As you know from Chapter 7, Section E, you
must either provide in your will for each living child (and any children of a
deceased child) or specifically disinherit them to be sure to avoid state law rules
which provide that overlooked children are entitled to inherit an automatic share
of your estate. To avoid these rules, it's enough to leave a child $1.00.

○   I am married to _____ and all references in this will to my

spouse are to _____. I was previously married to _____. That
                    him/her

marriage was terminated by _____.

[repeat as needed]

I have _____ children now living, whose names and dates of birth are:
          number

_____   _____
Name   Date of Birth

_____   _____
Name   Date of Birth

_____   _____
Name   Date of Birth

_____   _____
Name   Date of Birth

_____   _____
Name   Date of Birth

_____   _____
Name   Date of Birth

[repeat as needed]

There are _____ living children of my deceased child, _____:
              number   name

_____   _____
Name of grandchild   Date of Birth

_____   _____
Name of grandchild   Date of Birth

_____   _____
Name of grandchild   Date of Birth

[repeat as needed]

☐ Clause e.   Disinheritance Clause—Optional

If you don't plan to leave something (even $1.00, or an heirloom, or a share of your residuary estate) to each of the children you've listed above, you must specifically disinherit that child or risk a successful will challenge. To disinherit a child, check the box in the margin and number this clause with the next available number. Otherwise, leave both box and circle blank and simply skip this clause:

○   I specifically direct that _____ be disinherited and receive nothing

from my estate.

[repeat as needed]

☐ Clause f.   Specific Gifts of Cash—Optional unless you're making a cash gift in your will

If you desire to make one or more cash gifts, including money in checking, savings and money market accounts and certificates of deposits, treasury bills and notes, etc., check the box. Otherwise, proceed to Clause g.

Here you enter each cash gift you listed in Chapter 6 along with the names of the primary and alternate beneficiaries you named to receive these gifts.

○   I make the following gifts of cash:

I give _____ to _____ or, if
              amount   beneficiary

_____ doesn't survive me, to
                  beneficiary

_____ .
                  beneficiary

I give _____ to _____ or, if
                    amount   beneficiary

_____ doesn't survive me, to
                    beneficiary

_____ .
                    beneficiary

I give _____ to _____ or, if
                    amount   beneficiary

_____ doesn't survive me, to
                    beneficiary

_____ .
                    beneficiary

I give _____ to _____ or, if
                    amount   beneficiary

_____ doesn't survive me, to
                    beneficiary

_____ .
                    beneficiary

I give _____ to _____ or, if
                    amount   beneficiary

_____ doesn't survive me, to
                    beneficiary

_____ .
                    beneficiary

I give _____ to _____ or, if
                    amount   beneficiary

_____ doesn't survive me, to
                    beneficiary

_____ .
                    beneficiary

☐ **Clause g. Specific Gifts of Personal Property—Optional unless you make specific gifts of personal property in your will**

> Here you complete the clause necessary to make specific gifts of your personal property other than cash gifts, which you just covered. Don't use this clause for gifts of real estate, which are covered in Clause i. Assuming you wish to make specific gifts of personal property, check the box and keep reading. Otherwise leave the box blank and proceed to clause h.
>
> You made your decisions regarding these components in Chapters 5 and 6. Now, you only need transfer the descriptions of your property set out in Chapter

5^2 and the beneficiaries (and alternate beneficiaries) you've selected to receive it set out in Chapter 6 to the appropriate lines below. Remember, you can include more than one item of property in a single gift, if you desire.

○   I make the following specific gifts of personal property:

I give _____ to

description of gift

_____ or, if _____

beneficiary   beneficiary

doesn't survive me, to _____ .

alternate beneficiary

I give _____ to

description of gift

_____ or, if _____

beneficiary   beneficiary

doesn't survive me, to _____ .

alternate beneficiary

I give _____ to

description of gift

_____ or, if _____

beneficiary   beneficiary

doesn't survive me, to _____ .

alternate beneficiary

I give _____ to

description of gift

_____ or, if _____

beneficiary   beneficiary

doesn't survive me, to _____ .

alternate beneficiary

I give _____ to

description of gift

_____ or, if _____

beneficiary   beneficiary

doesn't survive me, to _____ .

alternate beneficiary

---

[2]If you didn't use the property inventory chart in Chapter 5 because of the simplicity of your desires and/or property situation, review our guidelines for describing property provided in that chapter (Section A) prior to describing the property here.

I give _____ to
                                          description of gift

_____ or, if _____
                beneficiary   beneficiary

doesn't survive me, to _____ .
                                          alternate beneficiary

I give _____ to
                                          description of gift

_____ or, if _____
                beneficiary   beneficiary

doesn't survive me, to _____ .
                                          alternate beneficiary

I give _____ to
                                          description of gift

_____ or, if _____
                beneficiary   beneficiary

doesn't survive me, to _____ .
                                          alternate beneficiary

I give _____ to
                                          description of gift

_____ or, if _____
                beneficiary   beneficiary

doesn't survive me, to _____ .
                                          alternate beneficiary

I give _____ to
                                          description of gift

_____ or, if _____
                beneficiary   beneficiary

doesn't survive me, to _____ .
                                          alternate beneficiary

I give _____ to
                                          description of gift

_____ or, if _____
                beneficiary   beneficiary

doesn't survive me, to _____ .
                                          alternate beneficiary

I give _____ to
                                          description of gift

_____ or, if _____
                beneficiary   beneficiary

doesn't survive me, to _____ .
                                          alternate beneficiary

I give _____ to
description of gift

_____ or, if _____
beneficiary   beneficiary

doesn't survive me, to _____ .
alternate beneficiary

I give _____ to
description of gift

_____ or, if _____
beneficiary   beneficiary

doesn't survive me, to _____ .
alternate beneficiary

I give _____ to
description of gift

_____ or, if _____
beneficiary   beneficiary

doesn't survive me, to _____ .
alternate beneficiary

I give _____ to
description of gift

_____ or, if _____
beneficiary   beneficiary

doesn't survive me, to _____ .
alternate beneficiary

Clause h.   Debts Forgiven—Optional unless you forgive debts

You can use your will to forgive debts. If you wish to, return to Chapter 6 where you described the debts to be forgiven and enter the information below. If you do, check the box. Otherwise leave it blank.

Reminder: If you're married and wish to use your will to forgive a debt, be sure you have full power to do so. This may not be the case if the money is owed to both you and your spouse. (See Chapter 4.)

I forgive my interest in the following debts, including all interest accrued as of the date of my death:

Person(s) or organizations	Date of loan	Approximate amount of debt plus interest at date of will signing
_____	_____	_____
_____	_____	_____
_____	_____	_____

Clause i.   Gifts of Real Estate—Optional unless you want to leave real property in your will

Assuming you own some real estate, check the box in the margin. Then complete the real estate clauses by transferring the property description information from the chart in Chapter 5[3] and your choice of a beneficiary (and alternate beneficiary) from Chapter 6 to the clause below. Each parcel of real estate you own, including any condominiums or co-ops, should be listed in your will separately.

 Using the Will Book, all real estate must be left outright to some person(s) and/or organization(s). As previously discussed, if you want to leave a "life estate" interest in any of your real estate, see a lawyer.

Now, complete the clauses.

I make the following gifts of real estate:

I give the property commonly known as _____
address or description of property

_____

to _____ or, if _____
beneficiary   beneficiary

doesn't survive me, to _____ .
alternate beneficiary

I give the property commonly known as _____
address or description of property

_____

to _____ or, if _____
beneficiary   beneficiary

doesn't survive me, to _____ .
alternate beneficiary

I give the property commonly known as _____
address or description of property

_____

to _____ or, if _____
beneficiary   beneficiary

doesn't survive me, to _____ .
alternate beneficiary

---

[3]See the previous footnote.

I give the property commonly known as _____
                                              address or description of property

_____

to _____ or, if _____
            beneficiary   beneficiary

doesn't survive me, to _____ .
                              alternate beneficiary

I give the property commonly known as _____
                                              address or description of property

_____

to _____ or, if _____
            beneficiary   beneficiary

doesn't survive me, to _____ .
                              alternate beneficiary

I give the property commonly known as _____
                                              address or description of property

_____

to _____ or, if _____
            beneficiary   beneficiary

doesn't survive me, to _____ .
                              alternate beneficiary

BUT IF SHE DOESN'T SURVIVE ME .. WHO TO LEAVE IT TO ..?

☐ **Clause j.   Encumbrances (Mortgages) on Real Property—Optional**

When you give a gift of real property, the recipient is responsible for all encumbrances (e.g., mortgages, deeds of trust, liens) unless you specify differently in your will. Occasionally, however, a person wants to leave a piece of real estate free of all encumbrances because the recipient cannot pay them or would be hard pressed to do so. If you want to vary the general rule and relieve the beneficiary of this obligation, you must put a clause in your will saying so. Of course, you must be sure there's enough money elsewhere in your estate to pay the encumbrances. Usually, if a person wishes to relieve a beneficiary of real property of the obligation to pay mortgage debts, tax liens, etc., they indicate that these should be paid from your residuary estate.

Note that the clause below applies to one specific gift of real estate only. If you want to give more than one gift of real estate free of encumbrances, repeat this clause for each such gift. Two additional clauses are provided for this purpose. Also, this clause shouldn't be used for any real property that you plan to leave as part of your residuary estate. If you use this clause, remember to check the box in the margin.

○   I direct that the gift of real estate, _____
address or description of property

given to _____, be made free of all encumbrances
beneficiary

on that property at my death, including but not limited to any mortgages, deeds of trust, real

property taxes and assessments, and estate and inheritance taxes, and that such encumbrances

shall be paid by my executor from _____.
source

I direct that the gift of real estate, _____
address or description of property

given to _____, be made free of all encumbrances
beneficiary

on that property at my death, including but not limited to any mortgages, deeds of trust, real

property taxes and assessments, and estate and inheritance taxes, and that such encumbrances

shall be paid by my executor from _____.
source

I direct that the gift of real estate, _____
address or description of property

given to _____, be made free of all encumbrances
beneficiary

on that property at my death, including but not limited to any mortgages, deeds of trust, real

property taxes and assessments, and estate and inheritance taxes, and that such encumbrances

shall be paid by my executor from _____.
source

✔ **Clause k.   Residuary Clause—Mandatory**

As previously discussed, the "residue" of your estate is exactly what it sounds like—all that remains after all cash gifts, specific gifts of personal property and gifts of real estate have been distributed. Whether your residue consists of a significant amount of property obviously depends on whether you've given most of your property away via specific gifts. Sometimes people make only a few specific gifts, and leave the bulk of their property as part of their residue. Also, if you get a windfall shortly before you die—win a lottery, receive a surprise inheritance—and don't make specific provision to leave it to a named beneficiary, it becomes part of your residue.

As you know from reading Chapter 6, the person who gets your residue is called "the residuary beneficiary," and they receive it under the terms of the "residuary clause" in your will. In addition to providing for your primary and alternate residuary beneficiaries, the residuary clause set out below also provides that:

• Alternate beneficiaries of shared gifts (both specific and residuary) only take the gift if all the primary beneficiaries fail to survive you by the time period specified in your will; and

• Specific gifts shall pass into your residuary estate in the event all the primary and alternate beneficiaries you name to receive the gift fail to survive you by the time period specified in your will. You will have the opportunity to choose a survivorship period in clause l.

Reminder: You should always name at least one alternate residuary beneficiary. Even if you decide to leave your residue to more than one residuary beneficiary (e.g., to my children Ben, Aaron and Sally Jones), name an alternate beneficiary anyway. If one of the residuary beneficiaries fails to survive you by the period specified in the will, the surviving residuary beneficiaries take that beneficiary's share. Only if all the residuary beneficiaries fail to survive you by your survivorship period will your named alternate receive the residue. Thus, if you name your three children as residuary beneficiaries and a cousin as the alternate residuary beneficiary, and one of your children predeceases you, the two surviving children will inherit all of your residuary estate and your cousin will inherit nothing.

You've already named the beneficiary, or beneficiaries, for your residue, and the alternate(s), in the chart in Chapter 6. Turn back to that chart now and transfer that information to the clause below.

○

I give my residuary estate, i.e., the rest of my property not otherwise specifically and validly

disposed of by this will or in any other manner, to _____,
                                                              beneficiary

or, if _____ fails to survive me, to
                          beneficiary

_____.
            beneficiary

If any primary beneficiary of a shared residuary gift or shared specific gift made in this will fails

to survive me by the period specified in this will, the surviving beneficiaries of that gift shall

equally divide the deceased beneficiary's share. If all primary beneficiaries of a shared residuary gift

or shared specific gift fail to survive me by the period specified in the will, that gift shall pass in

equal shares to the alternate beneficiaries named to receive that gift. If the alternate beneficiaries

named by this will to receive a specific gift don't survive me by the period specified in this will, or

there are no such named alternate beneficiaries, that gift shall become part of my residuary estate.

☑ **Clause I.   Survivorship Period Clause—Optional**

> As discussed in Chapter 6, a "survivorship period" clause requires a beneficiary to
> survive you by a specified time. If the named beneficiary doesn't survive you by
> this period, the property goes to whoever you've specified as your alternate
> beneficiary (or to the surviving beneficiaries if you've named more than one), or if
> they fail to survive you, the gift then becomes part of the residue.
>
> As discussed in Chapter 6, survivorship clauses can be valuable to prevent the
> possibility of your property from being tangled up in two probates—yours and
> that of the beneficiary who's to receive that property should that person die soon
> after you do. I recommend a 45 day survivorship period, at a minimum, and 180
> days at a maximum. If you desire a longer period see an attorney. If you don't
> desire any period at all, simply put zero in the indicated blank.

○   All primary, alternate and residuary beneficiaries named in this will are required to survive me

by _____ days as a condition of receiving any gift under the terms of this will.

☐ **Clause m. Abatement Clauses—Optional**

> These two optional clauses specify what happens if at your death you don't own
> property of sufficient value to cover all your cash gifts after your debts and taxes
> are paid. This issue is discussed in Chapter 6. If you don't include one of these
> clauses, the laws of your state govern this issue. If you do wish to include one of
> these clauses, remember to check the box and number the clause you choose
> (only choose one).

Alternative 1 · Abatement First from Residue

If my estate isn't sufficient to pay in full all cash gifts I've made in this will, my executor shall first sell the personal property, and then the real property, in my residuary estate, in the amount necessary to pay these gifts.

Alternative 2 · Abatement Pro-Rata from Cash Gifts First

If my estate isn't sufficient to pay all cash gifts I've made in this will in full, the executor shall make an appropriate pro-rata reduction of each cash gift.

Clause n.   Payment of Death Taxes and Debts Clause—Optional

Your estate is obligated to pay your debts and taxes, including all death taxes. These may be minimal, or even non-existent, and thus not worth bothering about in your will. Routine debts for charge accounts and personal services (e.g., the gardener or housekeeper) are normally paid by a surviving spouse or family member out of liquid assets left in a checking or savings account and don't need to be separately provided for. However, if your debts are substantial, or if your estate has a net worth over $600,000 and is therefore subject to federal estate taxes (see Chapter 8), you may want to specify that certain assets be used to pay your debts and taxes. If you don't, the cost of paying your debts and taxes may be paid from the residue or be pro-rated against all property in your estate, depending on the laws of your state.

You may also want to give some gifts of personal property free of all liability for debts and taxes (encumbrances on real estate aren't included here, as they were covered in Clause j). Similarly, you may want your debts and taxes paid from certain assets, such as a bank account you specify.

To achieve these desires, check the box and use or adapt one of the following clauses:

Alternative 1 · Residue Pays for Debts and Death Taxes

Except as otherwise specifically provided in this will, I direct that my executor shall pay all my debts and inheritance, estate or other death taxes out of the residue of my estate.

Alternative 2 - Debts and Taxes Paid for Out of Specific Assets

◯   Except as otherwise specifically provided in this will, I direct that my executor shall pay all my

debts and all inheritance, estate or other death taxes assessed against my estate from

_____
identify asset

> **Note:** In this clause, don't specify any item of real property which you're
> giving free of encumbrances under Clause j; you've already left this property free
> of encumbrances.

Alternative 3 - Exempting Specific Gifts from Liability for Debts and Taxes

◯   I direct that the gift _____ given to

_____ be given free of any liability for debts
name beneficiaries

or inheritance, estate or other death taxes assessed against my estate.

[Repeat as often as needed]

☑ **Clause o.   Executor(s) Clause—Mandatory**

> You already decided upon your executor(s) and successor executor(s) in Chapter
> 3. Now select an executor clause from the two alternatives below and enter your
> choices from Chapter 3.

Alternative 1 - Sole Executor Clause

◯   I nominate _____ as executor, to serve without bond.
executor

If _____ shall for any reason fail to qualify or cease to
executor

act as executor, I nominate _____, also to serve without bond.
alternate executor

I direct that my executor take all actions legally permissible to have the probate of my estate

done as simply as possible, including filing a petition in the appropriate court for the independent

administration of my estate.

Alternative 2 - Dual Executors

◯ I nominate _____ and _____
            executor   executor

to serve as executors without bond. If either of these persons fails to survive me, or is otherwise

unavailable to serve, the remaining surviving executor shall function as a sole executor also without

bond. If both of these persons fail to survive me, or are otherwise unavailable to serve, I nominate

_____ to serve as executor without bond.
      alternate executor

I direct that my executors take all actions legally permissible to have the probate of my estate

done as simply as possible, including filing a petition in the appropriate court for the independent

administration of my estate.

☑ **Clause p.   Executor's Powers Clause—Mandatory**

In the clause below, you'll find the standard Nolo Will clause for executor's powers. This clause must be included in all wills drafted in this chapter. It gives your executor a good deal of flexibility, which is generally desirable.

 Occasionally people wish to limit the power of their executor or give her special instructions or duties. If you find yourself in this situation, see a lawyer.

◯ **Executor's Powers**

Except as otherwise provided in my will, I hereby grant to my executor the following powers,

to be exercised as he or she deems to be in the best interests of my estate:

(a) To retain property without liability for loss or depreciation resulting from such retention.

(b) To dispose of property by public or private sale, or exchange, or otherwise, and receive or

administer the proceeds as a part of my estate.

(c) To vote stock, to exercise any option or privilege to convert bonds, notes, stocks or other

securities belonging to my estate into other bonds, notes, stocks or other securities, and to exercise

all other rights and privileges of a person owning similar property in his own right.

ASSEMBLE THE CLAUSES WILL

(d) To lease any real property that may at any time form part of my estate.

(e) To abandon, adjust, arbitrate, compromise, sue on or defend and otherwise deal with and settle claims in favor of or against my estate.

(f) To continue, maintain, operate or participate in any business which is a part of my estate, and to effect incorporation, dissolution or other change in the form of organization of the business.

(g) Except as otherwise provided in this will, to pay all my debts, and all taxes that may, by reason of my death, be assessed against my estate or any portion of it, whether passing by probate or not, provided that such debts and taxes shall be first satisfied out of my residuary estate.

(h) To do all other acts, which in his or her judgment may be necessary or appropriate for the proper and advantageous management, investment and distribution of my estate.

The foregoing powers, authority and discretion granted to my executor are intended to be in addition to the powers, authority and discretion vested in him or her by operation of law by virtue of his or her office, and may be exercised as often as is deemed necessary or advisable, without application to or approval by any court in any jurisdiction.

Clause q. Personal Guardian of Minor Children Clause—Mandatory If You Have Minor Children

Of course, if you don't have minor children, omit this clause.

You've already named your preferences for the primary and successor personal guardians of your minor children (if there's no living person entitled to legal custody who's available to assume it). See Chapter 7, Section B. Now is the time to put these choices in your will.

Alternative 1 - Guardian Appointment Clause for Use by Member of a Couple, or Single Parent Where Other Natural Parent Not Involved (e.g., Is Deceased, Has Formally Abandoned Child)

If at my death any of my children are minors and a personal guardian is needed, I nominate

_____ as guardian of the person(s) of
name

my minor children. If _____ cannot serve as guardian,
name

I nominate _____ as personal guardian.
name

I direct that no bond be required of any personal guardians.

Optional Addition - Statement of Reasons For Designating of Guardian

I believe it's in the best interests of my children for _____ to
name

be their personal guardian because _____

_____

_____

_____

_____

Alternative 2 - Personal Guardian Appointment Clause for a Parent With Other Parent Living but Not Desired as Child(ren)'s Guardian[4]

If at my death any of my children are minors and a personal guardian is needed, I nominate

_____ as guardian of the person(s) of my
name

minor children. If _____ cannot serve as guardian,
name

I nominate _____ as personal guardian. I direct
name

that no bond be required of any personal guardian.

---

[4]Reread the discussion in Chapter 7, Section B before using this alternative. The other natural parent usually gets custody (unless he or she is unfit or unavailable), regardless of your desires.

I believe it's in the best interests of my children for _____

name

to be their personal guardian, rather than _____

natural parent's name

because _____

_____

_____ .

Alternative 3 - Different Personal Guardians for Different Children

If at my death any of my children are minors and a personal guardian is needed:

I nominate _____ as guardian of my

name

child(ren) _____, _____, and

_____ . If _____ cannot

name

serve as guardian, I nominate _____ as personal

name

guardian for these children.

I nominate _____ as guardian of my

name

child(ren) _____, _____, and

_____ . If _____ cannot

name

serve as guardian, I nominate _____ as personal

name

guardian for these children.

I direct that no bond be required of any personal guardian.

I believe these people are the best personal guardians for the respective children because

_____

_____

_____ .

☐   **Clause r.   Gifts Under the Uniform Transfers to Minors Act—Optional**

In Chapter 7, Sections C(3) and D(7) you recorded your decisions as to which children you made gifts to would have those gifts supervised under your state's UTMA. You listed each such child's name and the adult "custodian" and "successor custodian" for each child listed. To actually make use of the Act for gifts made in your will, you simply transfer this information to clause "r," and complete the clause by filling in the name of your state.

Clause "r" itself states that "All property given in this will … " to the named minor is given under the Act. To remind you, you've already made your gift in clauses "f," "g" and "i." Here you're simply plugging the Act into your will for those minors you want to use the Act for.

You must complete a separate clause for each minor whose gifts are supervised under the Act. You can appoint only one custodian and one successor custodian per clause. You cannot appoint joint or shared custodians.

Reminder: You can only make gifts using the Act if it has been adopted in your state. If you don't live in one of the states listed below, you cannot make gifts in your will using the Act.

Alabama, Alaska, Arizona, Arkansas, California, Colorado, District of Columbia, Florida, Georgia, Hawaii, Idaho, Illinois, Iowa, Kansas, Kentucky, Maine, Massachusetts, Minnesota, Missouri, Montana, Nevada, New Hampshire, New Jersey, North Carolina, North Dakota, Ohio, Oklahoma, Oregon, Rhode Island South Dakota, Utah, Virginia, West Virginia, Wisconsin, Wyoming.

Most states which have adopted the Act specify a set age of either 18 or 21, when the minor receives property outright. (See list in Chapter 7, Section C(1).) However, a few states allow a will writer to vary this basic statutory age. If you live in one of the states listed below, and you've decided to vary the age at which a minor is to receive a gift you make from the basic age to a permissible one, complete the additional portion of clause "r" applicable for your state.

STATE	STATUTORY AGE FOR FOR RECEIVING GIFT	CAN BE CHANGED BY WILL WRITER TO AN AGE
Alaska	18	up to 25
Arkansas	21	down to 18
California	18	up to 25
Maine	18	up to 21
New Jersey	21	down to 18
North Carolina	21	down to 18
Virginia	18	to 21

◯   All property given in this will to _____ shall be given to
                                              minor's name

_____ as custodian for _____
           custodian's name   minor's name

under the Uniform Transfers to Minors Act of _____. If
                                                      your state

_____ cannot serve as custodian _____
           custodian's name   successor custodian's name

shall serve as custodian.

[repeat as needed]

Additional clause varying age at which minor receives gift, in states where permitted.
(Add to above clause if desired.

Alaska

The gift shall be transferred to _____
                                                      minor's name

when _____ becomes age _____
            he/she   (specify age from 19 to 25)

Arkansas

The gift shall be transferred to _____
                                                      minor's name

when _____ becomes age _____
            he/she   (specify age from 20 to 18)

California

The gift shall be transferred to _____
                                                      minor's name

when _____ becomes age _____
            he/she   (specify age from 19 to 25)

Maine

The gift shall be transferred to _____
                                                      minor's name

when _____ becomes age _____
            he/she   (specify age from 19 to 21)

New Jersey or North Carolina

The gift shall be transferred to _____
                                                      minor's name

when _____ becomes age _____
            he/she   (specify age from 20 to 18)

Virginia

The gift shall be transferred to the _____

minor's name

when _____ becomes age 21.

he/she

☐ **Clause s. Trusts for Property Left to Children—Optional**

In Chapter 7, Sections C(4) and D(7), you recorded your decisions of which children you wanted to make gifts to using a children's trust. You listed each such child's name, the age each child must reach to receive his or her property outright, and the trustee and successor trustee for each child's trust. If you wanted to name different trustees for different children's trusts, you also recorded that information. To create trusts in your will, you transfer this information into clause "s." Note that each trust provides that all property left to each child listed in Section A is to be turned over to him or her at age 35, unless you specify a different age.

Section B of this trust clause allows you to name different trustees, or successor trustees, for trusts for different children. If you named one trustee and one successor trustee for all the children listed (or for more than one child), simply list all those children's names together in Section B, and name that trustee and successor trustee once.

Trust for Property Left to Your Minor Children Clause

○ All property I give in this will to any of the children listed in Section A below shall be held for each of them in a separate trust, pursuant to the following trust terms, which shall apply to each trust:

A. Age Limit

Each trust shall end when the following beneficiaries become 35, except as otherwise specified:

Trust for   Shall end at age

_____   _____

_____   _____

_____   _____

B. Trustees

The trustee for _____ shall be

name of child or children

_____, or, if _____

trustee's name   trustee's name

cannot serve as trustee, the trustee shall be _____.

name

The trustee for _____ shall be

name of child or children

_____, or, if _____

trustee's name   trustee's name

cannot serve as trustee, the trustee shall be _____.

name

The trustee for _____ shall be

name of child or children

_____, or, if _____

trustee's name   trustee's name

cannot serve as trustee, the trustee shall be _____.

name

I direct that no bond shall be required of any trustee.

C. Beneficiary Provisions

(1) As long as a child is a beneficiary of this trust, the trustee may distribute from time to time

to or for the benefit of the beneficiary as much, or all, of the net income or principal of the trust, or

both, as the trustee deems necessary for the beneficiary's health, support, maintenance, and

education.

"Education" includes, but isn't limited to, college, graduate, postgraduate, and vocational

studies, and reasonably related living expenses.

(2) In deciding whether to make a distribution to the beneficiary, the trustee may take into

account the beneficiary's other income, resources, and sources of support.

(3) Any trust income which isn't distributed to a beneficiary by the trustee shall be accumulated

and added to the principal of the trust administered for that beneficiary.

D. Termination of Trust

The trust shall terminate when any of the following events occur:

(1) The beneficiary becomes the age specified in Paragraph A of this trust;

(2) The beneficiary dies before becoming the age specified in Paragraph A of this trust;

(3) The trust is exhausted through distributions allowed under these provisions.

If the trust terminates for reason (1), the remaining principal and accumulated net income of the trust shall pass to the beneficiary. If the trust terminates for reason (2), the remaining principal and accumulated net income of the trust shall pass to the trust beneficiary's heirs.

E. Powers of Trustee

In addition to other powers granted the trustee in this will, the trustee shall have:

(1) All the powers generally conferred on trustees by the laws of the state having jurisdiction over this trust;

(2) In respect to property in the trust, the powers conferred by this will on the executor; and

(3) The authority to hire and pay from the trust assets the reasonable fees of investment advisors, accountants, tax advisors, agents, attorneys, and other assistants for the administration of the trust and for the management of any trust asset and for any litigation affecting the trust.

F. Trust Administrative Provisions

(1) It's my intent that this trust be administered independent of court supervision to the maximum extent possible under the laws of the state having jurisdiction over this trust.

(2) The interests of trust beneficiaries shall not be transferable by voluntary or involuntary assignment or by operation of law and shall be free from the claims of creditors and from attachment, execution, bankruptcy, or other legal process to the fullest extent permissible by law.

(3) Any trustee serving hereunder shall be entitled to reasonable compensation out of the trust assets for ordinary and extraordinary services, and for all services in connection with the complete or partial termination of any trust created by this will.

(4) The invalidity of any provision of this trust instrument shall not affect the validity of the remaining provisions.

☐ **Clause t.   Guardian for Property of Your Minor Children—Optional unless you have minor children**

As discussed in Chapter 7, Section C, if you have minor children, you should always name a property guardian, and alternate property guardian in your will. You chose those people in Chapter 7, Section C(5). Here you simply transfer that information into your will.

Alternative 1 - Property Guardian Appointment

◯   If at my death any of my children are minors, and a property guardian is needed, I appoint

_____ as property guardian of my minor children. If
                    name

If _____ cannot serve as property guardian, I appoint
                         name

_____ as property guardian.
                    name

I direct that no bond be required of any property guardian.

Alternative 2 - Different Property Guardians for Different Children Clause

◯   If at my death any of my children are minors, and a property guardian is needed, I appoint

_____ to be property guardian for my children
                    name

_____ , _____ , and

_____ . If _____ cannot serve as
                                              name

property guardian, I appoint _____ as property guardian for
                                         name

these children.

I believe these are the best property guardians for these children because:

_____

_____

_____

If at my death any of my children _____ ,

_____ , and _____

are minors, and a property guardian is needed, I appoint _____
                                                                                          name

to be property guardian for these children. If _____
                                                                              name

cannot serve as property guardian, I appoint _____ as
                                                                        name

property guardian for these children.

I believe these are the best property guardians for these children because:

_____

_____

_____

I direct that no bond be required of any property guardian.

Clause u.   No Contest Clause—Optional

A no contest clause is designed to discourage will contests by disinheriting anyone who unsuccessfully challenges your will. (Obviously, a successful challenge to a will sets it aside, including a no contest provision.) The gift that was to go to the contesting beneficiary goes to the alternate beneficiary or, if no alternate was named, to the residuary beneficiary. If you believe there's any likelihood someone may challenge your will, or if you're just cautious, include a no contest clause in your will (remember to check the box).

Generally, courts enforce such a clause, but you should also see a lawyer before finalizing your will.

No Contest Clause

○   If any beneficiary under this will in any manner, directly or indirectly, contests or attacks this

will or any of its provisions, any property, share or interest in my estate given to the contesting

beneficiary under this will is revoked and shall be disposed of in the same manner provided herein

as if that contesting beneficiary had predeceased me without issue.

☐   **Clause v. Simultaneous Death—Optional**

> People often wonder and worry about what happens if they die at the same time
> as their spouse (or mate or lover). Who's a primary beneficiary under their will?
> Who gets what? As discussed in Chapter 6, Section J, survivorship clauses usually
> provide an orderly method for determining which heirs inherit a spouse's property
> when it's impossible to tell which spouse died first. Under the will you're drafting
> in this chapter, assuming you chose a survivorship period under clause 1, all
> property you left to your spouse (or mate or lover) will pass to the alternates in
> the event of a simultaneous death. Only if there's no survivorship period, or some
> property isn't successfully disposed of under the will, is this clause likely to come
> into operation. However, if you wish to include this clause in your will (it can't
> hurt), complete the following:

Simultaneous Death

○   If my _____ and I should die simultaneously, or under such circumstances
              wife/husband/mate

as to render it difficult or impossible to determine by clear and convincing evidence who

predeceased the other, I shall be conclusively presumed to have survived my _____
                                                                            wife/husband/mate

for purposes of this will.

☐   **Clause w. Pets Clause—Optional**

> You can't leave property directly to your pets, obviously. Also, generally, property
> cannot be left in a trust for a pet. However, you can provide for your pets in your
> will.[5] The simplest way is by leaving a sum of money (and whatever directions are
> appropriate) to a friend (who has agreed to take on the responsibility) to provide
> that care. For a thorough discussion of providing for pets, see *Dog Law* by Mary
> Randolph (Nolo Press).

---

[5]In many areas of the country, you cannot legally direct that your healthy pet be destroyed.
For example, a will provision requiring a woman's dog to be killed after her death was held
unenforceable by a San Francisco court.

○   I want my pet _____ to be well cared for, and direct that:
pet's name

_____
insert your instructions

_____

_____.

To achieve proper care for my pet, I leave the sum of $_____ to

_____, _____
name   address

_____.

☐   **Clause x.   Body Parts Donation Clause—Optional**

You may want your body to be available for medical research and/or organ transplant purposes. If so, include one or both of these alternate clauses. In many states, such as California, this clause meets all legal requirements. Because it often takes some time to locate and read a will, you also need to be sure you've arranged for the legal authorization necessary in your state, and immediate implementation of organ donation upon death.

Alternative 1 - Donation of Body to Medical Institution Clause

○   I declare that I want to donate my body to any medical institution which will accept it, for research purposes, and I direct my executor to take all steps necessary to carry out such donations of my body.

Alternative 2 - Donation of Body Parts for Organ Transplants Clause

○   I declare that, pursuant to the Uniform Anatomical Gift Act, I want to donate any and all of my body parts, organs, etc., to any medical facility or institution which will accept them, and I direct my executor to take all steps necessary to carry out such donation of my body parts, organs, etc.

Clause y. Burial Instructions Clause—Optional

You can include a clause regarding disposition of your body in your will. In many states, such a clause is legally binding. However, you shouldn't rely only on your will to establish a plan to dispose of your remains. Why? Because wills are often not located and read immediately after death. It's accordingly wise to leave specific instructions to those who will take responsibility for your funeral arrangements. But because putting your burial/body disposition instructions in your will gives them increased validity if someone challenges them, it's a good idea to also do this.

Note: If you want to assure that your plans are carried out, make sure your executor knows about them and has a copy of your will to back him up, should your plans be disputed after you die. It's also wise to both arrange and pay for funeral, burial or cremation details in advance.

Alternative 1 - Burial/Funeral Arrangement Clause

I've made and paid for funeral arrangements with _____

for burial at _____, and I direct my executor to take all steps

necessary to carry out such arrangements.

Alternative 2 - Cremation Clause

I've made arrangements and paid for the cremation of my remains with

_____ and I direct my executor to take all steps necessary

to carry out such arrangements.

☑ **Clause z.   Signature and Witnessing Clause—Mandatory**

This is the final clause of your will. It isn't actually numbered in your will.

I subscribe my name to this will this _____ day of _____, 19____,

at _____, _____, _____.
                  city   county   state

and do hereby declare that I sign and execute this instrument as my last will and that I sign it

willingly, that I execute it as my free and voluntary act for the purposes therein expressed, and that

I'm of the age of majority or otherwise legally empowered to make a will, and under no constraint

or undue influence.

_____
                                 your signed name

On this _____ day of _____, 19__, _____
                                                          your name

declared to us, the undersigned, that this instrument was _____ will and requested us
                                                  his/her

to act as witnesses to it. _____ thereupon signed this
                                      your name

will in our presence, all of us being present at the same time. We now, at _____
                                                             his/her

request, in _____ presence, and in the presence of each other, subscribe our names as
               his/her

witnesses and declare we understand this to be _____ will, and that to the best of our
                                          his/her

knowledge the testator is of the age of majority, or is otherwise legally empowered to make a will,

and under no constraint or undue influence.

We declare under penalty of perjury that the foregoing is true and correct, this _____ day of

_____ at _____.

_____
                witness' signature

_____, residing at _____
            witness' typed name   street address

_____, _____, _____.
                city   county   state

_____
                        witness' signature

_____ residing at _____,
        witness' typed name   street address

_____, _____, _____
            city   county   state

_____
                        witness' signature

_____ residing at _____,
        witness' typed name   street address

_____, _____, _____.
            city   county   state

D. Checklist

By now you should have:
- reviewed each clause in this chapter;
- where a mandatory clause provides alternatives, selected one of them;
- checked the boxes for each optional clause you wish to include and selected an alternative where appropriate; and
- sequentially numbered the clauses where circles are provided.

   Now it's time to follow the instructions in Section A of this chapter to cross out instructional language and make such technical changes as are obviously appropriate.

E. Next Steps

YOU'VE NOW PREPARED A WORKING DRAFT of your will ready for final typing, signing, and witnessing. For instructions on how to accomplish these tasks (and, if you wish, make your will "self proving"), proceed to Chapter 13. Act.

CHAPTER 13

FORMALITIES OF WILL DRAFTING

A.	Type Your Will	13/1
B.	Staple Your Will	13/2
C.	Requirements for Signing and Witnessing Your Will	13/2
D.	'Self-Proving' Wills: Using a Notary Public	13/3
E.	After Your Will Is Completed	13/4

LET'S FOCUS NOW ON THE FORMAL REQUIREMENTS necessary to make your will legal, and where to keep it once it's done. Fortunately, the formalities are easy. All you need to do is:

• make sure your will is neatly typed, and
• sign it in front of three witnesses and have them sign it as well.

Below I examine both of these formalities in detail. If your will doesn't comply with these technical requirements—say it was typed but not witnessed—the will cannot be validated by the probate court, and your property will pass as if no will existed. It's not hard to prepare a will correctly. But it's essential to check and double check to be sure you do.

A. Type Your Will

THE FINAL WILL YOU PREPARE from the Will Book must be completely typewritten. The typing machine can be an old portable or a sophisticated computer printer, as long as it prints clearly. This means you must take the draft will you've prepared (whether a basic form will from Chapter 11 or one you've assembled from Chapter 12) and either type the entire document yourself or have it typed. It isn't advisable and may not be legal to use a typewriter to fill in the blanks of a will form in this book and sign and witness that document as your will.

If you cannot type yourself, you obviously must arrange to have the will typed by someone else. Typing services can be located through the yellow pages or, if you want a typing service familiar with the wills in this book, through the National Association for Independent Paralegals at 800-542-0034. Most charge about $25 per hour, which means that unless your will is very long, you shouldn't pay more than about $50 to have it typed.

Your will should be typed on regular 8-1/2" x 11" white bond typing paper. It's preferable not to use erasable typing paper. Paper with a high rag content looks nicer, but cheap paper is just as legal. I recommend double spacing, although single spacing is permissible. Spacing should be uniform throughout the will. Normal side and top margins are acceptable (one inch on all sides is recommended), and no abnormal gaps should be present. Pages should be numbered sequentially, at the bottom of each page.

Once your will is complete you may want to staple it to a heavy sheet of backing paper that identifies it as your will. You can purchase a backing sheet from a stationery store.

Typing mistakes can be machine corrected, but there can be no handwritten corrections or cross-outs.

If you X out, or type over, a mistake, you may invalidate your will. Allowable machine corrections include use of self-correcting typewriters, and careful use of white-out, or correcting tape, and then retyping. However, don't do this extensively. If there are more than a few minor changes, retype your will.

Common Sense Note: Your primary mission when you type your will is to avoid any remote suspicion that you or anyone else changed your will after you engaged in the formal signing and witnessing ceremony. Accordingly, if a mistake is made on a sensitive item, say a beneficiary's name, you should retype the whole page rather than using white-out or something similar. You don't want to create the possibility that a beneficiary, a would-be beneficiary, or the probate judge, will question whether the change was valid.

B. Staple Your Will

ONCE YOUR WILL IS TYPED, simply staple it together in the upper lefthand corner with one or two heavy duty staples.

C. Requirements for Signing and Witnessing Your Will

NOW LET'S BRIEFLY REVIEW the proper procedures for signing and witnessing your will.

1. Signing Your Will

In legalese, signing your will is called the "execution" or the "acknowledgment" of the will. This means that you must date the will and sign it at the end in the presence of witnesses. The date is the day, month and year you sign the will. Your signature should be made in ink and should be in exactly the same form of your name you used in your will. In other words, if you commonly use a middle initial (or full middle name) and type your name that way in your will, sign it the same way. For example, if you start your will with the name of Elissa T. James, sign your will the same way,

not in another form, such as "E. T. James," or "Elissa Thelma James."

Be sure you sign your will in the state of your residence—otherwise, there might be problems regarding use of the correct self-proving affidavit (see Section D).

You aren't legally required to sign or initial every page of your will. However, if you're the cautious type, feel free to do so. The purpose of initialing every page of a will is to protect against the remote chance that some evil-doer will remove a page from your will and substitute a fraudulent page after you die. If you want to gain whatever added protection initialing or signing each page provides, do so on the lower right margin.

2. Witnessing Your Will

Under the law of every state, your signature on a formal typed will must be witnessed to be valid. This means that your witnesses must watch you sign the will and then sign their names, below your signature. Here's a step-by-step breakdown of how to accomplish this:

a. Use Three Witnesses

While state laws vary as to witnesses' requirements, having three people witness a will meets the legal requirements of all states. Even if the law of your state only requires two witnesses, three is better because it provides one more person to establish that your signature is valid should this become necessary during probate.

b. Who to Select as Your Witnesses

Here are the guidelines you should follow in selecting your witnesses. Each witness must be:

- A legally competent adult (i.e., over age 18);
- Not a beneficiary of your will. This is important—if you leave property to a witness he may be disqualified from inheriting, or the entire will may be invalidated. Relatives and family members who do not receive gifts in your will may be witnesses. But since your children must receive gifts, or be expressly disinherited, (see Chapter 7, Section E) You cannot use any of your children as witnesses;
- If possible, a person likely to be easy to locate when you die. This usually means choosing people who know you and who live in your area, don't move around a lot and are younger than you are. Using witnesses who live far away doesn't invalidate your will, but it can make it more difficult for your executor to produce the witnesses in court should this be required as part of probating your estate. Many states have substantially eliminated the requirement that a witness actually appear in court and testify in the probate proceeding, unless a will is contested. Instead, a written affidavit from the witnesses is deemed sufficient. However, a minority of states still require witness testimony in court. Also in rare circumstances, such as a will contest, the court testimony and character of your witnesses could be crucial. It's also a sensible idea to keep track of the location of your witnesses, and record their current addresses so your executor can readily locate them.

c. The Witnesses Must Witness You Signing Your Will

When you're ready to sign your will, assemble all your witnesses. There's absolutely no requirement that the witnesses read your will or that you read it to them. However, they must all realize that you intend the document to be your will. Traditionally, there's a ritual dialogue engaged in which sounds like something from a Gilbert and Sullivan operetta, but it does satisfy the technicalities of the law:

You say: "This is my will."

Your witnesses say (in unison or individually): "He says it's his will."

Then you sign your will, and immediately after that the witnesses sign it in ink with their normal handwritten signatures. The witnesses' addresses

aren't legally required, but it's a good idea to list them for identification and possibly to help locate them after your death.

D. 'Self-Proving' Wills: Using a Notary Public

IN NO STATE DOES A WILL LEGALLY HAVE TO BE NOTARIZED.[1] However, in most states you can potentially simplify the probate process if you and your witnesses sign a simple affidavit in front of a notary public declaring that the document is your will and that it was properly executed. This affidavit is then attached to your will. This whole process is called creating a "self-proving" will. It's important to reiterate that self-proving your will doesn't affect its validity.

The reason for self-proving your will is to eliminate the requirement that a witness appear at the probate proceeding after your death. This of course is particularly useful if your witnesses can't be found. However, there's now a strong national trend among the states to allow witnesses to a will to declare in an affidavit prepared after your death that they in fact witnessed the will (as opposed to actually appearing and testifying to this in court). Accordingly, including a self-proving affidavit with your will may not be the only way you can free your witnesses from the necessity of appearing in court.

If you desire to make your will self-proving, take the following steps:

Do not use a self-proving affidavit if you're a resident of California,[2] Maryland, Michigan, Ohio, Vermont, Wisconsin, or Washington D.C. These states don't recognize the self-proving option.

 Also, if you're in New Hampshire or Texas, see a lawyer for the precise language needed for your state's self-proving will.

1. Sign your will, and have it witnessed.

---

[1]Except Louisiana. Louisiana law is substantially different from all the others. This book doesn't apply to and shouldn't be used in Louisiana.

[2]The declaration that the witnesses sign is sufficient to make the will self-proving in California.

1. Sign your will, and have it witnessed.
2. Either have a notary present at the will signing, or find a notary at a later time. Either way, you and your three witnesses must personally appear before the notary and be prepared to identify yourselves.
3. Tell the notary that you want to make your will self-proving and ask whether he or she has a form for doing that. If so, use that form and follow the notary's instructions.
4. If the notary doesn't have the form, select the correct one for your state, between the two provided on the following pages. Tear the form out and type the final form, deleting the extraneous material on the book's form (the page caption, "Formalities of Will Drafting" and page number) and the Title ("Form 1" or "Form 2").

    People in the following states should use Form 1: Alabama, Alaska, Arizona, Arkansas, Colorado, Connecticut, Hawaii, Idaho, Illinois, Indiana, Maine, Minnesota, Mississippi, Montana, Nebraska, Nevada, New Mexico, New York, North Dakota, Oregon, South Carolina, South Dakota, Tennessee, Utah, Washington, and West Virginia.

    People in the following states should use Form 2: Delaware, Florida, Georgia, Iowa, Kansas, Kentucky, Massachusetts, Missouri, New Jersey, North Carolina, Oklahoma, Pennsylvania, Rhode Island, Virginia, and Wyoming.

5. Put your name and your witnesses' names in the spaces indicated in the affidavit, and give it to the notary. He or she will have you and your witnesses swear to the truth of the statement in the affidavit (that are basically the same statements you used when the will itself was being signed and witnessed) and will then date and sign the affidavit and put his or her notary seal on it.
6. Staple the affidavit to your will. If you ever make a new will or codicil, you should also redo your affidavit.

    Reminder: Both you and your witnesses must sign your will in addition to signing this affidavit. The affidavit and will are two separate documents.

E. After Your Will Is Completed

ONCE YOUR WILL IS TYPED, double-checked, then signed and witnessed (in front of a notary if you want it to be self-proving), you're done. Congratulations! You've completed an important job. For some, a party celebrating the completion of the will can be fun. Why not gather those you love, break out some good brandy (or soda, if you prefer) reveal as much (or as little) of your will as you want to, and enjoy? Your next concern is normally where to keep your will, and, perhaps, who to give copies to.

1. Storing Your Will

After you've prepared a valid will, what do you do with it? Your main consideration should be that upon your death the right people—at a minimum, your executor—know that your will exists and where it's located.

Your will should be left in a safe, accessible location. There's no one best place. It can be stored in a safe deposit box if you're sure your executor will have access to it after your death. Check with your bank about this. In a number of states, safe deposit boxes, even joint tenancy ones, of a person who died are "sealed" under state law until taxing authorities make an inventory, and aren't therefore instantly accessible by your executor. If a safety deposit box might cause problems, you can store it in a safe place in your home or office, such as a fireproof metal box.

Despite good intentions, it's often hard to find a will at death, and even harder to find other types of important personal property such as bank books and insurance policies. One good way to save your loved ones the hassles of searching for your will and other important papers when they're already dealing with the grief of losing you is to make a clear record of your will and all other property, its location as well as the location of any ownership documents.[3] Also, in some states, such as Ohio and Texas, the local court clerk's office will store your will for a small fee.

---

[3]Nolo offers a computer program to help you accomplish this: *For The Record* by Warner & Pladsen.

FORM 1

AFFIDAVIT

We, _____, _____, and
_____, and _____, the testator and the
witnesses, whose names are signed to the attached or foregoing instrument in
those capacities, personally appearing before the undersigned authority and being
first duly sworn, declare to the undersigned authority under penalty of perjury that:
1) the testator declared, signed and executed the instrument as his/her last will; 2)
he/she signed it willingly or directed another to sign for him/her; 3) he/she
executed it as his/her free and voluntary act for the purposes therein expressed;
and 4) each of the witnesses, at the request of the testator, in his/her hearing and
presence, and in the presence of each other, signed the will as witness and that to
the best of his/her knowledge the testator was at that time of full legal age, of
sound mind and under no constraint or undue influence.

Testator: _____

Witness: _____

Address: _____

Witness: _____

Address: _____

Witness: _____

Address: _____

Subscribed, sworn and acknowledged before me by
_____, the testator, and by _____ ,
_____, and _____, the witnesses, this
_____ day of _____, 19__.

SIGNED: _____

_____
OFFICIAL CAPACITY OF OFFICER

FORM 2

AFFIDAVIT

STATE OF _____

COUNTY OF _____

I, the undersigned, an officer authorized to administer oaths, certify that
_____, the testator, and _____,
_____, and _____ , the witnesses,
whose names are signed to the attached or foregoing instrument and whose
signatures appear below, having appeared together before me and having been
first duly sworn, each then declared to me that: 1) the attached or foregoing
instrument is the last will of the testator; 2) the testator willingly and voluntarily
declared, signed and executed the will in the presence of the witnesses; 3) the
witnesses signed the will upon request by the testator, in the presence and hearing
of the testator, and in the presence of each other; 4) to the best knowledge of
each witness the testator was, at that time of the signing, of the age of majority (or
otherwise legally competent to make a will), of sound mind and memory, and
under no constraint or undue influence; and 5) each witness was and is competent
and of the proper age to witness a will.

Testator: _____

Witness: _____

Address: _____

Witness: _____

Address: _____

Witness: _____

Address: _____

Subscribed, sworn and acknowledged before me by _____
the testator, and by _____, _____, and
_____ witnesses, this _____ day of _____, 19____.

SIGNED: _____

_____
OFFICIAL CAPACITY OF OFFICER

2. Making Copies

A copy of your will is a photocopy of the original signed and witnessed document. It isn't the equivalent of another original of your will. Some people wonder if it's sensible to prepare more than one separately typed, signed and executed original of their will in case one is lost or somehow inaccessible. I strongly advise against it, although in most states, preparation of duplicate originals is legal. If you later decide to change your will by adding a codicil (see Chapter 14, Section B), you have to change every original. Likewise, if you want to revoke your will (see Chapter 14, Section D), you'd have to locate and revoke each original. Tracking down all original versions of your will can be quite a burden. Or, worse, you might forget one or more of the duplicate original wills, and wind up changing or revoking some but not others, thus creating a confusing mess and potentially a legal disaster.

By contrast, making photocopies of your original will may well be a good idea. If you decide it's wise, you can give unsigned photocopies of your original will to people who you want informed of its contents, such as your executor, spouse or children. These copies, of course, aren't legal wills, but are provided for information only. On the other hand, your will is your own business. You don't have to reveal its contents to anyone, even your witnesses. Giving close family members or other loved ones a summary of your will may be a good idea if all is peace and harmony, but there are sometimes lots of practical reasons not to.

CHAPTER 14

CHANGING OR REVOKING YOUR WILL

A.	Revising and Updating Your Will	14/1
B.	Making Simple Changes in Your Will by Codicil	14/2
C.	Codicil Form	14/3
D.	Revoking Your Will	14/3

ONCE YOU'VE PREPARED YOUR WILL by using *Nolo's Simple Will Book,* it's extremely important that you not alter it by inserting handwritten or typed additions or changes. If you decide you want to change or revoke your will, you must do so in a legally permitted manner. You cannot simply cross out something in your will, or write in a change. Doing so will very probably invalidate your entire will. The laws of most states require that any additions or changes in a will, even clerical ones, be done in a formal way. This means either making a new signed and witnessed will, or adding a witnessed codicil (formal addition) to the existing one (see Section B below). And revocation must also be properly done, as explained in Section D.

A. Revising and Updating Your Will

THERE'S NO BLANKET RULE covering when you should make a new will or add a formally-witnessed codicil. By now it should be clear to you that what your will contains is heavily dependent on circumstances. The state of your residence, your marital status, the property you own, whether you have (minor) children, and whether a child predeceases you, leaving children of his or her own, are all examples of variables that determine what should be included in your will. As

these or other variables change, you'll want to update your will.

Simple changes, such as a change of one beneficiary, the addition of a gift, or a change in an executor or alternate executor, can be accomplished by codicil (see Section C below). More extensive changes require revocation of your existing will and creation of a new one. You should definitely consider making a new will:

- If you change your mind about who you want to have a significant portion of your property.
- If you're married and move from a community property state to a common law property state, or vice versa. For a list of which states fall into which category, see Chapter 4, Section D. The reason you may need a new will in this circumstance is that community property and common law property states view the ownership of property by married couples differently. This means the amount of property both you and your spouse have to leave may change if you move from one type of state to the other. Of course, if you plan to leave all or the bulk of your property to your spouse, this change will probably not have any real significance. If you move from one community property state or one common law state to another in the same category, it's probably not necessary for you to change your will.

- If your marital status changes, especially if you marry after making your will. If you don't do this, your new spouse will automatically inherit a share of the property that may be different than you would have wished.
- If you have or adopt children. Each time a child is born or legally adopted into your family, you should review your will. The new child should be named in your new will and provided for according to your wishes. If you don't do this, the child will automatically be entitled to a share that may be different than you would have wished (see Chapter 7, Section E(1).
- If one of your children dies.
- If any of your children die before you, leaving children of his or her own. As I discuss in Chapter 7, these children (your grandchildren) may be entitled to receive a share of your estate (in some states) unless they receive property under the will or you've specifically disinherited them.
- If any of your beneficiaries die, and you haven't named an alternate beneficiary. If a beneficiary you've named to receive either a specific gift or the residue dies before you, check your will to be sure it reflects your current desires. Do you still want the alternate beneficiary to receive that gift? If you didn't name an alternate in the first place, do you want the gift to go to the residuary beneficiary? If not, change your will.
- If the property you leave in your will either expands or shrinks substantially after you've made out your will. In this case you should review your will to make sure it realistically reflects your current situation. This is especially true if there are changes in your ownership of real estate or expensive personal property items. For example, if you leave your 1988 Cadillac to your son and then trade it in and buy a 1990 Buick, your son will get nothing, unless you update your will. On the other hand, if you leave your son "my car," he'll get whatever car you own at your death, even though it's a different one than you owned when you made your will.
- If anyone you named to care for your children or your or other children's property are no longer available to serve. Revise your will if any of the people you choose for the following can't do the job: your children's personal guardian(s) and

successor personal guardian(s); the custodian(s) and successor custodian(s), for any gifts under the Uniform Transfers to Minors Act; the trustees and successor trustees for any children's trust created in your will; your children's property guardian(s) and alternate property guardian(s) (see Chapter 7). If any of these persons moves away, becomes disabled, or simply turns out to be not the kind of people you wish to care for your children or property, make a new will naming somebody more suitable.
- If the person(s) you named as your executor is no longer able to serve.

As you know, the executor of your estate is the person charged with making sure your wishes are faithfully complied with. You may discover that the person or institution you originally named would really not be the best person for this task. For example, if you originally named your spouse, who has subsequently become seriously ill, you may want to substitute one of your children. If so, you should write a new will and change executors.

B. Making Simple Changes in Your Will by Codicil

YOU CAN MAKE SIMPLE CHANGES in your will by means of a "codicil"—the legal name for a written amendment to the terms of a will, made after the original will has been witnessed and signed. Codicils are frequently used for minor matters such as changes of individual gifts. In a codicil, the will writer can revoke a clause in the will he wants to change and then add a new clause, or the will writer can simply add a new provision, such as making a new specific personal property gift.

Example: John's (the will writer) brother Jim has died. John now wants to give the player piano he left to Jim to Jim's son Fred. Here's the Codicil John executes.

First: I revoke the provision of clause 4 of my will that provided that I give my player piano to my brother Jim.

Second: I add the following provision to clause 4: I give my player piano to my nephew Fred.

Example: The will writer buys a new gold necklace that she wants to leave to her favorite niece, Maria: "I add the following provision to Clause 4 of my will:

- I give my gold necklace to my niece, Maria Wallace, or, if she fails to survive me by 45 days, to Tom Wallace."

Again, if a major revision of the will is desired, don't use a codicil. A will that has been substantially re-written by a codicil is a confusing document and awkward to read. It may not be clear what the relationship of the codicil to the original will provision means. For major revisions, draft a new will and revoke the old one.

A codicil, being a sort of legal "P.S." to the will, must be executed with all of the formalities of a will that were discussed in Chapter 13. This means that the codicil must be typed, then dated and signed by you in front of three witnesses. These witnesses don't have to be the same people who witnessed the will, but it's advisable to use them if they're available. As with your original witnesses, these shouldn't be named as beneficiaries in your will. If your will is "self-proved" with a notarized affidavit, another affidavit for the codicil should also be executed. Once the codicil is completed, it should be stored with the original will.

Important: Be sure anyone with an unsigned copy of your will receives an unsigned copy of the codicil. This may be a nuisance, but will prevent confusion, or even conflict, later. The codicil doesn't have to be made part of the signature page of the original will. It must, however, refer to that will. This can be simply accomplished by labeling the codicil document "first codicil of the will of [your name] , dated [giving date will was originally prepared] ." The entire will is now considered to have been prepared as of the date of the codicil.

C. Codicil Form

FOLLOWING IS A SAMPLE FORM you can use or adapt if it becomes necessary to make a codicil to your will. You can adapt the form, for example, to make two or three minor changes in your will. In other words, you aren't stuck with this precise form. To use this form, follow the instructions for completing your draft will contained in Chapter 11, Section B: fill in the blanks and any additional sections you need, cross out all instructional language, and delete unwanted clauses. Then have the codicil form typed for you and your witnesses' signatures. If you need a self-proving affidavit, use the same form and follow the same instructions found in Section D of Chapter 13.

D. Revoking Your Will

ANYONE WHO WRITES A WILL should understand how it can be revoked. There are only two ways: first, by deliberate act of the will writer; second, by operation of law. Let's look at each of these.

1. A Deliberate Act to Revoke a Will

A will writer who wants to revoke a prior will should do so by express written statement, as provided for in all wills in this book. In many states, an existing will (or codicil) is also revoked by being "burnt, torn, concealed, defaced, obliterated or destroyed" if the will writer intended to revoke it. This can be legally accomplished by someone other than the will writer at his or her direction. The problem with destroying a will, or having someone else do so, is that this only serves to revoke the will if you intend it to. After your death this can become a matter of controversy, especially if you've distributed copies of your original will. So if you want the satisfaction of destroying a revoked will, go right ahead, but be sure you've also revoked it in writing in your new will. This is the only good way to make your intention clear.

FIRST CODICIL TO THE WILL OF

I, _____ , a resident of _____ ,

_____ declare this to be the first codicil to my will dated

_____ , 19___ .

FIRST: I revoke the provision of Clause ___ , of my will that provided:

(Include the exact language you wish to revoke)

and substitute the following : (Add whatever is desired.)

SECOND: I add the following provision to Clause __ : (Add whatever is desired.)

THIRD: In all other respects I confirm and republish my will dated

_____ , 19___ .

Dated _____ , 19___ _____

I subscribe my name to this codicil this _____ day of _____ , 19__ ,

at _____ , _____ ,
         city   county

_____ and do hereby declare that I sign and
         state

execute this codicil willingly, that I execute it as my free and voluntary act for the

purposes therein expressed, and that I am of the age of majority or otherwise

legally empowered to make a codicil and under no constraint or undue influence.

_____

On this _____ day of _____, 19 ____,
declared to us, the undersigned, that this instrument was the codicil to
_____ will and requested us to act as witnesses to it.
_____ thereupon signed this
codicil in our presence, all of us being present at the same time. We now, at
_____ request, in _____ presence, and in the presence of each
other, subscribe our names as witnesses and declare we understand this to be
_____ codicil and that to the best of our knowledge _____ is of the age
of majority, or is otherwise legally empowered to make a codicil and is under no
constraint or undue influence.

We declare under penalty of perjury that the foregoing is true and correct, this
_____ day of _____ at _____.

_____
witness' signature

_____ residing at _____,
witness' typed name   street address

_____, _____ _____
city   county   state

_____
witness' signature

_____ residing at _____,
witness' typed name   street address

_____, _____ _____
city   county   state

_____
witness' signature

_____ residing at _____,
witness' typed name   street address

_____, _____ _____
city   county   state

The revocation of a subsequent will doesn't revive an earlier one, unless the terms of the revocation state that it's the will writer's intent to revive the first will, or if the first will is "republished" (i.e., signed and witnessed anew). Thus, if Marguerite makes one will and then sometime later makes a second will expressly revoking the first will, the first will doesn't become valid if Marguerite tears up the second.

2. Revocation of a Will by Act of Law

This refers to spouses not suitably provided for, or children not mentioned in, your will. As is discussed in Chapter 4, in common law states, a spouse has a statutory right to a certain percentage of the other spouse's estate, unless that right has been waived by a written marital agreement. And, as discussed in Chapter 7, Section E, children not mentioned in a will have statutory rights to a part of a parent's estate. So the law looks upon the will as being revoked as far as a spouse not provided for or unmentioned children are concerned, but not as to any other provisions. With a will drafted from the Will Book, you shouldn't have to concern yourself with this, because if you followed instructions, you've suitably provided for your spouse and mentioned all your children in your will, and have either given something to each of your children, or expressly disinherited them.

GLOSSARY

ABATEMENT: Cutting back certain gifts under a will when it's necessary to create a fund to meet expenses, pay taxes, satisfy debts, or to have enough to take care of other bequests that are given a priority under law or under the will.

ACKNOWLEDGMENT: A statement in front of a person who's qualified to administer oaths (e.g., a Notary Public) that a document bearing your signature was actually signed by you.

ADEMPTION: The failure of a specific bequest of property to take effect because the property is no longer owned by the testator at the time of his death.

ADMINISTRATION: (of an estate): The court-supervised distribution of the probate estate of a deceased person. The person who manages the distribution is called the executor if there's a will. If there's no will, this person is called the administrator. In some states, the person is called "personal representative" in either instance.

ADOPTED CHILDREN: Any person, whether an adult or a minor, who's legally adopted as the child of another in a court proceeding.

ADULT: Basically, any person over the age of 18.

AUGMENTED ESTATE: A method used in a number of states following the common law ownership of property system to measure a person's estate for the purpose of determining whether a surviving spouse has been adequately provided for. Generally, the augmented estate consists of property left by the will plus certain property transferred outside of the will by such devices as gifts, joint tenancies and living trusts. In the states using this concept, a surviving spouse is generally considered to be adequately provided for if he or she receives at least one-third of the augmented estate.

BENEFICIARY: A person or organization who's legally entitled to receive benefits under a legal document such as a will or trust. Except when very small estates are involved, beneficiaries of wills only receive their benefits after the will is examined and approved by the probate court. Beneficiaries of trusts receive their benefits as provided in the trust instrument.

BEQUEST: An old legal term for a will provision leaving personal property to a specified person or organization. In this book it's called a "gift."

BOND: A document guaranteeing that a certain amount of money will be paid to those damaged if a person occupying a position of trust doesn't carry out his or her legal and ethical responsibilities. Thus, if an executor, trustee or guardian who's bonded (covered by a bond) wrongfully deprives a beneficiary of his or her property (say by blowing it during a trip in Las Vegas), the bonding company will replace it, up to the limits of the bond. Bonding companies, which are normally divisions of insurance companies, issue a bond in exchange for a premium (usually about 10% of the face amount of the bond). Under the Will Book, executors and guardians are appointed to serve without the necessity of purchasing a bond. This is because the cost of the bond would have to be paid out of the estate, and the beneficiaries would accordingly receive less. Using the Will Book, you should take care to select trustworthy people in the first place.

CHILDREN: For the purpose of the Will Book, children are: (1) the biological offspring of the will maker, (2) persons who were legally adopted by the will maker, (3) children born out of wedlock if the will maker is the mother, (4) children born out of wedlock if the will maker is the father and has acknowledged the child as being his as required by the law of the particular state, or (5) children born to the will maker after the will is made, but before his or her death.

CODICIL: A separate legal document that changes an existing will after it has been signed and properly witnessed.

COMMUNITY AND SEPARATE PROPERTY: Eight states follow a system of marital property ownership called "community property," and Wisconsin has a very similar law. Very generally, all property acquired after marriage and before permanent separation is considered to belong equally to both spouses, except for gifts to and inheritances by one spouse, and, in some community property states, income from property owned by one spouse prior to marriage.

In most marriages, the main property accumulated is a family home, a retirement pension belong to one or both spouses, motor vehicles, a joint bank account, a savings account, and perhaps some stocks or bonds. So long as these were purchased during the marriage with the income earned by either spouse during the marriage, they're usually considered to be community property, unless the spouses have entered into an agreement to the contrary. If the property was purchased with the separate property of a spouse, it's separate property, unless it has been given to the community by gift or agreement.

If separate property and community property are mixed together (commingled) in a bank account and expenditures made from this bank account, the goods

purchased will usually be treated as community property unless they can be specifically linked with the separate property (this is called "tracing").

Under the law of community property states, a surviving spouse automatically receives one-half of all community property. The other spouse has no legal power to affect this portion by will or otherwise. Thus, the property that a testator actually leaves by will consists of his or her separate property and one-half of the community property.

CONDITIONAL GIFT: A gift that only passes under certain specified conditions or upon the occurrence of a specific event. For example, if you leave property to Aunt Millie provided she's living in Cincinnati when you die, and otherwise to Uncle Fred, you've made a "conditional gift." *Nolo's Simple Will Book* doesn't encourage or provide clauses for conditional bequests.

CUSTODIAN: A person named to care for property left to a minor under the Uniform Gifts (or Transfers) to Minor's Act.

DEATH TAXES: Taxes levied on the property of a person who died. Federal Death Taxes are called Estate Taxes. State Death Taxes (if any) go by various names, including Inheritance Tax.

DECEDENT: A person who has died.

DEVISE: An old English term for real estate given by a will. In this book, it's called a "gift."

DOMICILE: The state, or country, where one has his or her primary home.

DOWER AND CURTESY: The right of a surviving spouse to receive or enjoy the use of a set portion of the deceased spouse's property (usually one-third to one-half) in the event the surviving spouse isn't left at least that share and chooses to take against the will. Dower refers to the title that a surviving wife gets, while curtesy refers to what a man receives. Until recently, these amounts differed in a number of states. However, since discrimination on the basis of sex is now considered to be illegal in most cases, states generally provide the same benefits regardless of sex.

ENCUMBRANCES: Debts (e.g., taxes, mechanics liens, judgment liens) and loans (e.g., mortgages, deeds of trust, security interests) which use property as collateral for payment of the debt or loan are considered to encumber the property because they must be paid off before title to the property can pass from one owner to the next. Generally, the value of a person's ownership in such property (called the "equity") is measured by the market value of the property less the sum of all encumbrances.

ESTATE: Generally, all the property you own when you die. There are different ways to measure your estate, depending on whether you're concerned with tax reduction (the taxable estate), probate avoidance (the probate estate), or net worth (the net estate).

ESTATE PLANNING: The art of dying with the smallest taxable estate and probate estate possible while continuing to prosper when you're alive and yet passing your property to your loved ones with a minimum of fuss and expense.

ESTATE TAXES: Federal taxes imposed on your property as it passes from the dead to the living. The federal government exempts $600,000 in 1987 and thereafter. Also, all property left to a surviving spouse is exempt under the marital exemption. Taxes are only imposed on property actually owned by you at the time of your death. Thus, estate planning techniques designed to reduce taxes usually concentrate on the legal transfer of ownership of your property while you're living, to minimize the amount of such property you own at your death.

EQUITY: The difference between the fair market value of your real and personal property and the amount you still owe on it, if any.

EXECUTOR: The person named in your will to manage your estate, deal with the probate court, collect your assets and distribute them as you've specified. In some states this person is called the "personal representative." If you die without a will, the probate court will appoint such a person., who's then called the "administrator" of the estate.

FINANCIAL GUARDIAN: See Guardian of the Minor's Property.

GIFTS: As used in the Will Book (except in Chapter 8 on estate planning), all property you leave to people, or organizations, on your death. A specific gift means an identified piece of property given to an inheritor.

GUARDIAN OF THE MINOR'S PROPERTY: Termed "property guardian" in this book. The person (or institution) appointed or selected in your will to care for property of your minor child. Also sometimes called "the Guardian of the Minor's Estate," or "Financial Guardian." Usually the same person will serve as guardian of the person and property guardian. However, it's also possible to split these tasks.

GUARDIAN OF THE PERSON: An adult appointed or selected to care for a minor child in the event no biological or adoptive parent (legal parent) of the child is able to do so. If one legal parent is alive when the other dies, however, the child will automatically go to that parent, unless the best interests of the child require something different, or (in some states) the court finds the child would suffer detriment.

HEIRS: Persons who are entitled by law to inherit your estate if you don't leave a will, and any person or institution named in your will.

HOLOGRAPHIC WILL: A will that's completely handwritten by the person making it. While legal in many states, it's never advised except as a last resort.

INHERIT: To receive property from one who dies.

INHERITORS: Persons or organizations who you leave property to.

INTER VIVOS TRUSTS: See Living Trusts.

INTESTATE: To die without a will.

INTESTATE SUCCESSION: The method by which property is distributed when a person fails to distribute it by a will or other estate planning device. In such cases, the law of each state provides that the property be distributed in certain shares to the closest surviving relatives. In most states, these are a surviving spouse, children, parents, siblings, nieces and nephews, and next of kin, in that order. The intestate succession laws are also used in the event an heir is found to be pretermitted (i.e., not mentioned or otherwise provided for in the will).

JOINT TENANCY: A way to take title to jointly owned real or personal property. When two or more people own property as joint tenants, and one of the owners dies, the other owners automatically become owners of the deceased owner's share. Thus, if a parent and child own a house a joint tenants, and the parent dies, the child automatically becomes full owner. Because of this "right of survivorship," a joint tenancy interest in property doesn't go through probate, or, put another way, isn't part of the probate estate. Instead it goes directly to the surviving joint tenant(s) once some tax and transfer forms are completed.

Placing property in joint tenancy is therefore a common tool used in estate planning designed to avoid probate. However, when property is placed in joint tenancy, a gift is made to any persons who become owners as a result. Thus, if Tom owns a house and places it in joint tenancy with Karen, Tom will have made a gift to Karen equal to one-half the house's value. This may have gift tax consequences.

LIVING TRUSTS: Trusts set up while a person is alive and which remain under the control of that person during the remainder of his or her life. Also referred to as "inter vivos trusts," living trusts are an excellent way to minimize the value of property passing through probate. This is because they enable people (called "trustors") to specify that money or other property (called the "trust corpus") will pass directly to their beneficiaries at the time of their death, free of probate, and yet allow the trustors to continue to control the property during their lifetime and even end the trust or change the beneficiaries if they wish.

MARRIAGE: A specific status conferred on a couple by the state. In most states, it's necessary to file papers with a county clerk and have a marriage ceremony conducted by authorized individuals in order to be married. However, in a minority of states called "common law marriage" states you may be considered married if you've lived together for a certain period of time and intended to be husband and wife. These states are: Alabama, Colorado, District of Columbia, Georgia, Idaho, Iowa, Kansas, Montana, Ohio, Oklahoma, Pennsylvania, Rhode Island, South Carolina and Texas.

Unless you're considered legally married in the state where you claim your marriage occurred, you aren't married for purposes of the Will Book.

MARITAL EXEMPTION: A deduction allowed by the federal estate tax law for all property passed to a surviving spouse. This deduction (that really acts like an exemption) allows anyone, even a billionaire, to pass his or her entire estate to a surviving spouse without any tax at all. This might be a good idea if the surviving spouse is young and in good health.

If the surviving spouse is likely to die in the near future, however, your tax problems will very likely be made worse by relying on the marital exemption. This is because the second spouse to die will normally benefit from no marital deduction, which means the combined estate, less the standard estate tax exemption, will be taxed at a fairly high rate. For this reason, many older couples with adequate resources don't leave large amounts of property to each other, but rather, leave it directly to their children so that each can qualify for a separate tax exemption.

MINOR: In most states, persons under 18 years of age. A minor isn't permitted to make certain types of decisions (e.g., enter into most contracts). All minors are required to be under the care of a competent adult (parent or guardian) unless they qualify as emancipated minors (in the military, married, or living independently with court permission). This also means that property left to a minor must be handled by a guardian or trustee until the minor becomes an adult under the laws of the state.

NET TAXABLE ESTATE: The value of all your property at death less all encumbrances and your other liabilities.

PERSONAL PROPERTY: All property other than land and buildings attached to land. Cars, bank accounts, wages, securities, a small business, furniture, insurance policies, jewelry, pets, season baseball tickets, etc., are all personal property.

POWER OF ATTORNEY: A legal document where you authorize someone else to act for you. A durable power of attorney allows someone to act for you if you become incapacitated, to make health care and financial decisions for you.

PRETERMITTED HEIR: A child (or the child of a deceased child) who's either not named or (in some states) not provided for in a will. Most states presume that persons want their children to inherit. Accordingly, children, or the children of a child who has died before the person making the will (the "testator") who aren't mentioned or provided for in the will (even by as little as $1.00) are automatically given a share of the estate unless such children are specifically disinherited in the will.

PROBATE: The court proceeding in which: (1) the authenticity of your will (if any) is established, (2) your executor or administrator is appointed, (3) your debts and taxes are paid, (4) your heirs are identified, and (5) your property in your probate estate is distributed according to your will (if there's a will).

PROBATE ESTATE: All of your property that will pass through probate. Generally, this means all property owned by you at your death less any property that has been placed in joint tenancy, a living trust, a bank account trust, or in life insurance.

PROBATE FEES: Because probate is so laden with legal formalities, it's usually necessary to hire an attorney to handle it. Under the law of some states, an attorney handling probate is entitled to be paid a percentage of the overall value of the probate estate. This can mean that the attorney will take a substantial fee of the estate before it's distributed to the heirs.

PROVING A WILL: Getting a probate court to accept the fact after your death that your will really is your will. In many states this can be done simply by introducing a properly executed will. In others, it's necessary to produce one or more witnesses (or affidavits of such witnesses) in court, or offer some proof of the testator's handwriting. Having the testator and witnesses sign a sworn statement (affidavit) before a notary public stating that all will-making formalities were complied with usually allows the will to "prove" itself without the need for the witnesses to testify, or other evidence.

QUASI-COMMUNITY PROPERTY: A rule in Idaho and California that requires all property acquired by people during their marriage in other states to be treated as community property at their death in the event the couple has moved to one of these states.

REAL ESTATE: A term used by the Will Book as a synonym for "real property."

REAL PROPERTY: All land and items attached to the land, such as buildings, houses, stationary mobile homes, fences and trees as considered as "real property" or "real estate." All property that isn't "real property" is personal property.

RESIDUE, RESIDUARY ESTATE: All property given by your will to your residuary beneficiary after all specific gifts of property (real and personal) have been made, i.e., "what's left."

SPOUSE: In the Will Book, your spouse is the person to whom you're legally married at the time you sign the will. If you later remarry, you'll need to make a new will if you wish to leave property to your new spouse.

TAKING AGAINST THE WILL: The ability of a surviving spouse to choose a statutorily allotted share of the deceased spouse's estate instead of the share specified in his or her will. In most common law property states, the law provides for a surviving spouse to receive a minimum percentage of the other spouse's estate (commonly between one-third and one-half). If the deceased spouse leaves the surviving spouse less than this in, or outside of, the will, the surviving spouse may elect the statutory share instead of the will provision (i.e., take against the will). If the spouse chooses to accept the share specified in the will, it's called "taking under the will."

TAXABLE ESTATE: The portion of your estate that's subject to federal and/or state estate taxes.

TENANCY IN COMMON: A way of jointly owning property in which each person's share passes to his/her heirs. The ownership shares needn't be equal.

TESTATOR: The person making the will.

TOTTEN TRUST (ALSO CALLED PAY-ON-DEATH BANK ACCOUNTS): Simple bank trust account enabling the depositor to name a beneficiary to receive the fund in the account after the beneficiary dies.

TRUST: A legal arrangement under which one person or institution (called a "trustee") controls property given by another person for the benefit of a third person (called a "beneficiary"). The property itself can be termed the "corpus" of the trust.

UNIFORM GIFTS/TRANSFERS TO MINORS ACT: A series of statutes that provide standard guidelines for transferring property to minors. Enacted into law by most states, the Uniform Gifts (or Transfers) to Minors Act is used by Chapter 12 of the Will Book to govern how property left to minors other than your own children is handled.

WILL: A legal document in which a person states various binding intentions about what he/she wants done after his/her death.

INDEX

A

Abandonment, 7/3n

Abatement, 6/18-19

Abatement clauses, 6/19, 12/15-16

Acknowledgment, of out-of-wedlock children, 7/24

Acknowledgment of the will, 13/2

Additions to will. *See* Changes; codicil(s)

Adopted children, 7/2, 7/3n, 7/23-24

Ademption, 6/18

Adult children, bequests to, 7/1, 7/5. *See also* Children

Affidavits. *See* Self-proving affidavit

Afterborn children, 7/23

Age of minor child, and children's trust, 7/7, 7/9, 7/17-18, 7/20, 8/9

Age of minor child, and UTMA, 7/6-7, 7/8, 7/15, 7/19-20, 11/8, 12/22

Age requirement, to make a will, 2/1-2

Alternate beneficiary: definition, 6/2, 7/15; for individual gifts, 6/7-9; for shared gifts, 6/9; naming, 6/7-9

Alternate personal guardian, 7/2

Alternate property guardian, 7/11, 7/14

Alternate residuary beneficiary, 6/15, 7/5, 12/14

Ancillary executor, 3/3

Animals, as beneficiaries, 12/29-30

Appraisals, 5/5-6

Appreciated property, 4/7-8

Assemble-it-yourself will clauses. *See* Will forms

Assets, to pay estate taxes, 8/6, 12/16

Attorney in fact, and durable power of attorney8/10

Augmented estate, 4/12-13

B

Backing for will, 13/1

Bank account trust. *See* Informal bank trust account

Bank: as executor, 3/2; as trustee, 7/17

Basic will forms. *See* Will forms

Beneficiary, 6/1-19, 7/5; definition, 6/2; of life insurance, 4/1-2, 4/3, 8/6, 8/7-8; of living trust, 4/3. *See also* names of specific types of beneficiaries

Beneficiary chart, 6/9-16

Bequests. *See* Gift(s)

Body/body parts donation clause, 12/30

Bond, 3/2, 7/16

Borrowed funds, as property, 4/8

Burial instructions clause, 12/31

Business, as property, 4/8

C

California Statutory Will, 2/4

Caption clause, 12/4

Cash gift shortfalls, 6/18-19

Cash gifts clause, 12/6-7

Changes, to will, 11/3, 12/3, 13/1-2, 14/1-5

Charitable gifts, 4/3-4

Charities, and estate taxes, 8/9

Child custody, 7/1-5

Children, 7/1-24; bequests to, and adult supervision, 7/6-11; definition, 6/1; disinheriting, 6/5, 7/5, 7/23, 11/4, 12/6; financial care, 7/5-18; not mentioned in will, 14/6; personal care, 7/1-5; and property ownership, 7/5

Children's trust, 7/7, 7/9-10, 7/11-13, 7/15-18, 7/20, 11/8-9; definition, 7/7; and estate planning, 8/9; and gifts to others' children, 7/20-21, 7/22; and insurance proceeds, 7/10

Children's trust clause, 11/8-9, 12/24-26

Closely held business, and estate taxes, 8/7n

Co-executors, 3/2-3

Codicil(s), 13/7, 14/1, 14/2-3; form, 14/4-5

Commingling, of property, 4/5

Common law marriages: and family protection, 4/11-14; and property ownership, 4/2, 4/4, 4/9-14

Common law property states: list, 4/4, 4/9; and property ownership, 14/1

Community property, 5/4, 5/5; defined, 4/5

Community property states, 4/2, 4/4-8; list, 4/4; and property ownership, 14/1
Computer drafted will, 2/3n
Conditional gift, 6/4
Contingent gift, 2/5, 6/4
Contract, to make a will, 2/5
Contractual agreements, and property, 4/3
Co-owners, 6/6, 8/5. See also Joint tenancy property; Tenancy in common property; etc.
Copies of will, 13/7, 14/3
Corporate executor, 3/2
Couples. See Married people; Person living with lover/mate
Cremation clause, 12/31
Curtesy, 4/11
Custodian, 7/6-7, 7/14, 7/19, 7/20. See also Uniform Transfers to Minors Act (UTMA)
Custody, of children, 7/1-5

D
Death and dying, 1/2; intestate, 2/3; legal steps afterward, 2/6; simultaneous, 5/4, 6/16-17; without a will, 1/2, 2/3
Death taxes, 12/16; and probate avoidance, 8/6. See also Federal estate taxes; State death taxes
Death taxes clause, 12/16-17
Debts: forgiving, 6/3; as property, 4/8
Debts clause, 12/16-17
Debts forgiven clause, 12/10
Decree, of divorce, 4/2
Devises. See Gift(s)
Directive to Physicians, 2/5
Disinheritance clause, 12/6
Disinheritance, 6/4-5; of children, 6/5, 7/15, 7/23, 11/4, 12/6; of grandchild, 6:5, 7/23; of spouse, 4/11, 6/4
Divorce: and property ownership, 4/2-3; and will, 6/4
Dollar (single) bequest, 6/5, 11/4
Domicile, definition, 2/1
Donation of body/body parts clause, 12/30
Dower, 4/11
Durable power of attorney, 2/5, 8/10-11
Dying. See Death and dying

E
Emancipated minor, 2/1, 7/2n
Encumbrances on real property clause, 12/13-14
"Equitable Distribution" law, 4/9n
Equity powers of court, 4/9n
Escheating, 1/2
Estate: definition, 1/2; value, and taxes, 8/7
Estate planning, 1/4, 1/7, 8/1-11; to reduce taxes, 8/6-9. See also Probate avoidance
Estate taxes. See Death taxes; Federal estate taxes; State death taxes
Execution of the will, 13/2
Executor, 2/2, 14/2; choosing, 3/1-3; fee, 3/1
Executor's powers clause, 12/18-19
Executor(s) clause, 11/6, 12/17-18

F
Family allowances, 4/11n
Family farmland, and estate taxes, 8/7n
Family pot trust, 7/10
Family protection, in common law states, 4/11-14
Federal estate taxes, 8/6-9
Felon, as inheritor, 6/4
Film will, 2/3
Flexible trust, 8/10
Fraud, 2/2
Funeral arrangements clause, 12/31

G
Generation-skipping trusts, 8/8-9
Gift(s): 6/1-19; and accompanying explanation in will, 6/2-3; to charities, 4/3-4; contingent, 2/5; definition, 1/3, 6/1, 8/6; and estate taxes, 8/7-8; and gift taxes, 8/6-8; to married persons, 6/3; outright to children, 7/10-12, 7/21; to parents of minor child, 7/19; and probate avoidance, 8/6-7; restrictions on, 6/4; shared, 6/5-6, 6/9; between spouses, 4/5n; under the UTMA clause, 11/7-8, 12/22-23
Gifts clauses, 11/5-6, 12/6-10, 12/11-12
Grandchildren: disinheriting, 6/5, 7/23; and generation-skipping trusts, 8/8-9
Group legal plans, 9/3

Guardian. *See* Personal guardian; Property guardian

H

Handwritten will, 2/4
Holographic will, 2/4
Husband, sample wills. *See* Married person

I

"Illegitimate" children. *See* Out-of-wedlock children
Incapacity, 2/2
Informal bank trust account, 4/4, 5/4, 8/5
Initialing, of will pages, 13/2
Insurance. *See* Life insurance
Inter vivos trust. *See* Living trust
Intestacy laws, 2/3, 8/2
Intestacy proceedings, 8/2
Intestate share, 4/12n
Intestate succession laws, 2/3, 8/2
Inventory of property, 5/1-18
IRAs, 2/6, 4/3, 5/4; and probate avoidance, 8/6
Irrevocable trust, 8/8-9

J

Joint personal guardian, 7/2
Joint tenancy property, 2/6, 4/1, 4/3, 5/4, 5/5; and probate avoidance, 8/5; and simultaneous death, 6/17
Joint tenancy with right of survivorship (JTWROS), 4/9n, 5/4
Joint wills, 2/4-5
JTWROS. *See* Joint tenancy with right of survivorship

K

Keoghs, 5/4; and probate avoidance, 8/6

L

Law clinics, 9/3
Law libraries, 9/4

Lawyer(s), 1/7-8, 9/1-4; fees, 9/2; hired by executor, 2/5; probate, 3/1, 8/2
Legal referral services, 9/3-4
Legal research, 9/4
Letters of administration, 2/6
Libel, in will, 6/3
Life estate gift, 6/4
Life estate trust, 6/17-18, 8/9. *See also* Marital life estate trust
Life insurance, 2/6, 4/1-2, 4/3, 5/4; and federal estate taxes, 8/7-8; and minor children, 7/10; and probate avoidance, 8/6
Life support systems, 2/5, 8/10
Living trust, 2/6, 4/3, 7/9, 7/21, 8/8; and probate avoidance, 8/4, 8/5. *See also* names of specific types of living trusts
Living trust property, 5/4
Living will, 2/5
Louisiana, 1/1, 2/2, 13/3n

M

Marital deduction, 8/8
Marital joint tenancy, 8/5
Marital life estate trust, 2/5, 8/8, 8/9. *See also* Life estate trust
"Marital Property Agreement," 4/6
Marital property ownership laws, 4/4-14
Marriages and children clause, 11/4, 12/5-6
Married person with minor children: sample will form, 11/2, 11/43-51; sample completed will, 11/10-19
Married person with no minor children, sample will form, 11/2, 11/37-42
Married persons, and property ownership, 4/2-3, 4/4-14
Mental state, definition, 2/2
Mexican divorces, 4/2
Minor children: as beneficiaries of life insurance, 7/10; bequests to, 7/1, 7/5-18; definition, 7/1. *See also* Children
Mistakes, in will preparation, 13/1-2. *See also* Changes
Monetary recovery for personal injuries, as property, 4/8
Mortgage(s) on real property clause, 12/13-14

Moving from state to state: and marital property, 4/13; and will, 2/1

Municipal bonds, 7/19

N

Name, in will, 11/3-4, 12/4

Net value of property, definition, 5/5-6

No contest clause, 12/28-29

Notarization, of will, 2/3

Notary public and notarization of will, 2/3, 10/4, 13/3-4, 13/5-6, 14/3

Nuncupative will, 2/4

O

Oral will, 2/4

Organ donation clause, 12/30

Out-of-wedlock children, 7/23-24

P

Paper, for will, 13/1

Partnership agreement, 4/3

Partnership property, 4/1

Pay-on-death bank account. *See* Informal bank trust account

Payment of death taxes and debts clause, 12/16-17

Pensions, 4/1-2, 4/3, 5/4; as community property, 4/6

Person living with lover/mate with minor children, sample will form, 11/2, 11/5, 11/59-67

Person living with lover/mate with no minor children, sample will form, 11/2, 11/5, 11/53-58

Personal guardian, 7/2-5, 7/16-17; other than parent, 7/3-4, 7/16-17

Personal guardian of minor children clause, 11/7, 12/19-21

Personal guardians (different), for different children, 7/4

Personal guardians (different) clause, 11/7, 12/21

Personal identification clause, 11/3-4, 12/4

Personal injury awards, as property, 4/8

Personal property: definition, 5/2, 5/3; inventory of, 5/1-18

Personal property gifts clause, 12/7-10

Personal representative. *See* Executor

Pets clause, 12/29-30

Postnuptial agreement, 4/12. *See also* "Marital Property Agreement"

Power of attorney, 8/10-11

Prenuptial contract, 4/4, 4/12

Prepaid legal insurance plan, 9/3

Pretermitted heirs, 7/23

Probate, 8/2-6, 10/4; and children's trust, 7/9, 7/21; and creditors, 2/6; definition, 2/3, 2/5, 8/2; drawbacks, 8/2; fees, 8/2; length of process, 6/16, 8/2; and state law exemptions, 8/3; when desirable, 8/3

Probate attorney. *See* Lawyer(s)

Probate avoidance, 8/3-4; methods, 8/4-6. *See also* names of specific methods of avoidance

Probate estate, 8/3; definition, 3/1

Probate homesteads, 4/11n

Professional executor, 3/2

Professional management firm, as executor, 3/2

Property bequests: and adult supervision, 7/6-11; to other children, 7/18-22; to own children, 7/5-18; to spouse, for benefit of children, 7/6

Property custodian, 7/11. *See also* Property guardian

Property guardian, 7/10-13, 7/14, 7/18, 7/21

Property guardian clause, 11/9, 12/27-28

Property inventory, 5/1-18

Property no longer owned, and bequests, 6/18

Property owned in other states, and probate, 3/3

Property ownership, 4/1-14; by children, 7/5

Property that can be willed, 5/4

Property that cannot be willed, 4/3, 5/4-5

Pro-rata option clause, and cash gift shortfall, 6/19, 12/15

Q

Quasi-community property, 4/13

R

Real estate gifts clause, 12/11-12
Real property, definition, 5/3
Recording of will, 2/3
Residuary beneficiary, 6/7, 6/15-16, 7/5, 12/14; definition, 6/2
Residuary clause, 11/6, 12/14-15
Residuary estate, definition, 6/2
Residuary option clause, and cash gift shortfall, 6/19, 12/15
Residue of estate, definition, 6/2, 6/19n, 11/6, 12/14
Retirement accounts/benefits/plans, 4/1-2, 4/3, 8/6
Revising will, 14/1-3
Revocable living trust. *See* Living trust
Revocation clause, 11/4, 12/4-5
Revoking will, 13/7, 14/3; by act of law, 14/6
Right of survivorship, 4/9n, 8/5. *See also* Joint tenancy with right of survivorship

S

Savings bonds, 7/19
Second marriages, and trusts, 8/9
"Second tax" problem, 8/8
Self-proving affidavit, 2/3, 10/4, 13/3-4, 13/5-6; and codicils, 14/3
Separate property, 4/5-8; definition, 4/5-6
Settlor, 8/4
Settlor trustee, 8/4
Shared gifts, 6/5-6, 6/9
Shared ownership, of property, 4/1. *See also* names of types of shared ownership
Shared-ownership business, 5/3
Signature, 2/2, 10/4, 13/2
Signature clause, 11/9, 12/32
Simultaneous death, 6/16-17; of joint tenants, 5/4, 6/17
Simultaneous death clause, 6/16-17, 11/7, 12/29
Single person with minor children, sample will form, 11/2, 11/27-35
Single person with no minor children, sample will form, 11/2, 11/21-26
Single persons, and property ownership, 4/1-2
Sole ownership property, 5/4
"Sound mind," definition, 2/2
Special needs trust, 8/10

Specific gift, definition, 6/2
Spendthrift trusts, 8/10
Spouse: disinheriting, 4/11, 6/4; not mentioned in will, 14/6; waiver of statutory inheritance rights, 4/12, 4/14
State death taxes, 8/6-7
Statutory inheritance rights, 7/23, 14/6; waiver of, 4/12, 4/14
Statutory will, 2/4
Stepparent adoption, 7/3n
Storage of will, 13/4, 14/3
Successor custodian, 7/7, 7/14, 7/19, 7/20. *See also* Uniform Transfers to Minors Act (UTMA)
Successor executor, 3/1, 3/2
Successor trustee, 7/7, 7/16-17, 7/21, 8/4. *See also* Children's trust
Survivorship period, 6/7n; definition, 6/2; establishing, 6/16
Survivorship period clause, 12/15

T

Taking against the will, 4/12
Taking under the will, 4/12
Tax-deferred bonds, 7/19
Tax rate, 7/19
Taxes, 7/19, 8/6-9, 12/16
Tenancy by the entirety property, 4/9n, 5/4, 5/5, 8/5
Tenancy in common property, 4/1, 4/9n, 5/4, 5/5, 8/5
Testator, definition, 2/2
Totten trust. *See* Informal bank trust account
Trust, for disadvantaged person, 8/10
Trust, living. *See* Living trust
Trust beneficiaries, of living trust, 8/4
Trust instrument, 8/4
Trustee, of children's trust, 7/7, 7/16-17, 7/21; compensation, 7/17. *See also* Children's trust
Trustee, of living trust, 4/3, 8/4. *See also* Living trust
Trustees (different), for different trusts, 7/17
Trustor, 8/4
Trusts for property left to children clause, 11/8-9, 12/24-26
Typed will, 2/4. *See also* Will
Typing of will, 11/3, 13/1-2
Typing service, 9/3

U

Undue influence, 2/2
Uniform Gifts to Minors Act, 7/19
Uniform laws, 7/6n
Uniform Transfers to Minors Act (UTMA), 1/1,
    7/6-9, 7/10, 7/11-15, 7/19, 11/8; definition,
    7/7; and gifts to others' children, 7/19-20,
    7/21-22; and insurance proceeds, 7/10; states
    adopting, 7/8
Unmarried people. *See* Single person(s)
UTMA. *See* Uniform Transfers to Minors Act
    (UTMA)

V

Validity, of will, 2/1-3
Video will, 2/3

W

Wife, sample wills. *See* Married person
Will: changing, 11, 3, 12/3, 13/1-4, 14/1-5;
    drafting, 13/1-7; forms, 10/1-4, 11/1-67, 12/1-
    33; legal requirements, 2/1-3; limitations, 2/5-
    6; need for, 1/2, 8/3-4; percent of Americans
    without, 1/2; recording, 2/3; revising, 14/1-3;
    revocation by act of law, 14/6; revoking, 13/7,
    14/3; sample completed, 1/4-6, 11/10-19;
    technical requirements, 2/2-3, 10/4, 13/1-7;
    types, 2/3-5
Will caption clause, 12/4
Will formalities, 2/2-3, 10/4, 13/1-7; copies,
    13/7, 14/3; signing, 2/2, 10/4, 13/2; storing,
    13/4, 14/3; typing, 11/3, 13/1-2; witnessing,
    2/3, 10/4, 13/2-3
Will forms: assemble-it-yourself, 10/3-4, 12/1-33;
    basic, 10/1-2, 11/20-67; completed sample,
    1/4-6, 11/10-19
Will identification provision, 11/3-4, 12/4
Witnesses: to codicils, 14/3; to holographic will,
    2/4; to self-proving affidavit, 13/4; to will, 2/3,
    10/4, 13/2-3
Witnessing clause, 12/32
Wooded land, and estate taxes, 8/7n
WROS. *See* Joint tenancy with right of
    survivorship

GET 25% OFF
YOUR NEXT PURCHASE

RECYCLE YOUR OUT-OF-DATE BOOKS

It's important to have the most current legal information. Because laws and legal procedures change often, we update our books regularly. To help keep you up-to-date we are extending this special offer. Cut out and mail the title portion of the cover of any old Nolo book with your next order and we'll give you a 25% discount off the retail price of ANY new Nolo book you purchase directly from us. For current prices and editions call us at 1-800-992-6656.

This offer is to individuals only.

CATALOG

...more books from Nolo Press

Estate Planning & Probate

Plan Your Estate
Attorney Denis Clifford. National 2nd ed.
Covers every significant aspect of estate planning and gives detailed, specific instructions for preparing a living trust. Includes all the tear-out forms and step-by-step instructions to let you prepare an estate plan designed for your special needs. Good in all states except Louisiana.
$19.95/NEST

Make Your Own Living Trust
Attorney Denis Clifford. National 1st ed.
Find out how a living trust works, how to create one, and how to determine what kind of trust is right for you. Contains all the forms and instructions you need to prepare a basic living trust to avoid probate, a marital life estate trust (A-B trust) to avoid probate and estate taxes, and a back-up will. Good in all states except Louisiana.
$19.95/LITR

Nolo's Simple Will Book
Attorney Denis Clifford. National 2nd ed.
It's easy to write a legally valid will using this book. Includes all the instructions and sample forms you need to name a personal guardian for minor children, leave property to minor children or young adults and update a will when necessary. Good in all states except Louisiana.
$17.95/SWIL

Who Will Handle Your Finances if You Can't?
Attorneys Denis Clifford & Mary Randolph. National 1st ed.
Give a trusted person legal authority to handle your financial matters if illness or old age makes it impossible for you to handle them yourself. Create a durable power of attorney for finances with the step-by-step instructions and fill-in-the-blank forms included in this book.
$19.95/FINA

The Conservatorship Book
Lisa Goldoftas & Attorney Carolyn Farren. California 1st ed.
Provides forms and all instructions necessary to file conservatorship documents, appear in court, be appointed conservator and end a conservatorship.
$24.95/CNSV

How to Probate an Estate
Julia Nissley. California 7th ed.
Save costly attorneys' fees by handling the probate process yourself. This book shows you step-by-step how to settle an estate. It also explains the simple procedures you can use to transfer assets that don't require probate. Forms included.
$34.95/PAE

LAW FORM KITS

Nolo's Law Form Kit: Wills
Attorney Denis Clifford & Lisa Goldoftas. National 1st ed.
All the forms and instructions you need to create a legally valid will, quickly and easily.
$14.95/KWL

AUDIO CASSETTE TAPES

Write Your Will
Attorney Ralph Warner with Joanne Greene. National 1st ed. 60 minutes
This tape answers the most frequently asked questions about writing a will and covers all key issues.
$14.95/TWYW

5 Ways to Avoid Probate
Attorney Ralph Warner with Joanne Greene National 1st ed. 60 minutes
Provides clear, in-depth explanations of the principal probate avoidance techniques.
$14.95/TPRO

SOFTWARE

WillMaker®
Version 5.0

Make your own legal will and living will (healthcare directive)—and thoroughly document your final arrangements—with WillMaker 5. WillMaker's easy-to-use interview format takes you through each document step-by-step. On-line legal help is available throughout the program. Name a guardian for your children, make up to 100 property bequests, direct your healthcare in the event of coma or terminal illness, and let your loved ones know your wishes around your own final arrangements. Good in all states except Louisiana
WINDOWS $69.95/WIW5
DOS $69.95/WI5
MACINTOSH $69.95/WM5

Nolo's Personal RecordKeeper
Version 3.0

Finally, a safe, accessible place for your important records. Over 200 categories and subcategories to organize and store your important financial, legal and personal information, compute your net worth and create inventories for insurance records. Export your net worth and home inventory data to Quicken®.
DOS $49.95/FRI3
MACINTOSH $49.95/FRM3

Nolo's Living Trust
Version 1.0

Put your assets into a trust and save your heirs the headache, time and expense of probate with this easy-to-use software. Use it to set up an individual or shared marital trust, transfer property to the trust, and change or revoke the trust at any time. Its manual guides you through the process, and legal help screens and an on-line glossary explain key legal terms and concepts. Good in all states except Louisiana.
MACINTOSH $79.95/LTM1

Going to Court

Represent Yourself in Court: How to Prepare & Try a Winning Case
Attorneys Paul Bergman & Sara Berman-Barrett National 1st ed.
Handle your own civil court case from start to finish without a lawyer with the most thorough guide to contested court cases ever published for the non-lawyer. Covers all aspects of civil trials including lining up persuasive witnesses, presenting testimony, cross-examining witnesses and even picking a jury.
$29.95/RYC

Fight Your Ticket
Attorney David Brown. California 5th ed.
Shows you how to fight an unfair traffic ticket—when you're stopped, at arraignment, at trial and on appeal.
$18.95/FYT

Everybody's Guide to Small Claims Court
Attorney Ralph Warner.
National 5th ed.. California 11th ed.
These books will help you decide if you should sue in Small Claims Court, show you how to file and serve papers, tell you what to bring to court and how to collect a judgment.
National $16.95/NSCC
California $16.95/CSCC

Everybody's Guide to Municipal Court
Judge Roderic Duncan. California 1st ed.
Sue and defend cases for up to $25,000 in California Municipal Court. Step-by-step instructions for preparing and filing forms, gathering evidence and appearing in court.
$29.95/MUNI

Collect Your Court Judgment
Gini Graham Scott, Attorney Stephen Elias & Lisa Goldoftas. California 2nd ed.
Contains step-by-step instructions and all the forms you need to collect a court judgment from the debtor's bank accounts, wages, business receipts, real estate or other assets.
$19.95/JUDG

How to Change Your Name
Attorneys David Loeb & David Brown. California 5th ed.
All the forms and instructions you need to change your name in California.
$19.95/NAME

The Criminal Records Book
Attorney Warren Siegel. California 3rd ed.
Shows you step-by-step how to seal criminal records, dismiss convictions, destroy marijuana records and reduce felony convictions.
$19.95/CRIM

AUDIO CASSETTE TAPES

Winning in Small Claims Court
Attorney Ralph Warner with Joanne Greene.
National 1st ed. 60 minutes
Strategies for preparing and presenting a winning small claims court case.
$14.95/TWIN

Business/Workplace

The Legal Guide for Starting & Running a Small Business
Attorney Fred S. Steingold. National 1st ed.
An essential resource for every small business owner. Find out how to form a sole proprietorship, partnership or corporation, negotiate a favorable lease, hire and fire employees, write contracts and resolve disputes.
$22.95/RUNS

Sexual Harassment on the Job: What it is and How To Stop it.
Attorneys William Petrocelli & Barbara Kate Repa.
National 1st ed.
An invaluable resource for both employees experiencing harassment and employers interested in creating a policy against sexual harassment and a procedure for handling complaints.
$14.95/HARS

Marketing Without Advertising
Michael Phillips & Salli Rasberry. National 1st ed.
Outlines practical steps for building and expanding a small business without spending a lot of money on advertising.
$14.00/MWAD

Your Rights in the Workplace
Barbara Kate Repa. National 2nd ed.
The first comprehensive guide to workplace rights —from hiring to firing. Covers wages and overtime, parental leave, unemployment and disability insurance, worker's compensation, job safety, discrimination and illegal firings and layoffs.
$15.95/YRW

How to Write a Business Plan
Mike McKeever. National 4th ed.
This book will show you how to write the business plan and loan package necessary to finance your business and make it work.
$19.95/SBS

The Partnership Book
Attorneys Denis Clifford & Ralph Warner.
National 4th ed.
Shows you step-by-step how to write a solid partnership agreement that meets your needs. It covers initial contributions to the business, wages, profit-sharing, buy-outs, death or retirement of a partner and disputes.
$24.95/PART

Software Development: A Legal Guide
Book with Disk-DOS
Attorney Stephen Fishman
National 1st ed.
A reference bible for people in the software industry. This book explores the legal ins and outs of copyright, trade secret and patent protection, employment agreements, working with independent contractors and employees, development and publishing agreements and multi-media development. All contracts and agreements included on disk.
$44.95/SFT

How to Form a Nonprofit Corporation
Attorney Anthony Mancuso.
National 1st ed.
Explains the legal formalities involved and provides detailed information on the differences in the law among all 50 states. It also contains forms for the Articles, Bylaws and Minutes you need, along with complete instructions for obtaining federal 501(c)(3) tax exemptions and qualifying for public charity status.
$24.95/NNP

The California Nonprofit Corporation Handbook
Attorney Anthony Mancuso.
California 6th ed.
Shows you step-by-step how to form and operate a nonprofit corporation in California. It includes the latest corporate and tax law changes, and the forms for the Articles, Bylaws and Minutes.
$29.95/NON

How to Form Your Own Corporation
Attorney Anthony Mancuso
California 7th ed.. New York 2nd ed..
Texas 4th ed.. Florida 3rd ed.
These books contain the forms, instructions and tax information you need to incorporate a small business yourself and save hundreds of dollars in lawyers' fees.
California $29.95/CCOR
New York $24.95/NYCO
Texas $29.95/TCOR

How to Form Your Own Corporation is also available with incorporation forms on disk for these states:
New York 1st ed. DOS $39.95/NYCI,
MACINTOSH $39.95/NYCM
Texas 4th ed. DOS $39.95/TCI
Florida 3rd ed. DOS $39.95/FCCO

The California Professional Corporation Handbook
Attorney Anthony Mancuso.
California 5th ed.
Health care professionals, lawyers, accountants and members of certain other professions must fulfill special requirements when forming a corporation in California. Contains up-to-date tax information plus all the forms and instructions necessary.
$34.95/PROF

The Independent Paralegal's Handbook
Attorney Ralph Warner.
National 2nd ed.
Provides legal and business guidelines for anyone who wants to go into business as an independent paralegal helping consumers with routine legal tasks.
$24.95 PARA

Getting Started as an Independent Paralegal

Attorney Ralph Warner. National 2nd ed.
Two tapes, approximately 2 hours
Practical and legal advice on going into business as an independent paralegal from the author of *The Independent Paralegal's Handbook.*
$44.95/GSIP

How to Start Your Own Business: Small Business Law

Attorney Ralph Warner with Joanne Greene. National 1st ed. 60 minutes
What every small business owner needs to know about organizing as a sole proprietorship, partnership or corporation, protecting the business name, renting space, hiring employees and paying taxes.
$14.95/TBUS

Nolo's Partnership Maker

Version 1.0
Attorney Tony Mancuso & Michael Radtke
Prepare a legal partnership agreement for doing business in any state. Select and assemble the standard partnership clauses provided or create your own customized agreement. Includes on-line legal help screens, glossary and tutorial, and a manual that takes you through the process step-by-step.
DOS $129.95/PAGI1

California Incorporator

Version 1.0 (good only in CA)
Attorney Tony Mancuso
Answer the questions on the screen and this software program will print out the 35-40 pages of documents you need to make your California corporation legal. A 200-page manual explains the incorporation process.
DOS $129.00/INCI

The Neighborhood

Neighbor Law: Fences, Trees, Boundaries & Noise

Attorney Cora Jordan. National 1st ed.
Answers common questions about the subjects that most often trigger disputes between neighbors: fences, trees, boundaries and noise. It explains how to find the law and resolve disputes without a nasty lawsuit.
$14.95/NEI

Safe Homes, Safe Neighborhoods: Stopping Crime Where You Live

Stephanie Mann with M.C. Blakeman. National 1st ed.
Learn how you and your neighbors can work together to protect yourselves, your families and property from crime. Explains how to form a neighborhood crime prevention group; avoid burglaries, muggings and rapes; combat gangs and drug dealing; improve home security and make the neighborhood safer for children.
$14.95/SAFE

Dog Law

Attorney Mary Randolph. National 1st ed.
A practical guide to the laws that affect dog owners and their neighbors. Answers common questions about biting, barking, veterinarians and more.
$12.95/DOG

Money Matters

Stand Up to the IRS

Attorney Fred Daily. National 2nd ed.
Gives detailed strategies on surviving an audit, appealing an audit decision, going to Tax Court and dealing with IRS collectors. It also discusses filing delinquent tax returns, tax crimes, concerns of small business people and getting help from the IRS ombudsman.
$21.95/SIRS

How to File for Bankruptcy

Attorneys Stephen Elias,
Albin Renauer & Robin Leonard. National 4th ed.
Trying to decide whether or not filing for bankruptcy makes sense? This book contains an overview of the process and all the forms plus step-by-step instructions you need to file for Chapter 7 Bankruptcy.
$25.95/HFB

Money Troubles: Legal Strategies to Cope with Your Debts

Attorney Robin Leonard. National 2nd ed.
Essential for anyone who has gotten behind on bills. It shows how to obtain a credit file, negotiate with persistent creditors, challenge wage attachments, contend with repossessions and more.
$16.95/MT

Simple Contracts for Personal Use

Attorney Stephen Elias & Marcia Stewart. National 2nd ed.
Contains clearly written legal form contracts to buy and sell property, borrow and lend money, store and lend personal property, release others from personal liability, or pay a contractor to do home repairs. Includes agreements to arrange child care and other household help.
$16.95/CONT

Nolo's Law Form Kit: Personal Bankruptcy

Attorneys Steve Elias, Albin Renauer & Robin Leonard and Lisa Goldoftas. National 1st ed.
All the forms and instructions you need to file for Chapter 7 bankruptcy.
$14.95/KBNK

Nolo's Law Forms Kit: Rebuild Your Credit

Attorney Robin Leonard. National 1st ed.
Provides strategies for dealing with debts and rebuilding your credit. Shows you how to negotiate with creditors and collection agencies, clean up your credit file, devise a spending plan and get credit in your name.
$14.95/KCRD

Nolo's Law Form Kit: Power of Attorney

Attorneys Denis Clifford & Mary Randolph and Lisa Goldoftas. National 1st ed.
Create a conventional power of attorney to assign someone you trust to take of your finances, business, real estate or children when you are away or unavailable. Provides all the forms with step-by-step instructions.
$14.95/KPA

Nolo's Law Form Kit: Loan Agreements

Attorney Stephen Elias, Marcia Stewart & Lisa Goldoftas. National 1st ed.
Provides all the forms and instructions necessary to create a legal and effective promissory note. Shows how to decide on an interest rate, set a payment schedule and keep track of payments.
$14.95/KLOAN

Nolo's Law Form Kit: Buy and Sell Contracts

Attorney Stephen Elias, Marcia Stewart & Lisa Goldoftas. National 1st ed.
Step-by-step instructions and all the forms necessary for creating bills of sale for cars, boats, computers, electronic equipment, and other personal property.
$9.95/K CONT

Family Matters

Nolo's Pocket Guide to Family Law

Attorneys Robin Leonard & Stephen Elias. Nat, 3rd ed.
Here's help for anyone who has a question or problem involving family law—marriage, divorce, adoption or living together.
$14.95/FLD

Divorce & Money

Violet Woodhouse & Victoria Felton-Collins
with M.C. Blakeman.
National 2nd ed.
Explains how to evaluate such major assets as family homes and businesses, investments, pensions, and how to arrive at a division of property that is fair to both sides.
$21.95/DIMO

The Living Together Kit

Attorneys Toni Ihara & Ralph Warner. National 6th ed.
A detailed guide designed to help the increasing number of unmarried couples living together understand the laws that affect them. Sample agreements and instructions are included.
$17.95/LTK

A Legal Guide for Lesbian and Gay Couples

Attorneys Hayden Curry, Denis Clifford & Robin Leonard. National 7th ed.
This book shows lesbian and gay couples how to write a living-together contract, plan for medical emergencies, understand the practical and legal aspects of having and raising children and plan their estates. Includes forms and sample agreements.
$21.95/LG

California Marriage & Divorce Law

Attorneys Ralph Warner,
Toni Ihara & Stephen Elias. California 11th ed.
Explains community property, pre-nuptial contracts, foreign marriages, buying a house, getting a divorce, dividing property, and more. Pre-nuptial contracts included.
$19.95/MARR

Divorce: A New Yorker's Guide to Doing it Yourself

Bliss Alexandra. New York 1st ed.
Step-by-step instructions and all the forms you need to do your own divorce and save thousands of dollars in legal fees. Shows you how to divide property, arrange custody of the children, set child support and maintenance (alimony), draft a divorce agreement and fill out and file all forms.
$24.95/NYDIV

How to Raise or Lower Child Support in California

Judge Roderic Duncan & Attorney Warren Siegal.
California 1st ed.
Appropriate for parents on either side of the support issue. All the forms and instructions necessary to raise or lower an existing child support order.
$16.95/CHLD

The Guardianship Book

Lisa Goldoftas & Attorney David Brown.
California 1st ed.
Provides step-by-step instructions and the forms needed to obtain a legal guardianship of a minor without a lawyer.
$19.95/GB

How to Do Your Own Divorce

Attorney Charles Sherman
(Texas ed. by Sherman & Simons)
California 19th ed. & Texas 5th ed.
These books contain all the forms and instructions you need to do your own uncontested divorce without a lawyer.
California $21,95/CDIV
Texas $17.95/TDIV

Practical Divorce Solutions

Attorney Charles Sherman.
California 2nd ed.
Covers the emotional aspects of divorce and provides an overview of the legal and financial considerations.
$12.95/PDS

How to Adopt Your Stepchild in California

Frank Zagone & Attorney Mary Randolph.
California 4th ed.
Provides sample forms and step-by-step instructions for completing a simple uncontested stepparent adoption in California.
$22.95/ADOP

Patent, Copyright & Trademark

Trademark: How to Name Your Business & Product

Attorneys Kate McGrath & Stephen Elias, With Trademark Attorney Sarah Shena. National 1st ed.
Learn how to choose a name or logo that others can't copy, conduct a trademark search, register a trademark with the U.S. Patent and Trademark Office and protect and maintain the trademark.
$29.95/TRD

Patent It Yourself

Attorney David Pressman.
National 3rd ed.
From the patent search to the actual application, this book covers everything including the use and licensing of patents, successful marketing and how to deal with infringement.
$36.95/PAT

The Inventor's Notebook

Fred Grissom & Attorney David Pressman.
National 1st ed.
Helps you document the process of successful independent inventing by providing forms, instructions, references to relevant areas of patent law, a bibliography of legal and non-legal aids and more.
$19.95/INOT

The Copyright Handbook

Attorney Stephen Fishman.
National 1st ed.
Provides forms and step-by-step instructions for protecting all types of written expression under U.S. and international copyright law. Covers copyright infringement, fair use, works for hire and transfers of copyright ownership.
$24.95/COHA

Landlords & Tenants

The Landlord's Law Book, Vol. 1: Rights & Responsibilities

Attorneys David Brown & Ralph Warner.
California 4th ed.
Essential for every California landlord. Covers deposits, leases and rental agreements, inspections (tenants' privacy rights), habitability (rent withholding), ending a tenancy, liability and rent control. Forms included.
$32.95/LBRT

The Landlord's Law Book, Vol. 2: Evictions

Attorney David Brown. California 4th ed.
Shows step-by-step how to go to court and evict a tenant. Contains all the tear-out forms and necessary instructions.
$32.95/LBEV

Tenants' Rights

Attorneys Myron Moskovitz & Ralph Warner.
California 11th ed.
This practical guide to dealing with your landlord explains your rights under federal law, California law and rent control ordinances. Forms included.
$15.95/CTEN

Homeowners

How to Buy a House in California

Attorney Ralph Warner, Ira Serkes & George Devine.
California 2nd ed.
Effective strategies for finding a house, working with a real estate agent, making an offer and negotiating intelligently. Includes information on all types of mortgages as well as private financing options.
$19.95/BHCA

For Sale By Owner

George Devine. California 2nd ed.
Everything you need to know to sell your own house, from pricing and marketing, to writing a contract and going through escrow. Disclosure and contract forms included.
$24.95/FSBO

Homestead Your House

Attorneys Ralph Warner,
Charles Sherman & Toni Ihara. California 8th ed.
Shows you how to file a Declaration of
Homestead and includes complete
instructions and tear-out forms.
$9.95/HOME

The Deeds Book

Attorney Mary Randolph.
California 2nd ed.
Shows you how to fill out and file the right
kind of deed when transferring property.
Outlines the legal requirements of real
property transfer.
$15.95/DEED

Nolo's Law form Kit: Leases & Rental Agreements

Attorney Ralph Warner & Marcia Stewart
California 1st ed.
With these easy-to-use forms and
instructions, California landlords can
prepare their own rental application, fixed
term lease and month -to-month rental
agreement.
$14.95/KLEAS

Just For Fun

Devil's Advocates: The Unnatural History of Lawyers

by Andrew & Jonathan Roth. National 1st ed.
A hilarious look at the history of the legal
profession.
$12.95/DA

29 Reasons Not to Go to Law School

Attorneys Ralph Warner & Toni Ihara. National 3rd ed.
Filled with humor, this book can save you
three years, $70,000 and your sanity.
$9.95/29R

Poetic Justice: The Funniest, Meanest Things Ever Said About Lawyers

Edited by Jonathan & Andrew Roth. National 1st ed.
A great gift for anyone in the legal
profession who has managed to maintain a
sense of humor.
$8.95/PJ

Nolo's Favorite Lawyer Jokes on Disk

Over 200 jokes and hilariously nasty
remarks about lawyers. 100% guaranteed
to produce an evening of chuckles and
drive every lawyer you know nuts.
DOS 3-1/2 $9.95/JODI
MACINTOSH $9.95/JODM

Older Americans

Beat the Nursing Home Trap: A Consumer's Guide to Choosing and Financing Long-Term Care (formerly Elder Care)

Joseph Matthews. National 2nd ed.
This practical guide shows how to protect
assets, arrange home health care, find
nursing and non-nursing home residences,
evaluate nursing home insurance and
understand Medicare, Medicaid and other
benefit programs.
$18.95/ELD

Social Security, Medicare & Pensions

Attorney Joseph Matthews with Dorothy Matthews
Berman. National 5th ed.
Offers invaluable guidance through the
current maze of rights and benefits for
those 55 and over, including Medicare,
Medicaid and Social Security retirement
and disability benefits, and age
discrimination protections.
$15.95/SOA

Research & Reference

Legal Research: How to Find and Understand the Law

Attorneys Stephen Elias & Susan Levinkind.
National 3rd ed.
A valuable tool on its own or as a
companion to just about every other Nolo
book. Gives easy-to-use, step-by-step
instructions on how to find legal
information.
$19.95/LRES

Legal Research Made Easy: A Roadmap Through the Law Library Maze

2-1/2 hr. videotape and 40-page manual
Nolo Press/Legal Star Communications. National 1st ed.
Professor Bob Berring explains how to use
all the basic legal research tools in your
local law library with an easy-to-follow six-
step research plan and a sense of humor.
$89.95/LRME

Consumer

Nolo's Pocket Guide to California Law

Attorney Lisa Guerin & Nolo Press Editors.
California 2nd ed.
Get quick clear answers to questions about
child support, custody, consumer rights,
employee rights, government benefits,
divorce, bankruptcy, adoption, wills and
much more.
$10.95/CLAW

Nolo's Pocket Guide to Consumer Rights

Barbara Kaufman.
California 2nd ed.
Practical advice on hundreds of consumer
topics. Shows Californians how and where
to complain about everything from
accountants, misleading advertisements
and lost baggage to vacation scams and
dishonored warranties.
$14.95/CAG

Legal Breakdown: 40 Ways to Fix Our Legal System

Nolo Press Editors & Staff.
National 1st ed.
Forty common-sense proposals to make
our legal system fairer, faster, cheaper and
more accessible.
$8.95/LEG

How to Win Your Personal Injury Claim

Attorney Joseph Matthews. National 1st ed.
Armed with the right information anyone
can handle a personal injury claim. This
step-by-step guide shows you how to avoid
insurance company run-arounds, evaluate
what your claim is worth, obtain a full and
fair settlement and save for yourself what
you would pay a lawyer.
$24.95/PICL

Nolo's Law Form Kit: Hiring Child Care & Household Help

Attorney Barbara Kate Repa & Lisa Goldoftas
National 1st ed.
All the necessary forms and instructions
for fulfilling your legal and tax
responsibilities. Includes employment
contracts, applications forms and required
IRS forms.
$14.95/KCHLD

Immigration

How to Get a Green Card: Legal Ways to Stay in the U.S.A.

Attorney Loida Nicolas Lewis with Len T. Madlanscay.
National 1st ed.
Written by a former INS attorney, this
book clearly explains the steps involved in
getting a green card. It covers who can
qualify, what documents to present, and
how to fill out all the forms and have them
processed. Tear-out forms included.
$19.95/GRN

order form

CODE	QUANTITY	ITEM		UNIT PRICE	TOTAL
			Subtotal		
			California residents add Sales Tax		
			Shipping & Handling ($4 for 1 item; $5 for 2-3 items; +$.50 each additional item)		
			2nd day UPS (additional $5; $8 in Alaska & Hawaii)		
			TOTAL		

Name

Address (UPS to street address; Priority Mail to P.O. boxes)

for faster service, use your credit card and our toll-free numbers

Monday-Friday, 8am to 5pm Pacific Time

ORDER LINE	1-800-992-6656	or	in (510) area call 549-1976
CUSTOMER SERVICE	1-510-549-1976		
FAX YOUR ORDER	1-800-645-0895	or	in (510) area call 548-5902

METHOD OF PAYMENT

☐ Check enclosed   ☐ VISA   ☐ Mastercard   ☐ Discover Card   ☐ American Express

Account #   Expiration Date

Authorizing Signature   Daytime Phone

Send to

NOLO PRESS, 950 PARKER STREET, BERKELEY, CA 94710
Allow 2-3 weeks for delivery. PRICES SUBJECT TO CHANGE.

visit our store in Berkeley

If you live in the Bay Area, be sure to visit the Nolo Press Bookstore

on the corner of 9th & Parker Streets in west Berkeley. You'll find

our complete line of books and software—all at a discount.

Call 1-510-704-2248 for hours.

FREE NOLO NEWS SUBSCRIPTION

When you register, we'll send you our quarterly newspaper, the *Nolo News,* free for two years. (U.S. addresses only.) Here's what you'll get in every issue:

INFORMATIVE ARTICLES

Written by Nolo editors, articles provide practical legal information on issues you encounter in everyday life: family law, wills, debts, consumer rights, and much more.

UPDATE SERVICE

The *Nolo News* keeps you informed of legal changes that affect any Nolo book and software program.

BOOK AND SOFTWARE REVIEWS

We're always looking for good legal and consumer books and software from other publishers. When we find them, we review them and offer them in our mail order catalog.

ANSWERS TO YOUR LEGAL QUESTIONS

Our readers are always challenging us with good questions on a variety of legal issues. So in each issue, "Auntie Nolo" gives sage advice and sound information.

COMPLETE NOLO PRESS CATALOG

The *Nolo News* contains an up-to-the-minute catalog of all Nolo books and software, which you can order using our toll-free "800" order line. And you can see at a glance if you're using an out-of-date version of a Nolo product.

LAWYER JOKES

Nolo's famous lawyer joke column continually gets the goat of the legal establishment. If we print a joke you send in, you'll get a $20 Nolo gift certificate.

We promise *never* to give your name and address to any other organization.

Your Registration Card

Complete and Mail Today

NOLO'S SIMPLE WILL BOOK
Registration Card

We'd like to know what you think! Please take a moment to fill out and return this postage paid card for a free two-year subscription to the *Nolo News.* If you already receive the *Nolo News,* we'll extend your subscription.

Name _____ Ph.( ) _____
Address _____
City _____ State _____ Zip _____
Where did you hear about this book? _____
For what purpose did you use this book? _____

	Yes	No	Not Applicable	
Did you consult a lawyer?				
Was it easy for you to use this book?	(very easy) 5	4	3 2 1	(very difficult)
Did you find this book helpful?	(very) 5	4	3 2 1	(not at all)

Comments _____

THANK YOU   SWIL 2.6

[Nolo books are]…"written in plain language, free of legal mumbo jumbo, and spiced with witty personal observations."

—ASSOCIATED PRESS

"Well-produced and slickly written, the [Nolo] books are designed to take the mystery out of seemingly involved procedures, carefully avoiding legalese and leading the reader step-by-step through such everyday legal problems as filling out forms, making up contracts, and even how to behave in court."

—SAN FRANCISCO EXAMINER

"…Nolo publications…guide people simply through the how, when, where and why of law."

—WASHINGTON POST

"Increasingly, people who are not lawyers are performing tasks usually regarded as legal work… And consumers, using books like Nolo's, do routine legal work themselves."

—NEW YORK TIMES

"…All of [Nolo's] books are easy-to-understand, are updated regularly, provide pull-out forms…and are often quite moving in their sense of compassion for the struggles of the lay reader."

—SAN FRANCISCO CHRONICLE

NO POSTAGE
NECESSARY
IF MAILED
IN THE
UNITED STATES

BUSINESS REPLY MAIL
FIRST-CLASS MAIL PERMIT NO 3283 BERKELEY CA

POSTAGE WILL BE PAID BY ADDRESSEE

NOLO PRESS
950 Parker Street
Berkeley CA 94710-9867